The
GARIA

The
GARIA

An ethnography of a
traditional cosmic system
in Papua New Guinea

Peter Lawrence

MANCHESTER UNIVERSITY PRESS
1984

Published by
Manchester University Press
Oxford Road, Manchester M13 9PL
and
51 Washington Street, Dover
New Hampshire 03820, U.S.A.

ISBN 0 7190 0980 4

Si meliora dies, ut vina, poemata reddit,
Scire velim, pretium chartis quotus arroget annus . . .

If age improves poetry as it does wine, how many
years should it take, I wonder, to seal the
reputation of one's written works?

Horace, *Epistolae* II: 34-5

In memory
of
Watutu Katiapu
Luluai of Iwaiwa 1952–1965

FOREWORD

I recollect very well my first encounter with the Garia thirty-two years ago.
When, fresh from the field, Peter Lawrence enthusiastically described Garia
social organization to me, my initial reaction was, shall we say, cautious.
What later came to be designated the African segmentary descent group
model was still a novelty and to many of us full of promise. Melanesia meant,
above all, the Trobriands, Dobu, Manus, the Solomon Islands, and descent
groups resembling those of the African Model seemed to occur in all of them.
The Garia were conspicuously different. Whether looked at from within or
from without, they seemed to have a structure without boundaries: no genealogical boundaries marking off one group of people from another, such as
we find in unilineal descent groups, no local boundaries fixing village sites
more or less permanently, no political boundaries with neighbouring peoples,
no closed ritual associations or exclusive access to economic resources — a
society based, in short, not on unilineal descent groups but on ramifying
cognatic kinship relations. Coupled with the absence of leadership offices
corresponding to chieftainship or headmanship, this fluidity of structure posed
the problem of how any sort of social continuity or cohesion could be maintained in Garia society.

The answer lay in the institution of the 'security circle' and the concept of
nanunanu, which Lawrence translates as to 'think on' or 'have concern for' a
kinsman or other member of the security circle. I was so taken with this idea
that I later adopted *nanunanu* as the most vivid expression known to me for
the mutual amity which I considered to be the distinctive mark of kinship in
all societies.

Coming back to the Garia in this book is an enlightening experience. It is the all-pervasive character of the cognatic structure and morality of Garia kinship institutions that must strike every reader. From land tenure to family organization and marriage, pig exchange ceremonies, transactions with gods and ghosts and the emergence of typical New Guinea big men — everything that goes on in Garia social life is linked with the core cognatic complex and mode of thought. Lawrence's earlier publications have made many features of this social system known to anthropologists; but we now have an integral picture of it as a going concern in its ecological setting and historical situation. And it is worth emphasizing, for both historical and theoretical reasons, that, as Professor Lawrence makes clear, it is a system that has resiliently survived over fifty years of assaults and upheavals. Japanese invasion during World War II, white administration and missionary enterprise both before and after the war, and now national independence, have introduced many social and economic changes which have resulted in the abandonment of some traditional beliefs and practices (for example warfare) but have not undermined the basic Garia social order. Even the period of cargo cult enthusiasm brilliantly recorded in Lawrence's (1964) *Road Belong Cargo* left no lasting disruption.

Lawrence's analysis of the Garia social system enables us to understand how they have been able to maintain their culture and social institutions in the face of strong external pressures. The built-in flexibility of their cognatic base might well have played a part in this. Such systems, we now know, are much more common in Papua New Guinea than would have been anticipated before the great expansion of field research in the past thirty years or so. I am reminded of Radcliffe-Brown's last statement of his kinship theory in *African Systems of Kinship and Marriage* (Radcliffe-Brown and Forde 1950: 1-85), in which he begins with an account of the cognatic system of the Anglo-Saxons, rather than with the example of a unilineal descent group, as the paradigm for the exposition of his theory. He considered cognatic systems to provide more cogent evidence of the fundamental role of sibling relations in what he called the construction of kinship systems than do unilineal descent groups. The Garia present us with an excellent example.

The essence of their social organization, Professor Lawrence shows, is the right of the individual to align himself, for all social and cultural purposes, freely with kin on the side of either of his parents, including antecedents of perhaps four generations back. This gives rise to the main problem that, as Radcliffe-Brown (loc. cit.) points out, confronts all such systems of social organization: how to counteract — how to put boundaries to — the outward extension of kinship ties to farther and farther zones of cousinship. The Garia solution is the security circle centred ideally on the sibling group. As a relatively limited selection of an individual's or a sibling group's close kin on both sides, within which there is maximum mutual trust and solidarity in accordance with the moral principle of *nanunanu,* it marks off something like a home community for each person.

A distinctive feature of cognatic systems, well exemplified in the security circle, as Freeman showed in his seminal paper of 1961, is the equality of jural status of brothers and sisters and, consequently, of husbands and wives. Among the Garia, as in some other New Guinea cognatic systems, there is, however, a patrilineal and patrilateral bias in that the most important land rights are vested in patrilineages. And it is easy to see that this serves as a stablizing factor, complementary to the security circle, providing something like areas of economic and jural anchorage for the individual. It is all the same indicative of the freedom of individual choice that is characteristic of cognatic systems that relatives through females are readily incorporated into patrilineages.

However, it is the security circle that appears to be the focal structure in Garia social organization, not the patrilineage. Neighbours cultivating land in the same general area are assimilated into a person's security circle as are even gods and ghosts. And we can see why. It is a way of extending the binding moral obligations of mutual trust and solidarity of *nanunanu* to people and agencies that are not by definition so bound but must, for the sake of everyone's well-being, be brought into this orbit. Indeed, this is the pay-off hoped for also from the ceremonial exchanges between non-kin. The classical opposition between 'status' (i.e. kinship relations) and 'contract' (i.e. non-kinship, most immediately affinal, relations) is thus in part, at least, resolved. The Garia, perhaps it is needless to add, also hold with the maxim first given prominence by Margaret Mead as a touchstone of Melanesian moral principle, that one must not eat one's own pigs.

I have dwelt on what is to me the central theme of Professor Lawrence's book for a particular reason. It has become fashionable to question whether field work is still necessary in social anthropology except as a passage rite to professional status for the novice or as a form of escapism from disillusionment with modern capitalist, industrial society. What is thus overlooked is that it is primarily through ethnographic field work that discoveries that open up new insights about culture and social organization are made. And this is what, to my mind, makes Lawrence's analysis of the Garia security circle, and its structural and moral significance, noteworthy. What I find particularly important is the analysis of how moral principles that rely, in the last resort, on the individual's sense of responsibility and not on legal or political sanctions, work in this society, linking fulfilment of the mundane rights and duties of kinship with the ritual fulfilment of the obligations to gods and ghosts on which the common well-being is believed to depend.

The case histories of dispute settlement bring this out clearly. In particular, they enable us to follow step by step the way kinship relations are reckoned by links of both patri- and matrifiliation.

Commenting on the part played by neutral kin in dispute settlement, Lawrence refers to parallels reported from the Plateau Tonga of Central Africa. This suggests that not all African models are inapplicable to New Guinea, or indeed vice versa. The moral principle summed up in the vivid Garia concept of *nanunanu* is, to my mind, the foundation of kinship organization, the ultimate *raison d'être* of the social and cultural recognition of kinship, in all human societies.

Such comparability applies also, I would suggest, to what Professor Lawrence sees as the overarching framework of order and cohesion in Garia social life. The essence of this is that Garia conceive of themselves and of their society as belonging to a single, unitary cosmos that embraces both the mundane order and the 'mystical' order of human existence. They see themselves as living in a universe in which there is no hard and fast separation between the sphere of the powers and agencies that are conventionally labelled 'supernatural' or 'sacred' or 'mystical' (what Lawrence calls superhuman) and the sphere of everyday, this-worldly existence. Gods, ghosts and demons, however they may be labelled by the outsider, are as much part of the 'terrestrial' life of the society as food production and pig-raising, marriage and the family, in regard to all of which success is believed ultimately to depend upon sustained reciprocity in the relationships between men and gods and between men and ghosts. It is of interest to add that Durkheim (1954), contrasting, in the first chapter of *The Elementary Forms of the Religious Life,* the world view of modern scientifically instructed peoples with that of peoples like the Australian Aborigines, concludes that the idea of the supernatural is characteristic of the former, having come about in opposition to the idea of a law-governed system of nature, and is not part of the latter type of world view.

I must resist the temptation to comment further on Professor Lawrence's absorbing book and merely draw attention to his treatment of such topics as the role of the typical New Guinea big man among the Garia and the replacement of more violent methods of settling disputes by means of football. But I cannot end without expressing my gratitude for the splendid charts, maps, tables and genealogies with which the argument is supported. I must confess that for all the elegant, straightforward style of the exposition, refreshingly free as it is of any trendy jargon, I would have found it hard to follow the details of this to me quite intricate New Guinea culture without these aids.

Last, but by no means least, there is a quality of this book that I wish most specially to commend. The time has long passed when anthropologists who have been privileged to live among a people like the Garia in friendship and trust can be content with addressing themselves to their professional colleagues and peers in what they write about their host societies. Today an ethnographic monograph must be meaningful to the people who are its subject-matter no less than to the outside world. Professor Lawrence's monograph is, I venture to say, a fine example of what I have in mind.

Meyer Fortes
King's College, Cambridge

CONTENTS

ILLUSTRATIONS

Plates

Maps

Figures

Genealogies

Tables

PREFACE

The substantive first draft of this work was my doctoral thesis, based on field research in the southern Madang Province, Papua New Guinea, between April 1949 and June 1950, and submitted to the University of Cambridge in September 1951. In the Introduction I indicate my reasons for late publication and refer to my studies in the area since 1950. These subsequent visits have been numerous, even if brief: October 1952 until February 1953, January 1958, August 1965, January and August 1968, January and August 1972, May 1975, January 1977, and annually thereafter until 1981. Although they have augmented my knowledge and matured my understanding, they have corroborated my initial analysis, which I now present with some embellishment but relatively little basic modification. Yet what is immediately important is that, after thirty years field work, I have incurred many debts that I must acknowledge.

First, I thank the institutions that funded my research: the Australian National University (until 1953), the Department of Territories, Canberra (in 1958), the Australian Research Grants Committee (in 1968 and 1972), and the Sydney University Research Grants Committee (in 1965, 1972 and 1975, and between 1977 and 1981). I could have achieved little without this support.

Second, the inhabitants of Papua New Guinea — indigenes and expatriates alike — are famous for their hospitality. In the Preface to a previous work, *Road Belong Cargo* (Lawrence 1964), I expressed my thanks to those who helped me before 1958. I can only repeat them now. Yet since then I am beholden to many more people.

Above all, I am grateful to the Garia as a whole. The older men of 1949-

50 accepted me as a 'son': I could not have wished for more tolerant and generous 'parents'. Their descendants have continued the relationship. It would be impossible to record all their names here, although many recur throughout these pages. I have dedicated this book to the memory of one of their number who must stand for all. Watutu Katiapu, *Luluai* of Iwaiwa from 1952 until his death in 1965, was one of the most decent men I have ever known. His people will always remember him for helping them meet the challenge of modern development.

Again, I acknowledge the kindness and interest of many individuals in Papua New Guinea during my frequent comings and goings. For Port Moresby alone the list is long: the late Sir Donald and Lady (now Dame Rachel) Cleland, Sir David and Lady Hay, Mr and Mrs Les Johnson, Sir John Guise, Sir John and Lady Gunther, the late Sir Alan and Lady Mann, Sir John and Lady Minogue, Sir Horace and Lady Niall, Jean and the late Keith McCarthy, David and Sue Chenoweth, and her sister Mary, Helen and the late David Fenbury, Friedegard and Bill Tomasetti, Christine and Tony Voutas, Joan and Nigel Oram and Louise and Mekere Morauta. In the Madang Province I made many friends: in government service, Des and Marie Clifton-Bassett, Benson Gegeyo, Jerry Nalau, Peter and Coline Colton, Des Pike, Bob Smith, Otto Alder, Ron Green, James and Korry Spencer, John O'Brien, Frank and Sue Cotton, John Banzak, Gigmai Apa, Magistrate Riri of Bahaur and Roland Lubett; in Provincial Government, the Rt Hon. the Premier Bato Bultin and the Hon. the Minister for Tourism Kaki Angi; in the Lutheran Church Gary and Jean Reitz (whom I have known since 1949), Dick Hueter and Liwa Kolau (for many years President of Ambenob Local Government Council); and, in the business community, Deane and the late Eric Snook (whom I first met in 1949), Jason and Barbara Garrett, John and Anna Middleton of Karkar, Ted Whitaker, Elizabeth Sowerby, John Tulloch, Bill Stanton and Margaret and John Perkins (one of the Province's best loved pilots), to name but a few. I shall never forget Wafun Kapudi of Bahaur, who cared for me in the field until he died in 1978.

I have many academic debts. My wife, both in and out of the field, has consistently injected her common sense and insight. I thank the Commonwealth Scientific and Industrial Research Organization, Canberra, for permission to reproduce as Figure 1 a diagram from its publication *Lands of the Ramu-Madang Area* (C.S.I.R.O. 1976: 32). I thank also Ian Edwards and Michael de B. Collins Persse of Geelong Grammar School, Victoria, for allowing me to reproduce as Figure 2 the excellent transverse sketch of the terrain between Madang and the Waghi Valley, which they published originally in *The Corian* (June 1972: 378). The late Edgar Ford, one of Australia's most distinguished cartographers, prepared the maps, figures and genealogies, and Ed Roper (Department of Anthropology, University of Sydney) solved a number of technical problems with considerable ingenuity as well as processing the photographic plates. Robyn Wood, Rhonda Porada, Angela Garside and Jayne Munro (all of the Department of Anthropology, University of Sydney) performed perhaps the most irksome task of all: they typed and retyped the final draft of the manuscript with the greatest skill and devotion.

Dr Charlotte Carr-Gregg (Deakin University), Dr Daryl Feil (University of Queensland), Associate Professor Michael Allen (University of Sydney), Professor Tom Harding (University of California, Santa Barbara), Professor Andrew Strathern (University College, London) and the late Emeritus Professor Meyer Fortes (University of Cambridge) read and criticized a somewhat cumbersome second draft.

Finally, Andrew Strathern and Meyer Fortes read and commented on the final draft. I shall always be grateful to them both for their unfailing encouragement and support. Meyer Fortes knew the Garia since 1951. His Foreword is a high compliment from a great friend — and a great man.

Peter Lawrence
University of Sydney

TERMINOLOGY AND ORTHOGRAPHY

Readers unfamiliar with anthropological usage should note the following technical terms throughout the text:

Ego: a shorthand term for a man or woman who is the reference point in any discussion — not to be confused with the Freudian ego.

Kinship symbols: F stands for Father, M for Mother, B for Brother, Z for Sister, S for Son, and D for Daughter. These symbols can be combined in any number of ways: for example, FF = Father's Father, FM = Father's Mother, MB = Mother's Brother, and FZS/D = Father's Sister's Son/ Daughter, and so forth.

Siblings: a general term for the children of any married couple — true brothers, true sisters, and true brothers and sisters.

Throughout the text I present, first, Garia terms and, second, Pidgin equivalents. I spell both languages phonetically and use my own orthography. Three points about my Garia orthography should be noted:

apostrophes separate vowels, indicating that there is no diphthong;

ä is pronounced as in German *Säge* (roughly as in English *air*);

vowels at the end of words are little stressed. The emphasis is always on preceding consonants.

Introduction

This book is an analysis of the traditional sociocultural system or, as I prefer, the total conceived cosmic order of the Garia of the southern Madang Province in Papua New Guinea: their generalized economic and sociopolitical structure, and their religion. It is the second in a series of three projected monographs on the ethnography of the region. The first (Lawrence 1964) described the local Cargo Movement from 1871 until 1950. The third will deal with a second language group, the Ngaing of the Rai Coast.

Although I have worked in the southern Madang Province periodically for thirty years, the research I now present was largely completed during my first two visits, between April 1949 and June 1950, and between October 1952 and February 1953. The delay in publication has been due to two factors: first, especially in the 1950s, my colleagues' lack of enthusiasm for my interpretation of Garia ethnography; and, second, the pressure of teaching and, certainly after 1966, administrative duties.

A dispassionate review of the first factor is essential to explain this book's position in recent social anthropology in Melanesia. For about a decade after the completion of my early field work, my approach to Garia ethnography

1

did not conform to a mode of analysis that had come into vogue in much of the British Commonwealth after World War II. At that time members of the British School had made considerable advances in ethnography and had argued cogently that large-scale stateless societies in Africa were structured on the basis of rigid unilineal segmentation, which provided the framework of both local and political organization. In the immediate post-war years, disciples at Australian universities began to apply this segmentary theory, as it was then known, in the Papua New Guinea Highlands, which the Australian Administration was just beginning to bring under its control. Initially, their reaction was understandable: as Barnes (1962) observed, they discovered relatively large and nominally patrilineal populations which they could easily regard as examples of what he now called the African Model.[1] But they proceeded with too little caution, espousing segmentary theory as if it were unchallengeable dogma for all Papua New Guinea. Any enthographer who did not endorse it as the cornerstone of analysis was in error: he or she had either misinterpreted his or her material or had been misled by his or her informants.

When I first went to Papua New Guinea my own outlook was implicitly the same. On the basis of the accounts then published, most, if not all, of the country's traditional societies could be construed as small, basically segmentary systems. I arrived in Madang in 1949 quite certain that I should quickly discover a miniature of Nuer or Tallensi society. In fact, I found the virtual antithesis: a cognatic society of some 2500 people without corporate territorial groups subdivided on the principle of unilineal descent and serving political functions on the basis of a neat system of confrontation and balance. Rather, there was a process of continual flux, convergence (a term suggested to me by Professor Fortes) and compromise: the manipulation of networks of interpersonal relationships which I could not define as discrete social units. After taking my Ph.D. at Cambridge in 1951 I returned to Australia, where I was to follow my professional career but where my analyses were received with polite but scarcely veiled scepticism. I was describing systems of relationships that seemed to be without ethnographic precedent. The general reaction was typified and endorsed by Sir Edmund Leach's (1956) review of my short monograph on Garia land tenure (Lawrence 1955).

With so little encouragement at that time, I decided to set aside my Garia studies in favour of my other field of research, the Cargo Movement, my account of which, as I have indicated, appeared some nineteen years ago. Yet, although I had never intended to abandon them, it has been only recently that I could give them the attention that they deserved. After 1966 I was held up by the second factor I have mentioned: heavy programmes of teaching and administration at the Universities of Queensland and Sydney, which gave me little opportunity for serious writing until after 1975.

Nevertheless, delay in publication has probably made this a better book for at least two reasons. In the first place, during the last twenty years there has been a radical change in our interpretation of Melanesian societies. I have already referred to Barnes's (1962; cf. Brown, P. 1971) well-known paper on the use of the African Model in the Papua New Guinea Highlands, which he found unjustified because the people's localized political groups were not exclusively derivatives of patrilineal descent. Although these groups consisted initially of bands of agnates, they were often augmented by affines and non-agnatic cognates who either drifted in or were invited to join. There was some over-reaction to this paper: Highlands societies, once accepted as impeccably patrilineal and segmentary, were attributed a degree of cognatic elasticity that may not have been entirely warranted. Yet the overall effect was salutary. There was a rush to reappraise much of the Papua New Guinean ethnographic corpus: the analysis of interpersonal kinship ties, so long neglected, began to take its place alongside that of unilineal descent groups. For me this was a measure of vindication: my Garia research could now be placed in a recognizable context. I was heartened when Langness (1972: 926) generously drew attention to it.

At the same time, although the Garia were becoming academically more respectable, Langness made a significant comment: they were possibly 'an extreme case' of Melanesian sociopolitical flexibility. So far, they seem to be exceptional in the literature of the area in that, as noted, they lack the territorially based political groups that appear as essential features of all other societies so far described, however pliant their internal organization. Such groups are reported among not only predominantly unilineal (cf. Lawrence 1971a: 1-30) but also cognatic societies studied by scholars other than myself: the To'ambaita (Hogbin 1939), Choiseul Islanders (Scheffler 1965), and Kwaio (Keesing 1971) of the Solomon Islands; the Huli (Glasse 1968) and Kunimaipa (McArthur 1971) of the southern Highlands, and Telefolmin (Craig 1969) of the western Highlands, of Papua New Guinea; the Kilenge of west New Britain (Zelenietz and Grant 1980); and the Molima of eastern Papua New Guinea (Chowning 1962).[2] I do not challenge these authors' arguments for the peoples about whom they write. I reject only the assumption that *no* stateless society can hold together without fixed territorial groups and that *no* account of a cognatic society can be complete until we can divide it into such units (cf. Freeman 1961: 200). The case I have argued for the Garia since 1949 is consistent with Fox's (1967: 146-56) reasonable comments: that cognatic groups cannot function in the manner of conventionally defined and presented lineages as discrete residential and political groups but are bound to overlap and create divided interests, thereby making what has been called a network analysis essential. We are now beginning to recognize that stateless societies throughout all Oceania are not discrete isolates but fall along a continuum, from the essentially bilateral through the cognatic to the predominantly unilineal. The Garia are just one version of the cognatic.

In the second place, because of this delay, I have been able to augment my early research through a number of short visits to the field since 1953. Although I am still satisfied with the general validity of my initial analyses (Lawrence 1955 and 1971b), I have been forced to give them greater balance by placing due weight on material to which I had previously paid too little attention. After 1972 — and, more particularly, after 1975 as a result of correspondence with Drs L. Conton and D. Eisler, who were studying the Sopu people at Usino — I began to realize that especially social structure among the Garia, although always rooted in common principles, was capable of more permutations than my previous publications had suggested. These two workers reported from Usino a structure of a basically patrilineal parish, originally consisting of two patrilineage carpels (Conton and Eisler 1976). Clearly, I had to check my earlier work, which, *mutatis mutandis,* might have been as mistaken as the stress on the African Model elsewhere: it might have pushed the Garia too far towards the other end of the continuum. In May 1975 I returned to the field and satisfied myself that Conton's and Eisler's findings did not apply in Garialand. Nevertheless, I realized that I had to offset the networks of purely interpersonal relationships on which I had so far based my argument by describing a number of territorial divisions whose significance I had previously underestimated. Although these divisions did not negate my earlier case in that they did not represent a system of conventional political groups, they perhaps made the Garia a less 'extreme case'. For this I am in Conton's and Eisler's debt.

Presentation and Analysis

In view of its nature, it would be at least premature to try to interpret my material in the light of several prominent current anthropological theories — such as French structuralism, symbolism, and neo-Marxism — certainly until it has been ordered and presented in its own right. I have deliberately restricted myself to an ethnography in the general field of network analysis — especially the constellations of interpersonal exchange and political relationships, which the term implies and about which there is now a considerable literature[3] — albeit in a far more extensive context than some scholars might consider warranted. Although I concentrate heavily on Garia secular or purely human society, I go well beyond it and treat it as essentially a part of the wider system I mentioned at the outset: the total cosmic order that the people conceive. The approach is substantially the same as that in my monograph on the Cargo Movement (Lawrence 1964). Traditionally, the people regard their cosmos as a finite terrestrial environment containing two realms, one inhabited by human beings, and the other by gods and spirits. They make no ontological distinction between these two realms: they place them both firmly on the earth, and do not equate them respectively with what Europeans call the natural and supernatural or transcendental. My aim is to demonstrate not only how these two realms are, or are believed to be, constituted but also how they impinge, or are believed to impinge, on each other in everyday social behaviour, land tenure, local organization and sociopolitical control.

More specifically, I am concerned with the pattern, maintenance and restoration of order in the total cosmos. Ideally, because the Garia do not conceive its human and superhuman realms as spatially or intrinsically separate, I should examine in turn each of the foregoing problems simultaneously in both realms. Yet this is methodologically cumbersome: inevitable cross-referencing leads to continuous and tedious repetition. Like McSwain (1977), who faced the same difficulty, I follow anthropological convention and, even though it is artificial in this instance, present the two realms as if they were discrete, discussing the three issues I have listed seriatim in the context of each one on its own. My analysis, therefore, is an attempt to provide answers to two sets of questions: First, *what is the structure of Garia human society? Why is local organization so irregular? How does so flexible a society with so little immediately visible cohesion maintain any degree of order and restore it when the rules are broken?* Second, *what is the conceived structure of the realm of deities and spirits of the dead? How are putative relationships between human and superhuman beings expressed and maintained? What happens when the rules defining these relationships are broken?*

My answers are contained in eight chapters. In the first I present background material: terrain, climate, population, economy, the annual cycle of events, and local history after European settlement in the Madang Province. The next five chapters concentrate on the human realm of the cosmos. In Chapter 2 I introduce the structural form of human society. I outline the mythological origins of the cosmos and then describe the main features of the social system: the territorial divisions I call bush god domains and the ego-centred networks of interpersonal relationships I call security circles. In Chapter 3 I detail the principles of land tenure — patrilineal inheritance combined with other forms of acquisition — and the composition and leadership of garden teams. In Chapter 4 I discuss local organization, which is not an

automatic function of any single feature of structural form but an epiphenomenon of the interaction between the security circle, the rules of land tenure,
and the influence of big men. Especially in northern Garialand, ego's holdings
are so fragmented and dispersed that, to make use of them, he is forced to be
migratory. Hence local organization is bound to be kaleidoscopic. In the
south, settlements are more stable.

Chapter 5 has a dual role. On the one hand, it initiates discussion of
sociopolitical control by describing the processes of self-regulation which help
to prevent the occurrence of wrong action and disputes. I pay particular
attention to the exchange of pigs and the acquisition of land rights from
outside the patriline (already described in Chapter 3), showing how they
strengthen specific categories of relationships within ego's security circle and
thereby his moral commitments to certain people. On the other, the chapter
also augments the earlier account of the form and dynamics of Garia society:
the pig exchange increases the social range of ego's security circle by creating
new relationships with erstwhile outsiders. This sort of doubling is inevitable
in a society in which sociopolitical control is only one function of its generalized structure. In Chapter 6 I turn to the forces that tend to restore social
order after offences have been committed: the kinds of retaliatory action
available to the plaintiff and the principles that govern the conduct of disputes.

I devote the last two chapters to the superhuman realm of the cosmos: that
of deities and other spirit-beings, with whom men try to establish relationships similar in form and moral imperative to those they enjoy among themselves. In Chapter 7 I describe beliefs about these superhuman beings and
the initiatory stages by which a youth is introduced to them.[4] I show that
initiation not only reinforces and even expands his human security circle by
buttressing old and creating new social ties but also enables him to establish
a superhuman security circle by forging advantageous relationships with specific deities and ghosts. In Chapter 8 I discuss the content of putative relationships between human and superhuman beings — ritual honour in return
for material benefits as an expression of reciprocal moral obligation — and
the types of retaliatory action taken by gods, ghosts and demons against
people who affront them. To end the chapter I discuss the roles of leaders,
whom I describe as men of both realms of the cosmos: with their monopoly
of religious knowledge, they mediate between human and superhuman beings.

Finally, in a short Epilogue, I summarize the reactions of the Garia to
contact with the west since the 1920s, particularly to the programmes of
economic, political and educational development that the Australian Administration pioneered after 1945 and that paved the way to independence thirty
years later. I suggest that their responses — like those of other peoples in

Papua New Guinea — have been consistent with the traditional sociocultural system I now describe.

1

The Environment and its Recent History

Despite certain variations in social process which I discuss in later chapters the Garia are culturally and linguistically homogeneous. In this chapter I present background information: terrain, climate, population, economic system, the annual cycle of events, and recent history since European contact. Historical material is obviously relevant because it helps demonstrate the tenacity and continuity of the Garia sociocultural system in the face of considerable external pressures. Broadly, despite the curtailment of traditional trade, inevitable losses in material culture, the prohibition of warfare and the introduction of Christianity, the old way of life was largely intact during the 1940s and 1950s and still quite recognizable in the 1970s. The greatest pressures have been on local organization which, particularly in northern and southwestern Garialand, was modified for some thirty years but thereafter was able to revert in many places to its traditional pattern. I explain how this could happen in a later context.

Terrain and Climate

Garialand is some 80 to 110 square kilometres of low mountain ranges about

8

thirty to fifty kilometres west-south-west of Madang, Papua New Guinea, and forms part of what, for reasons I give later, became known as the Bagasin Area. Its central map co-ordinates are approximately 145° 22' E and 5° 28' S.[1] The neighbours of the Garia are: to the north, the Girawa, Kein, and Yarue; to the east, the Yapa; to the east and south, the Kopoka; and to the south and west, the Sopu (see Map 1). Especially among the Garia and Sopu on the north-western border there is a high degree of sociocultural overlap and bilingualism.[2] Moreover, the Garia have always been linked by trade through Girawaland to Madang, through Yapa and Yarue country to Bogati, and through southern Sopu territory (especially Usino village) to Faita and Bundi in the Bismarck Mountains, and to the Ramu Valley (cf. Conton and Eisler 1976). For the Garia, therefore, the traditional cosmos consists of their own territory together with those places beyond it of which they are aware and with which they have contact.

The Garia mountains lie between the Madang coastal plain and the Ramu Valley. By Papua New Guinean standards they are not high. In comparison with the Bismarcks, which dominate them to the south, the Finisterres and the Adelberts, they would be classified as foothills. The highest peaks are about 920 metres, and the linking ridges about 460 metres, above sea level. Yet Garialand is rugged. To the north there is little or no flat land, although south of a line running east–west through Epu the ridges gradually fall away and level out in the Ramu Valley near the Garia–Sopu–Kopoka border. The whole area is covered with dense jungle except for occasional stretches of savannah and patches of secondary growth where gardens have been culti-vated. Of the higher peaks the most important, both in the people's estima-tion and from a geographical point of view, is Mount Somau. In traditional mythology Mount Somau saw the beginning of the cosmos. In geographical terms it is the central feature of a drainage system running through the rest of Garialand and consisting of three principal rivers whose valleys average from 300 to 370 metres above sea level. The first is the Pike, which flows south and west towards the Ramu from its source on the northern slopes of Mount Somau. The second is the Merimerigatai, which also has its source on the northern slopes of Mount Somau and flows north-west to the third, the Mobo, which in its turn runs south-west to join the Ob'ubule and Pike rivers just north of Kutulu in Sopu country. Traditionally, these rivers were a major communications system but there was also a network of foot tracks from settlement to settlement along the valleys and through the mountains (Fig-ures 1 and 2 give an impression).

As is usual in Papua New Guinea there are two more or less distinct seasons: the dry, which lasts from late February or early March until late October or early November, and the wet from October-November until

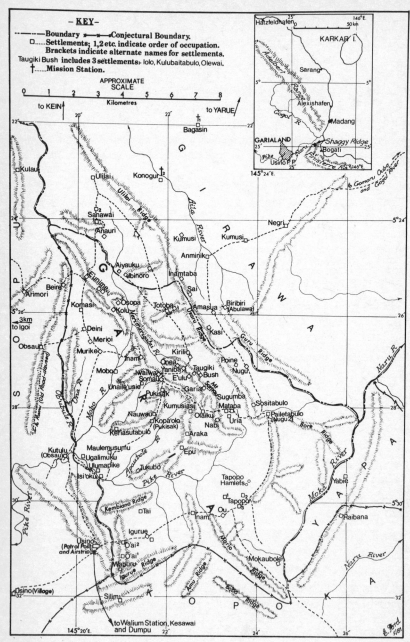

Map 1 Garialand

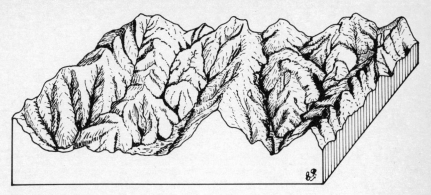

Figure 1 Bagasin land system

The area shown comprises the territories of the Garia and their immediate neighbours.

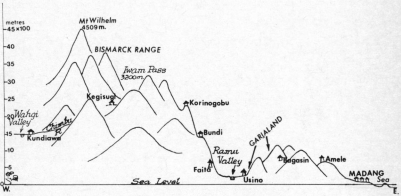

Figure 2 Transverse sketch from Madang to Kundiawa

February-March. During the dry season, midday temperatures average 26.7°C with a high degree of humidity. Rain does fall at this time, but at irregular intervals. Especially in northern Garialand these months are marked by a very strong wind from the coast every afternoon, from about 1600 hours until nightfall. During the wet season, midday temperatures are a little lower but both days and nights are very humid because of the rain that falls regularly in the late afternoon. The high wind from the north ceases but weather changes are less predictable.

Population

Since my first visit in 1949 the Garia population appears to have remained comparatively stable. In 1950, on the basis of my own and Administration figures (at that time inexact because of post-war conditions), I estimated it as 2435, a figure I revised as 2538 in 1953 on the basis of more reliable information. In May 1975 the official census listed 2627 persons, of whom 683 were thought to be away in commercial or government employment — probably rather more emigrants than twenty-five years before, when job opportunities were fewer. These figures suggest that, although there has been some increase since 1950, the population explosion reported from other areas under intense administration has not occurred in Garialand. In practical terms, I carried out my field work among a resident population ranging from about 2400 in 1949-53 to about 2000 in the 1970s.

Traditionally, the Garia were scattered in small hamlets, each with fewer than fifty persons. From the late 1920s until the early 1950s they were concentrated in fourteen large villages by the Australian Administration with backing from the Lutheran Mission, although in 1947 there was a further temporary reorganization as a result of cargo cult propaganda. Territorially, a village contained a number of wards or sections named after small bush areas which used to be cleared periodically as hamlet sites. Since the 1950s many of these large aggregations have broken up and the people have tended to revert to their original pattern of local organization based on intermittently shifting hamlets. I record the causes and history of this process later.

The Garia differ from seaboard peoples. Their language is non-Austronesian, although by 1949 nearly everyone, including children, was fluent in the lingua franca, Pidgin, and since the 1960s a few have learnt English. They are short of stature with an average height of 1.6 metres. Yet they are physically tough and, especially in their own terrain, can perform considerable feats and endure the greatest hardships. They have a reputation for austerity. Coastal people patronize them as bushmen but fear their sorcery. In their turn, Garia disdain coastal folk for their soft living.

The Economic System and Annual Cycle

As I have summarized the principles underlying the traditional economic systems of the southern Madang Province elsewhere (Lawrence 1964: 10-11), I pay here greater attention to Garia technology and important annual activities. Traditional economic principles are still intact: in Stanner's (1953: 10) terms, a broad lack of specialization, a stress on subsistence rather than profit and expansion, and a tendency to stasis. Recent critics, some of them Papua New Guineans, have warned that generalizations of this kind should not be regarded as absolute. Yet Stanner's summary is basically correct: it accentuates the obvious contrasts with the economic system of modern in- dustrialized society, which Europeans are bound to use as a yardstick, without eliminating common elements. Even in the 1970s the Garia economic system retained all the characteristics listed: the people were still largely generalized agriculturalists concerned with producing their own food. Commercial ven- tures introduced by the Australian Administration after 1945 — mainly the cultivation of rice and coffee — were only ancillary.

Unlike traditional economic principles, Garia material culture has not survived intact. It is impossible to give a complete account because many artefacts have been replaced by European counterparts. Those that remain are essentially simple and, apart from dance ornaments and pottery, have the stamp of utility rather than decoration.

There are three kinds of house (*ata*): the *yana* and *ui'ata,* dwellings for men and women respectively, about 3.7 by 2.4 metres in area and 1.8 metres high; the *libu'ata* or stilt-house, which is also a dwelling but varies in size; and the *äleata* or men's club, about 8.2 metres square and 4.6 metres high. *Yana, ui'ata* and *äleata* are traditional.[3] They have earth floors and are built of either leaf thatch on a beehive framework of withies or, more commonly, split log walls with a roof of palm or grass. The *libu'ata* was introduced from the coast in the 1920s by the Australian Administration: it has bark walls, a raised floor of black palm planks, and a roof of palm or grass thatch. Outside the men's club is the settlement slit-gong, a hollowed log about 1.8 metres long by 1 metre in diameter, with a long rectangular opening at the top. It is beaten with a short pole to send information to other settlements.

Clothing has changed radically since European contact. Traditionally, everyone went barefoot and children of both sexes naked but, after puberty, all males wore terracotta bark-girdles *(mali)* and all females skirts of bark- fibre *(soro)*. All adults were bare above the waist but men of consequence wore wigs of grass and fibre. By 1949 wigs had virtually disappeared and, although bark-girdles and fibre-skirts were retained as ceremonial dress, most men and a few women wore *laplaps* (cotton loin cloths or 'kilts') as everyday attire. Some men had short or long trousers, shirts, sweaters and hats (often surplus army issue), and a few women blouses for special occasions. By the 1970s most men had shirts and shorts, and some even socks and shoes, while many women had European skirts and blouses, and only very young children went naked.

Everyday artefacts include: netbags for carrying, made exclusively and used almost entirely by women; conical clay pots; boat-shaped wooden plates;

and round wooden bowls. The standard tools for agriculture are digging sticks (sharpened poles), axes and bush-knives. Adzes are used for wood-work. All these cutting tools originally had stone blades, but nowadays they are steel. They still rank among a man's most valued possessions. Since 1945 household inventories have been augmented by blankets, mosquito-nets, hurricane and pressure lamps, transistor radios and a wide range of carpen-ter's tools.

Certain artefacts have always accentuated male status: weapons for war, hunting and sorcery; and implements for eating betel-nut. Offensive weapons are bows, arrows, spears and daggers. Bows *(puriä)* are made of black palm and strung with bamboo strips. There are three types of reed-shafted arrows: one tipped with sharpened bamboo; another tipped with sharpened black palm; and a third with a multipronged head of black palm slivers or nowa-days steel wires. The first two were used in armed conflict and are still used for hunting large game. The third is used for wounding close relatives in disputes, and to shoot birds and fish. Spears have wooden shafts and points of black palm or nowadays steel. Daggers are made from cassowary leg-bones. Warriors carried also wooden shields. The bow and arrow are impor-tant in two other contexts: male initiation and sorcery. In initiation, penile incision is carried out by puncturing the glans penis with a small arrow shot from a miniature bow *(itete)*. The type of sorcery particularly feared *(ämale)* is said to be 'shot' into a victim's body by means of a standard bow *(puriä)* and arrow. Implements for chewing betel-nut are: dried and hollowed gourds and bamboo tubes (and nowadays European cigarette or tobacco tins) for storing lime; and serrated sticks for feeding lime into the mouth. The people have always planted their own tobacco, which they roll into cigars and smoke through bamboo tubes, although since contact many prefer European twist, loose tobacco, and ready-made cigarettes, all of which are now manufactured in Madang.

Artefacts used in the dance also are highly esteemed: hand-drums and body ornaments, which are traditionally monopolized by men, although women have limited access to them. The hand-drum, the principal musical instrument, is about 76 centimetres long and 18 centimetres in diameter at each end. It is made from a hollowed log tapered at the waist, where there is now a small handle for carrying, which, in 1949, informants claimed was a recent introduction. One end is covered with a lizard skin, kept taut by a number of resin nipples. The only other musical instruments are three kinds of *opu*: short bamboo tubes (18 centimetres long by 6 centimetres in diame-ter), which men beat on the ground to accompany the Abaiwala initiatory songs, the short bamboo flutes, which they blow during the Oitu (Nisiri) initiatory ceremony, and the *nali,* long bamboo pipes formerly used in the

Nalisägege. When dancing, men wear ornate head-dresses, shell and bone ornaments and floral decorations. The most prized head-dress is made from the plumes of the bird of paradise (sp. *raggiana*), although the feathers of the white cockatoo are also in great demand. The most valued shell ornament is the *kamu* — two white shells joined by a stick and held between the teeth. There are also cowrie shell necklaces and dogs' teeth crowns. Men wear bones of small animals in their nasal septa. As floral decorations, men and women place bunches of leaves, crotons and flowers in armbands, bark-girdles and skirts. They adorn their faces with black, red, white and yellow paint.

The main economic activities in which the Garia take part are pottery, trade, hunting and fishing, raising livestock, and agriculture. In this context, I describe each of these pursuits as it takes place within the annual cycle of events.

Pottery, by the coil method, is a task for the last months of the wet season (January to March). Although women collect the clay, men are the actual potters, and a good potter wins considerable renown. Trade, however, was mainly a perennial, if sporadic, undertaking. The Garia have always been linked to their immediate neighbours by extensive networks of trade ties (described in Chapter 2). They regard the route to Astrolabe Bay via the Naru River as specially important: it is their best source of shell valuables, and they claim that several of their deities journeyed up and down it, one of them to bring vital parts of their culture such as the Kanam dance, love philtres, and the custom of penile incision. In pre-contact days Usino in Sopu country was an inland entrepôt (Conton and Eisler 1976). Each area had its special products. Garia concentrated on making pots, which they traded for marine products from the Girawa and Naru peoples, and for sorcery medicines, tobacco, wooden plates and bowls, stone axes and knives, bows, and arrows from the Sopu and Kopoka. Individuals or parties could go away to trade at any time according to need or deal with their partners in the course of ordinary pig exchanges. Although the volume of articles traded has been considerably reduced as a result of the establishment of modern stores, the networks of partnerships have been maintained, especially along the Naru route.

Living as they do in rugged country and with limited game, Garia cannot be successful hunters. The most esteemed quarries are wild pig, cassowaries and, of course, birds of paradise and cockatoos. But there are also wallabies, possums, bandicoots, hornbills, bush pigeons, various types of edible snakes, land crabs and, near the Ramu, crested Goura pigeons. Apart from pig-pits, there are few traps. The main weapons are bows and arrows, and sometimes spears, although since 1965 some of the larger settlements have obtained shotguns under government licence.[4] Hunting is normally a perennial but casual and individual pursuit, for game drives are difficult in the mountains unless a man happens to flush out a wild pig or cassowary and can send word to kinsmen to help him. The same is broadly true of fishing, in which northern Garia do not pretend to be skilled: they eat fish mainly during the wet season, when the rivers rise. In southern Garialand, especially in riverain settlements, fish are more plentiful, better appreciated and part of everyday diet. Weapons are multipronged arrows and spears.

Domestic pigs are the people's most important livestock but must not be confused with wild pig. Raising them is a perennial activity. Even so, Garia have few pigs: a rich man claims four or five and an ordinary man one or two. In European terms, pigs have a high value: a fully grown beast fetched £A5 between 1949 and 1953, $A40 in 1972, from K50 to K60 in 1979, and from K120 to K150 in 1980.[5] They are not butchered and eaten casually but reserved for ceremonial occasions. Hence their importance quite clearly is more accurately rated by their role in sociopolitical life: as the principal units in bride-wealth and feast-exchanges, discussed in Chapters 2 and 5. Here I am concerned only with the techniques of breeding. Of any litter born in a settlement, some boars are allowed to run wild in the bush while others are castrated and domesticated with the sows. During the day gelts and sows root outside the settlement but return in the evening to be fed (mainly cooked taro) by their owners. Sows mate with wild boars. In addition, fowls, dogs and nowadays cats are bred and raised in the settlements. Cassowary chicks, although not bred in captivity, are caught in the bush and brought home to be domesticated.

Finally, the activity that concerns the people most is agriculture, which also is virtually a perennial task. I discuss land tenure in Chapter 3 and confine myself here to the methods of preparing gardens. According to Brookfield and Hart (1971: 40-2), Garia soil is of the Brown Forest variety. More specifically (CSIRO 1976: 32) soils range from 'predominantly brown residual' types in the higher and middle ranges to 'undifferentiated residual' and 'young alluvial' types nearer the Ramu. This appears to confirm informants' assertions that all Garia soil is relatively of the same quality. The form of agriculture is shifting cultivation: each year specific areas are cleared, fenced, planted, harvested, and then left fallow for about seven years. The people say that the purpose of the fallow period is to allow the trees on the site to grow again to a size big enough to be used for fencing against wild pig when it is cleared again. The obvious check on soil erosion — a vital issue because most gardens lie on steep mountain sides to ensure proper drainage — is a purely latent function. The following indigenous crops are cultivated: taro (the main staple), yam, native spinach, pit, cooking bananas and surgarcane. These are supplemented by other crops introduced since 1871: *Xanthosoma* taro, corn and various European vegetables. There are also fruit- and food-trees: banana, breadfruit, galip *(canarium polyphyllum)* and coconut (introduced by the Lutheran Mission). In contrast to coastal areas, taro in Garialand is a seasonal rather than a perennial crop, harvested only during certain months. This is due probably to regional differences in soil and rainfall which the people, although aware of them, cannot explain. They told me that in the 1930s indigenous Lutheran Mission personnel urged them to plant two crops a year, one in July and the other in November, to offset the yearly period of shortage discussed below. The second crop rotted in the ground.

The annual cycle of events is determined by the general weather pattern. The dry season is also the time of plenty *(sobule yausei),* and the wet season the time of shortage *(mausei).* The importance of this distinction is clear in the context of agricultural routines. Otherwise, there is one other irregular climatic phenomenon: the time of drought and dearth *(yabule yausei),* when no rain has fallen at any time in the year. I witnessed this to some extent in 1950 but more particularly in 1972: rivers ran low, creeks and small water courses dried up, crops failed, and the people faced the most serious food shortages.

The people set the beginning of the agricultural year in May, when the dry season is established, food is abundant, and they can start preparing their new gardens.[6] The work falls into four main stages: clearing undergrowth; felling trees; building fences; and planting. Yet in agriculture — as in other major activities — Garia do not distinguish between physical labour and the religious ritual associated with it. Before each of the above four stages, garden leaders must perform rites to guarantee the success of the purely physical or secular work. Without these rites, it is said, the whole enterprise would fail. This stresses at once a point that I made in the Introduction and shall repeat throughout this book: the conceived interdependence between the human and superhuman cosmic realms. As I have argued in other publications (especially Lawrence 1964, 1965 and 1971c), the people regard religion as of supreme technological importance: a primary operative force, the cornerstone of their universe. In the Garia language *saina* means any kind of work, although it is used mainly to designate a garden and the tasks, both physical and ritual, that bring it into being. Felling trees, building a fence and planting ritual are all *saina.* Work is a compound of secular and religious techniques — a compound because, in the people's view, the one cannot be divorced from the other.

The first stage in preparing new gardens is when, quietly and informally, garden leaders *(saina otaba'apu,* Pidgin *asman bilong wokgaten)* announce that they will cut bush in certain areas and perform ritual to drive out Siki-kiba, a snake deity harmful to crops. They may then invite individuals to work with them or, if they are well established, show Olympian impassiveness and wait for other people to seek permission to do so. During the next ten days garden teams gradually come together and start clearing undergrowth from the sites selected. This is the duty of women and older children, although men will often lend a hand. The second stage, tree-felling, which is essentially the job of men and youths, is preceded by ritual to protect them from falling timber. They cut every tree about a metre above the ground so that, when the crops have been harvested, the stumps will grow up again as trees that can be used for fencing in the future. They pile leaves and twigs around the stumps, and cut trunks and branches into lengths suitable for fence-building, which is the third stage. The leaders again perform ritual to ensure that the fence will be completed in time for planting to begin on schedule and be strong enough to keep out pigs. Men, women, youths and older children collaborate in its construction, women and children carrying the lighter branches, and men and youths the heavier logs. Men do the actual building.

Ideally, the workers should have prepared every garden site by early July and have completed its fence before August, so that the leaders can initiate the fourth and last stage, the division of the garden into individual plots by laying poles on the ground as markers. This is followed by planting, which also is preceded by ritual to ensure its success. Men and women plant together without any division of labour. There is no obvious plan in the placing of the different crops in the garden except that taro is always planted higher on the slope to give it drainage and sugarcane lower down so that it will be well watered. A few weeks later, when the taro shoots are about 15 centimetres high, the gardeners burn off the leaves and twigs previously piled around the stumps, so that the wind can scatter the ash and fertilize the soil. Then, without further ritual or any observable plan, they plant the subsidiary foreign crops.

About early October, with the wet season close, all heavy physical work in the gardens should be over although, for reasons I give later, in some cases planting drags on into November and even later. Yet normally the crops are now left to mature on their own except for periodical weeding. It is a period of tend-and-care, although the garden leaders must still carry out important ritual duties. When the taro is about 60 centimetres high, they have to guarantee its proper growth by means of special rites, and later perform others to ensure the maturity of sugarcane, promote an adequate supply of taro shoots and other seeds for next year's gardens, and prevent the theft of the current year's crops by means of sorcery. These rituals completed, the leaders place the gardens under a taboo: apart from those of recent foreign origin, no new crops may be harvested until they give permission about mid-January. I describe some of these rituals in greater detail in Chapter 8.

The agricultural cycle correlates closely with the patterns of both food consumption and the major social and religious activities throughout the oecological year. From the end of the wet season, which ushers in the time of plenty, gardens planted in the previous year provide all traditional and introduced crops. Indigenous crops are finished during November. Hence from the time the site is first cleared until it has been eaten out, a garden has a socioeconomic life of about eighteen months. As I shall show later, this is significant for social structure. Yet, during the wet season, when they have harvested their staple crops, the people's immediate problem is to find an alternative food supply. Before contact with the west, they relied on pandanus supplemented by roots and berries from the bush. Nowadays they enjoy also the European crops to which I have alluded and which continue well into January: corn, cucumbers, tomatoes and pumpkins.

The dry season and time of plenty are the period also of intense socioreligious activity and good health. Although agriculture takes up much time from May until October, other important tasks and ceremonies either precede or synchronize with it. During January, February and March the people concentrate on pottery and, about the same time, as soon as their new gardens are bearing, perform rituals in honour of the spirits of the dead, partly to thank them for the success of the agricultural year and partly to initiate young men. In the past they had the Nalisägege festival, which was specially dedicated to the ghosts, but had given it up by 1949, although they still staged the Abaiwala ceremony for the same purposes. From May (with the end of the heavy rains) until about late August (when the weather is again uncertain), they celebrate pig exchanges. Sores and illnesses are at a minimum.

The wet season and time of shortage are a period of make-and-mend and poor health. People build new houses or repair old ones, refurbish tools and weapons, weed their gardens and plan activities for the coming year. Life is unpleasant but not unendurable. Diet is monotonous and inadequate, and a perpetual worry is the increase of sickness. Boils and sores are now common, and old folk in particular succumb more frequently to pneumonia and other pulmonary diseases. Because of these factors, in the immediate post-war years, young men used to leave home at this time for casual work around Madang, returning in January when the leaders had given permission to harvest the new crops. They earned cash with which to buy European luxuries and helped conserve food supplies for old people, women and children still in Garialand. Since the 1960s, with the provision of medical aid posts and the opening of trade stores near Usino and along the new motor highway, these hardships have been somewhat alleviated. Moreoever, after 1950, Garia emigrant workers and casual visitors established three permanent settlements near Madang—Od, Maktaru and Gumbiris (near the bridge over the Gum River)—so that they could always live with kinsmen when away from home.

Recent History

Garia speak of two events as outstandingly important in their recent history. The first was a devastating earthquake and fall of ash, which have been reported also from other parts of the north-eastern Papua New Guinean mainland, and which destroyed their gardens and forced them to turn to cannibalism during the emergency.[7] My informants in 1952-53 placed the cataclysm towards the end of the nineteenth century, but recent expert research (Blong 1982) suggests that it was probably caused by the eruption of Long Island (Arop) more than two hundred years earlier. The implications of this for native historiography are obvious: the people recall actual events for longer periods than we have previously supposed, even if they have no techniques for dating them accurately. Nevertheless, as the earthquake appears to have occurred so long ago, it is impossible to assess its far-reaching socio-political effects on the Garia.

The second important event was contact with Europeans, which, in the southern Madang Province, began over a century ago and has left its mark on Garia society, especially in the field of local organization, a major theme in this book, in ways that we can assess. Contact started with a decade of tangential association. Between 1871 and 1883 the Russian scientist Mik-louho-Maclay spent nearly three years at Bongu on the Rai Coast. Yet, as he did not travel far inland, although his presence created traditions in which they still share, it had no direct impact on the Garia. Effective contact dates from 1884, when Germany annexed North-East New Guinea. For the next eighty-nine years the Garia were technically placed under seven different administrations: two German (1884-99 and 1899-1914); four Australian (1914-21, 1921-42, 1942-46 and 1946-73); and one Japanese (1942-44). They became part of a self-governing Australian territory in 1973 and of a fully independent nation-state within the Commonwealth of Nations in 1975.

We are not concerned with the history of European administration in the whole southern Madang Province, which is documented in other works (Hannemann n.d, Inselmann 1944, Lawrence 1964, Harding and Lawrence 1971, Morauta 1974, Lawrence and Lawrence 1976, McSwain 1977, Hempenstall 1978, and Moses 1977 and 1978). I detail here only the major events as they impinged on the Garia: the people's experiences before 1918, during the inter-war years (1918-42), during the Japanese occupation (1942-44) and during the period of post-war reconstruction and development. This is an essential introduction to my account of patterns of settlement and migration since the 1920s.

Initial contacts until 1918

The Garia had probably heard about Europeans before they encountered them. At Bongu, Maclay was called and believed to be a deity *(tibud* in the coastal languages). His name travelled inland and was corrupted to *Magarai,* which the Garia adopted as a synonym for deity *(oite'u,* Pidgin *masalai).* They used the word also to designate the first foreigners they met, although it is impossible to state exactly when this occurred. The two German administrations did not extend their political control much beyond 17 kilometres from the coast, although they sponsored three inland expeditions before the end of the nineteenth century. The first lasted from October to December 1890 and followed the Gogol River from its mouth near Bogati to its tributary the Naru to explore the inland plain lying between them. The second started in 1896 and lasted five years, following the route of the previous expedition and eventually reaching the Ramu. The third, begun in 1899, surveyed the Ramu from its mouth virtually to its source by means of a small steamship (von Beck 1911). In the same year the Imperial Administration conceived 'a land route' (presumably following the Naru) from the coast to the Ramu (Sack and Clark 1979: 181) — a project not realized until 1975.

As these three expeditions skirted their territory to the east and south the Garia could hardly have been unaware of them. Yet, unlike the coastal groups, nowadays they have only the vaguest memories of the first Europeans to come to them. Older informants in 1949 told me that these men (who could have belonged to the 1896 expedition) travelled along the Naru and distributed presents. Yet their most vivid recollections were of recruiters who visited them (again following the Naru) probably during World War I, about a decade before they were brought under administrative influence (cf. Rowley 1958: 128-31). The most memorable was a Chinese, who was carried on a litter, used his rifle to persuade young men to sign on, and shot at those who ran away.

The Garia interpretation of these experiences was in keeping with that already elaborated by the coastal peoples. They concluded that their visitors were deities *(oite'u/magarai,* Pidgin *masalai)* and called the Pidgin they now heard *oite'u kuna* ('language of the gods', Pidgin *tok masalai).* Yet they associated them also with the spirits of the dead: they called European goods red in colour *kaua po ulu* (goods from spirits of men killed by violence) and all other European articles *kopa po ulu* (goods from spirits of men who had died naturally).[8] By 1949 these phrases had become merely figures of speech, although *magarai* was still an accepted term for deity (see also Lawrence 1964: 67-8).

The inter-war years: 1918-42

Recruiting was intensified after 1918, when the Australian Administration was more firmly established and began to bring the inland peoples under control. After initiation and before marriage, three years in European employment became part of a young man's education. Garia worked on plantations and gold-fields, in stores, and as house servants in all the major centres of the then Mandated Territory. Some enlisted in the police. Many appear to have been well regarded by their employers, several rising to responsibility as plantation overseers and foremen of road gangs. From their own accounts, although typical of the pre-war colonial period, their relations with their employers were generally amicable. In outlying areas, villagers were still shy of Europeans and there was, of course, always discontent about low wages and the non-fulfilment of cargoist expectations, although this was ultimately directed at the missionaries (Lawrence 1964: 87 ff.). In fact, many employees spoke about their former employers with respect and affection. This relatively tranquil situation was due to the establishment of orderly administration and the surveillance of the Lutheran Mission.

The incorporation of the Garia and their neighbours in the Australian political organization cannot be dated precisely because of the loss of local records during the Pacific War. Yet it can be placed within a narrow time bracket. The Administration had brought the people under general influence by the end of the 1920s and under full control by 1936. Full political control meant four things. First, the Administration outlawed warfare and decreed that all cases of homicide went before its courts. Second, it discouraged hamlets and regrouped the people in fourteen large villages. Third, it installed three categories of headmen it had inherited from the German Administration—the *luluai,* the *tultul* and the medical *tultul*—and added a fourth of its own, the paramount *luluai.* The *luluai* and *tultul,* respectively first- and second-in-command of a village, had to keep the village book, liaise with District Headquarters, and supervise work on roads, houses and latrines, which the people had to carry out every Monday. The medical *tultul* was responsible for village health: he had to see to minor ailments and report serious epidemics to the European doctor in Madang. The paramount *luluai* was supposed to superintend all these activities in a cluster of villages. Fourth, again following the German model, the Administration inposed a head tax of ten shillings a year on all adult males save those under indenture, those who had worked ten months of the year for Europeans, those who had given fourteen days free labour to the District Office, and indigenous mission helpers and their students.

The Lutheran Mission moved into the Garia area soon after the end of World War I. Until 1914 its work had been confined to the coast. But now it began to win a large number of converts and, like the Administration, started to concentrate on the inland. In 1918 it established Amele Station overlooking the Gogol and, in 1922, Bagasin Station in Girawaland. From there it evangelized the whole region between the Gogol and the Ramu. It had placed indigenous helpers in Garialand by 1925 and in Usino (Sopu country) by 1931. In 1937 it held a large baptismal celebration in Somau and Iwaiwa villages. As a prerequisite the men had to renounce traditional religion by displaying to the women and children, and then destroying, the secret ritual paraphernalia (for agriculture, initiation, dancing, pig exchanges and sorcery) of which they had a monopoly. The Mission also set up its own organization, making the Garia part of a congregation based on Bagasin Station. It installed indigenous teachers and evangelists and built primary schools in the largest villages, and provided secondary schools at Bagasin and Amele. It also appointed in every village a congregational elder who, with his peers, belonged to a council that advised the European missionary. Finally, for obvious reasons, it supported the Administration's aim to concentrate the people in large villages: such a policy helped its own organization operate more effectively (cf. Lawrence 1956).

The Japanese occupation: 1942-44

By the end of 1941, notwithstanding the anti-European cargo propaganda of the period, the Garia had accommodated to the colonial order, which brought advantages that compensated for the irritations it imposed. This order was shattered on 21 January 1942, when the Japanese bombed Madang, the Civil Administration was withdrawn and ANGAU (the Australian New Guinea Administrative Unit) was put in charge. Only a small force of European volunteers and native police was left to defend the town, although the missionaries stayed at their posts. Its position was at best precarious and it quickly eroded any vestigial confidence in Australian administration when it organized the removal of as many goods as possible from the Madang stores to the Central Highlands to prevent them from falling into Japanese hands. The Japanese eventually landed in Madang on 18 December 1942, forcing all European personnel other than coastwatchers to withdraw. Some missionaries escaped, while others, like the Chinese residents, were captured, interned, humiliated and even executed. Allied troops drove out the Japanese on 25 April 1944.

The Japanese occupation did not greatly inconvenience the Garia. In fact, their greatest hardship at that time probably occurred before the Japanese arrived: their compulsory participation in the removal of the stores to the Highlands, for which the only available means of transport was human carriers. But this was a job to which they had grown used and which, by all accounts, they performed with at least outward good will. Thereafter they were in political limbo. The nearest European forces were in the mountains south of the Ramu. The Japanese manned the region with only light forces: a station on Ulilai Ridge in Girawaland, and forward posts at Nugu (Garialand) and Usino (Sopu country). At this stage they were interested only in buying food: they did not interfere in village affairs and left the existing village headmen in office (Lawrence 1964: 49 and 105-15).

During 1943 a few Garia enlisted in the Japanese police force, while others, out of loyalty to their previous European employers, joined the Allies. Indentured labourers began to trickle home. Otherwise life was tranquil and, for a while at least, most people remained in their pre-war villages. Probably their worst privation was the lack of medical attention, while the most significant change in their lives was in religion. The Lutheran Mission had ceased to exist, so that the old leaders, who had always resented their own eclipse at the hands of the Christians, reasserted themselves and openly reintroduced traditional ritual for agriculture, dancing and initiation, and also training in sorcery.

The situation changed in February 1944, when the Allies mounted their successful assault on Madang. Troops from Dumpu and the Highlands made a two-pronged attack, one force battling through Shaggy Ridge to the coast, and the other heading for the Naru through Garialand and Yapa territory. The Garia suffered from the fighting. Bombs destroyed some gardens and killed several people. Troops were quartered in their settlements. As a result, especially northern Garia, who had begun to hive off from their large villages towards the end of 1943 to live near their gardens, now deserted them entirely. They scattered in the bush, living miserably, until the fighting was over and it was safe to return.

After the recapture of Madang, ANGAU patrols went through the inland area with three objects in view. First, a party of European troops and native police had to put down the so-called Bagasin Rebellion, which was led by Kaum of Kalinam in Kein territory and in which a number of Garia from the E'unime-Kolu area were involved (Lawrence 1964: 110-15). Second, it seemed essential to regroup the people in their pre-war villages and see to their food supply, which had been disrupted by the recent campaign, and to their health which, after more than two years of neglect, was appalling. Third, once these issues had been resolved, the armed forces wanted to engage every available able-bodied man to help carry supplies to the troops who were now pushing the enemy to the north. At this time the Garia were heavily recruited. Once again they accepted the imposition with good grace. But this was virtually the last of their tribulations at the hands of white men, for there was now a turning point in race relations.

Reconstruction and development after 1945

Outwardly, after the Japanese surrender, the pre-war order seemed to return to the southern Madang Province. The Administration went on patrolling the villages, in which the most serious problem was an influenza epidemic that lasted from 1945 until 1949. Many deaths were reported. The missions gradually regrouped their congregations. The planters reoccupied their properties and tapped the villages for labour. Madang town rose from the ashes as businesses were re-established and expanded. Yet the old colonial system could not last, partly because of indigenous political forces and partly because of policies worked out in Canberra, both of which were to subject the people to pressures far more intense than those imposed by the pre-war Australian Administration.

First, in 1947 and 1948, the Garia were subjected to extensive cargoist propaganda. In 1947 a team of native ex-soldiers and cargoists predicted that, if they deserted their current settlements to live in really large villages or 'camps', they would receive substantial consignments of European goods. This led to a concentration of the Garia population in or around a few of the more important pre-war villages for about twelve months, although the process was arrested later in the same year by a new prophecy that, unless the people gathered at Igurue village in southern Garialand, they would be drowned in a great flood. The survivors would be rewarded with cargo. Many people from Tapopo and northern Garialand flocked to Igurue but went away again early in the new year when they realized that the augury was false. Also in 1948 messages derived from the pagan revival and cargo cult on the Rai Coast reached the Garia: they were to abandon Christianity in favour of their traditional religion, which was now seen as the key to European wealth. Although they seem to have wasted little time on cargo cult on this occasion, the people had already reintroduced their own religion for its original purposes when I arrived in 1949, so that I was able to learn many of its beliefs and observe many of its rituals (Lawrence 1964: 159-63 and 201-3).

Second, the Administration began to introduce its programmes of economic, political and educational development in conformity with the Australian Government's aim of promoting Papua New Guinean self-determination and its charter from the United Nations Organization. From one point of view, it meddled less in the people's daily lives than it had done before the war, abandoning its strategy of creating large villages and allowing the re-establishment of smaller settlements. Yet, from another, it began to impinge on them more heavily through these new programmes.

The Garia were introduced first to economic development. Even in 1949 they had planted a small amount of dry rice as a cash crop and by 1952, when they had increased the area under cultivation, had begun to regard it as a road to European wealth. But they were handicapped by three factors: their own lack of experience with this kind of crop; the Administration's inability to provide regular supervision; and the lack of proper transport. Hence, in late 1952, they responded enthusiastically to the District Office's suggestion that they help build a motor road from Madang to Goroka via Bundi. By means of voluntary rosters and using only their own tools, they cleared their section of the route from the Girawa border through western Garialand to the Pike. Several people in the northern area planned to move to the low country near the Ramu Valley and buy land from their relatives there because it would be more suitable for growing rice. The scheme had failed by 1956 because the District Office could not provide the funds and equipment for laying the road surface. The Garia were bitterly disappointed. They had openly renounced cargo cult in favour of secular economic development. Now their hopes, admittedly unrealistic, lay in ruins.

Eight years later the people's enthusiasm was rewarded. Encouraged by a sympathetic Administration officer, led by two energetic *luluais,* supervised by an experienced native policeman, and again with only voluntary labour and their own tools, they cleared and levelled an airstrip near Usino. Their sense of achievement was tremendous. What was more important, their fortunes changed at once for the better. With direct air transport to Madang, they could plant and market more cash crops than in the past. At first they tried rice once again but soon gave it up for coffee, which had proved very profitable throughout the whole country. Also, as trade stores opened at the airstrip, they had easier access to European goods.

Political and educational development soon followed. The people had already voted in 1964 in the first election for the House of Assembly (now the National Parliament) in Port Moresby. By 1965 the Administration had established a patrol post at the airstrip. In 1966 it proclaimed the Usino Local Government Council in which the Garia were incorporated. It replaced village medical *tultuls* with aid posts under trained orderlies and built a primary school at the station. In addition, despite the resurgence of the traditional religion in 1948, the Lutheran Mission, which had abandoned its station at Bagasin for a new one at Konogur (also in Girawaland), had by now reopened many of its village schools, while the Seventh Day Adventists had begun to work in southern Garialand.

The next decade saw even greater changes. Between 1973 and 1975 the indigenous Government financed the building of a motor road—probably first conceived by the German Imperial Administration in 1899 and then made an issue in the House of Assembly election of 1968—along the Naru River (the traditional Garia route to the sea) from Madang to Usino, where it joined the Ramu road, which in turn linked with the Lae–Highlands highway. This gave the Garia relatively easy access to many distant places and also brought a good deal of motor traffic, especially from the Highlands, through their territory. The enterprising opened stores along the highway to exploit this potentially lucrative trade and bought their own vehicles. In 1977 the Council planned a series of feeder roads from the highway to settlements in northern Garialand and Girawaland. Also, between 1974 and 1977, the Ramu Hydroelectric Scheme set up power lines to Madang along the same route as the highway. In 1977-78, with the establishment of relatively cheap and efficient road communications, the national Government closed the Usino Airstrip, which had outlived its purpose, and moved the station to a more suitable site at Walium in Kopoka country. Also in 1978 it introduced the Madang Provincial Government, which I ignore in this account because, by 1980, it had made no impact on the Garia.

Patterns of Settlement and Migration: c. 1925-80

The foregoing account of contact history delineates the major events to which Garia society has adjusted during the last sixty years. According to standard anthropological and administrative opinion in 1949 these external pressures should have seriously weakened if not destroyed it. Yet, despite several permanent losses (notably armed conflict and the Nalisägege festival), the socio-cultural system has proved remarkably durable. Its patterns of kinship, descent and land tenure are still intact and, although it was seriously threatened by Christianity and its by-product Christian cargo doctrine before 1942, traditional religion showed great resilience during the Japanese occupation and, more particularly, in and after 1948. In fact, European contact had its greatest impact on local organization (see Chapter 4). Nevertheless, so that the elasticity and adaptability of traditional social structure can be appreciated at once, I now summarize the general trends in Garia settlement formation and migration between about 1925 and 1980. Obviously, I cannot do this with total accuracy for the whole period but my outline should be sufficient to place the issue in perspective.

Informants told me that before contact the people were distributed throughout all Garialand, although then as now population density was greater in the north than in the south. After the establishment of the Lutheran Mission in 1922 and the beginning of political administration about three years later, Bagasin in Girawaland became the region's accepted centre. The main tracks to Madang did not follow the Naru route but went through Girawaland to the Gogol and Amele, one via Bagasin Mission Station and the other via Amasua, Negri, Gomuru and Ouba. The Administration's policy seems to have concentrated the Garia at this time in the northern area, especially in and around Somau and Iwaiwa, which became known as their principal villages, at the expense of the south-western area near the Pike, which was deserted. The Pike people moved north to Nauwau and Kopa'olo, on a ridge to the south of Somau and Iwaiwa but at some distance from their usual homes. Hamlets around Tapopo and Igurue in the south-east were grouped as two separate villages. The same pattern was repeated throughout the rest of Garialand.

As already recounted, this situation continued well into the Japanese occupation, although after the dry season of 1943, in the absence of either Australian or Japanese surveillance, the people began to break away from their pre-war villages to live in hamlets near their gardens. The Pike people especially began to drift back to their real homes. During the Shaggy Ridge campaign of February 1944, when the horror of modern war, albeit briefly, hit Garialand, the villages finally disintegrated and were re-established by ANGAU only several months after the Allied recapture of Madang. The Pike people were brought back to Nauwau and Kopa'olo.

Yet the reconstituted villages lasted only three years. Since then Garia local organization has been periodically unstable. Initially there were the two cargoist disturbances of 1947. The first had only a limited effect in the remote northern and southern areas, for it merely reinforced already existing village populations and brought in stragglers who had escaped the Administration's net. But in central and south-western Garialand it caused migration on a considerable scale. The villages of Yaniba, Kirili, Onea, Nauwau and Kopa'olo were concentrated at Somau and Iwaiwa. Together with that of neighbouring Inam the population of the new settlement was over six hundred, about five times as large as the biggest northern villages before the war. Again, later in the same year a number of its inhabitants deserted it for Igurue in response to the second cargo prophecy, although they came back after a short period. When I arrived in April 1949 most of the Yaniba, Kirili and Onea people had returned to their original villages, leaving the new houses they had built still standing, although most of those from Nauwau and Kopa'olo continued to live along Suaiyau Ridge adjacent to Somau and Iwaiwa. Even at this time there were still advocates of very large settlements: in May 1949 emissaries from Inam and Iwaiwa unsuccessfully urged Kolu and E'unime to come together.

Somewhat later, in the 1950s, when the cargoist disturbances had subsided and it was becoming obvious that the Administration was relaxing its previous policy, many village populations began to disperse. The most interesting case was again that of the Pike people, who once more moved back to their original homes in the south-west. They were encouraged to do this by the people of Obsau (a Sopu mountain village), who had migrated to Kutulu on the western bank of the Pike, claiming rights to the land of the original inhabitants, now extinct, through cognatic links. The previously deserted south-western lowlands now had a population of some importance. The Garia were once more distributed throughout their whole territory.

The events of the 1960s brought further changes in local organization. With the opening of Usino Patrol Post, the Garia at last saw their chance to engage in serious cash-cropping. In 1965, when I revisited them, many people from the north had built houses and planted rice gardens along the airstrip. But when rice was replaced by coffee they had to return to their homes to plant the trees on their own land. As a result of this continual migration, large settlements now tended to disappear and local organization to return to its traditional model of small scattered hamlets. The main exception was the village of Mobo built in 1971 by the river of that name due west from Iwaiwa, with immigrants from Kolu, Inam, Kirili, Onea and Yaniba. It attracted inhabitants for two reasons. On the one hand, in 1970 northern Garialand had been damaged by a serious earthquake, so that people were happy to move to an area that had not been affected. On the other, riverain life promised greater comforts than existence in the mountains.

Finally, the Madang–Usino highway seems to have had relatively little effect on local organization. Government officers expected that it would lead to a form of ribbon development. Yet, after several visits between 1975 and 1980, I was not persuaded that this had occurred. A few settlements along the route have moved a little closer to it and, as mentioned, some people have opened trade stores, but there has been no mass movement. Moreover, if it is successful, the Usino Council's current project of building feeder roads should encourage the people to remain in their own localities.

I now examine the theme I indicated above: the survival of the Garia sociocultural system (virtually all its values and beliefs, and most of its important customs) in the face of the pressures to which it has been subjected since the middle 1920s. In the next three chapters I concentrate on the general form of the sociopolitical structure, which, as I have continually stressed, is so supple that it has usually been able to adjust to the recurrent radical oscillations in local organization as long as the people have not been moved too far away from their permanent land interests. The Australian Administration's pre-war policy of regrouping small settlements as composite villages, probably unwittingly, did not greatly abuse this principle so that, although they preferred their own system of dispersed hamlets, the Garia could accept the new order with little resentment. The cargoists, however, ignored it: they lured the people too far away from their land. Hence, as soon as their promises of the imminent arrival of vast European wealth had been proved false, they could not hold together the swollen settlements for which they were responsible.

2

The Structural Form
of Human Society

For the Garia the cosmic order is an integrated system. As I have already remarked, they do not distinguish between the natural and the supernatural, and regard the cosmos as essentially terrestrial: their own small demesne together with those places outside it with which they have contact. Hence the total cosmic order that they conceive consists of two networks of relationships which they know or assert to exist within this geographical arena and of which man sees himself as the focal point: the objective and observable relationships between human beings themselves or the *actual sociopolitical structure;* and the subjective and putative relationships between men, gods, ghosts and other spirit-beings or *religion.* Although the people believe that they may have almost daily intercommunication with superhuman beings who live close to them on the earth, and although they use the same linguistic terms to describe the salient features of their relationships with them as they do for those between themselves, nevertheless, for the reasons already given, I describe these two conceptually intermeshed networks as if they were discrete.

I begin my investigation of this cosmic structure by describing in this chapter, first, its culturally accepted origins and, second, the form of one realm within it, human society, for which I set up a model initially divorced from much of its cultural content. Except for the next three sections, I set aside the investigation of the other realm, that of superhuman beings or religion, for the final chapters.

The Accepted Origins of the Cosmic Order

The Garia explain the origins of their cosmic order in a set of myths which tell how deities shaped the physical environment, created human beings, and invented social and material culture. They believe that, in a sense, the physical environment always existed, although they have vague myths for the appearance of the sun, moon and rainbow. Their initial concern was with the earth, which was originally bare rock except for a mound of soil on Mount Somau, guarded by the lizard god Sinatu and the python god Mubu, which had coiled itself around it. There was a rat under the soil seeking to burrow its way out. In doing so, it bit the python, which in its anger scattered the soil in all directions, so that virgin jungle (*urumo*) sprang up on the mountains and in the valleys. Human beings came into existence towards the west of Garialand, near the River Mobo, where a boulder was struggling to give birth to them. The snake goddess Obomwe took pity on it in its travail and herself performed the act of parturition. But she should not have intervened. Had she allowed the boulder to give birth in its own time, men and women would have been immortal. Through her haste she brought death as well as life into the world, so that she also presides over the three lands of the dead.

Thereafter other deities created social and material culture. Bush gods (*weisa po oite'u*) established their own domains, presiding normally over war, hunting and weather. Some have myths explaining their origins, while others are said just to have existed from the beginning. They attracted people to their domains, taught them their language (which they called Garia) and rules for kinship, marriage and land tenure, and in some cases, but not all, gave them descent names. Myths for the economy and important institutions are particularly detailed but lack chronological sequence. In no apparent order, other deities introduced artefacts, food plants, animals and vital customs. One set of deities invented the slit-gong, hand-drum, pottery and so forth; another set, taro, spinach, yam and other crops; another, pigs and dogs; and another, sorcery and the initiatory ceremonies. Deities from places outside Garialand, especially the coast, were periodically incorporated in the pantheon when they invented new dances which the people bought from other groups and then performed.

Yet the deities did not concern themselves solely with the genesis of the sociocultural system. They also showed men how to control it. In the period of antiquity each god or goddess appeared to human beings in dreams or even lived with them, teaching them four things: his or her open name; the secular procedures necessary to manufacture, grow, raise or perform his or her artefact, food plant, animal or ceremony; his or her myth of origin; and the secret of his or her power, the esoteric spell (usually based on his or her secret name), the repetition of which would ensure success in the relevant activity. This is another clear expression of the assumed integration of the total cosmic system to which I have referred in earlier contexts. Religion is important not merely as a form of explanation and validation: things are as they are because the gods made them so and hence they have to be right. Its role goes well beyond this: it is regarded as an essential force in everyday affairs. Ritual gives men the ability to create beneficial relationships with deities and spirits of the dead, harness their power, and thereby actuate the proper functioning of the cosmic order. This is the virtual monopoly of the leaders or big men (*kokai'apu,* Pidgin *bikpela man*), whose pre-eminence is seen to rest in large degree on their mastery of religious knowledge and who therefore belong, in a sense, to both realms of the cosmos and are regarded as its keystone. I elaborate this theme in Chapters 7 and 8.

Garia Society: the Problem of Structural Form

The problem in analysing Garia society stems from its lack of fixed territorial groups. Certainly it is possible to break up Garialand into a number of more or less discrete geographical divisions, the bush god domains. Yet these have little sociopolitical importance. The persons associated with a particular domain do not belong to any regular social category, are by no means invariably co-resident, and do not acknowledge automatic allegiance to each other. It is impossible to describe social structure and local organization simultaneously: indeed, it is essential to approach each separately. As I have mentioned and shall later argue in detail, local organization is not a function of any single feature of the social system, such as common land rights in a particular bush god domain or membership in a particular descent group. Populations of most settlements are irregular and unstable. They are aggregations of persons who are interrelated according to no set pattern — in some cases not interrelated at all — but who have come together because, at least for the time being, they have common economic interests in the same area or wish to associate with a particular leader. They often do not last very long: unless there are special reasons to the contrary, individuals move elsewhere as soon as they have exploited their economic interests or are attracted by another person. It is for this reason that I have already described local organization as an epiphenomenon of the interaction between the ego-centred networks of kinship, marriage and descent relationships which I call security circles, the rules of land tenure, and the influence of big men. These considerations govern the presentation of my argument. In this chapter I describe, first, the bush god domain and, second, the security circle.

The Bush God Domain

In Garialand every deity has a number of human devotees but, as is implicit in the previous paragraph, this in itself does not create a system of territorially defined political groups. None of these human associations has more than geographical significance. Certain deities are common to the whole population: the lizard Sinatu, the python Mubu, the snake goddess Obomwe, and the gods of betel-nut, sorcery and male initiation. They reflect cultural homogeneity but never reciprocal moral obligation or support. The same applies to deities presiding over material culture and the economy. Each has his or her sphere of influence but this does not delineate an exclusive territory because a man is not restricted to only one set of gods. For example, he may follow several taro goddesses or yam gods at the same time. Multiple spheres of influence and interest tend to cut across and neutralize each other. This, as will be seen, is a common Garia phenomenon that negates unquestioning allegiance in both realms of the cosmos.

Normally it might be supposed that the adherents of bush gods presiding over war, hunting, weather and nowadays football (a substitute for older forms of physical violence) would demonstrate this kind of unity. Yet this does not occur. There are twenty-five bush god domains, the approximate positions of which are marked on Map 2. The general pattern is for each domain to have only one senior deity, although there are two exceptions. In one case, there are two senior deities, Yabapunaku and Eimanaku, who are treated as equals. In the other, Pukusakunaku is said to have divided his domain into two areas, the northern supervised by Walalianaku and the southern by Yomanaku, although he retains final supremacy. Bush gods are the primary, but not the only, superhuman custodians in these domains. They delegate authority to minor deities to protect hamlets, potential hamlet sites, and nowadays village wards. When a hamlet's human inhabitants move to another site, they induce their local tutelary to go with them. Bush gods and tutelaries are said to have a variety of forms: men (but never women), py-

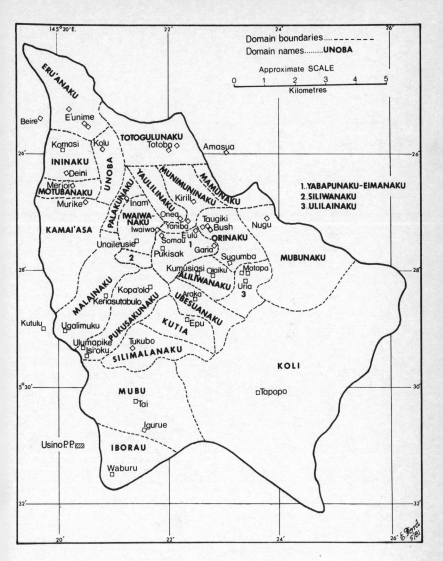

Map 2 Approximate positions of Garia bush god domains

thons, snakes, lizards, dogs or hawks (see Table 1). Men endeavour to secure their help either by invoking them audibly by their open names or, if they know them, by whispering or breathing their secret names as spells (see Chapter 8).

Table 1 Garia bush gods (see also Map 2)

Name	Corporeal form	Name	Corporeal form
Äliliwanaku	human	Munimuninaku	human
E'uruanaku	human	Orinaku	human
Iborau	snake	Palakunaku	human
Ininaku	human	Pukusakunaku	human
Iwaiwanaku	human	Silimalanaku	hawk
Kamai'asa	human	Siliwanaku	human
Koli	human	Totogulunaku	human
Kutia	hawk	Ubesuanaku	hawk
Malainaku	lizard	Ulilainaku	hawk
Mamunaku	dog	Unoba	hawk
Motubanaku	lizard	⎰ Yabapunaku	human
Mubu	python	⎱ Eimanaku	human
Mubunaku	python	Yaulilinaku	human

Each bush god domain is associated with a number of named cognatic stocks, of which there are about two hundred in all Garialand. Its total land area is divided into small strips, large blocks or huge tracts, each of which bears the name of one of these stocks. By the same token, the current inhabitants of a domain, however transitory, tend to be members of these stocks, although there are always exceptions, as will be clear in Chapter 4. Each domain may have from three to sixteen stock names associated with it and an average population of one hundred although, especially between the 1920s and 1950s, the northern domains have always been the most densely settled.

Nevertheless, despite the factors enumerated, members of cognatic stocks that have given their names to the land of any one bush god domain do not automatically owe one another political loyalty. Apart from acknowledging the custodianship of the bush god, they are not an exclusive group in any field of action, as is clear in a number of ways. First, they can be called members of the domain only in the loosest sense: some of them never live in it and those who do are by no means permanent residents. Second, they are neither an exogamous nor an endogamous group: with one exception (Malainaku, p. 120), they marry as much among themselves as with members of stocks with land in other domains. Third, they engage in no common activity: they do not all make gardens together, or hold communal hunts or fish drives. Fourth, they celebrate no common ritual to the bush god nor can they regard his support as spontaneous and guaranteed. They have to win it by their own individual ritual exercises: those who are most expert and assiduous can expect the greatest favours, while those who do not or cannot invoke him can expect no favours at all. I discuss this in detail in Chapter 8. In addition, some bush gods serve functions other than those already mentioned. For example, Yabapunaku presides over the Kanam dance and love philtres not only in his own domain but also in many others in northern Garialand. Fifth, domain boundaries are often vague. Unless they follow ridges and rivers, they may be so imprecise that some pieces of land are said to be under the protection of two or more bush gods. Sixth, especially in northern Garialand pieces of land bearing the name of a specific cognatic stock are not restricted to only one bush god domain. Of seventy-two stocks in the domains of Palakunaku, Iwainanaku, Yabapunaku-Eimanaku, Älili-wanaku, Yaulilinaku, Munimuninaku, Siliwanaku and Orinaku, twenty-four had land bearing their names in more than one domain: in most cases two, in several cases three, and in one case six. This situation is made more complex by a process of acquiring permanent land rights beyond normal patrilineal inheritance, which tends to fragment a man's personal holdings and disperse them through several domains. I describe this in Chapter 3.

Clearly, bush god domains are not the geographical framework of a system of conventional political groups. People associated with them through their landholdings do not feel constrained, through this common bond alone, to defend each other militarily or forensically, or to settle disputes among themselves by means of negotiation rather than bloodshed and lethal sorcery. Informants repeatedly insisted that, in major undertakings and conflicts, they would help other persons with land rights in their own domains only if they had personal ties with them based on kinship, marriage, descent or some other special partnership. Should circumstances warrant it, they would feel morally free to kill those not so linked to them equally within and outside their domains. Certainly it is technically possible for these purely interpersonal ties to be geographically so concentrated that all the current inhabitants of a domain are bound politically to each other, as was claimed to be true — or very nearly true — in twelve out of twenty-five cases in May 1975. Yet even this has little practical significance for two reasons. On the one hand, those who normally live in these twelve domains could never express their nominal solidarity in public because they had equally close relationships with people in neighbouring domains, which would inevitably divide their loyalties and force them to remain neutral in any foreseeable dispute. On the other, there are others who have rights in a domain but do not always live in it because of the dispersal of their land interests. They may not be related in any way to a number of the more permanent residents. Clearly this is a complex situation which I can explain more easily after I have presented the argument I have outlined: the structure of the security circle, followed by the principles of land tenure and the processes of local organization.

The Human Security Circle

As Garia express all political allegiances in terms of interpersonal ties rather than group membership, it is best to begin the analysis with the concept of ego's political region: the geographical arena in which he carries out his everyday affairs and which usually consists of several bush god domains. From his point of view, the human and superhuman inhabitants of this region can be classified as those who belong to his security circle and those who do not. For the present I am concerned almost entirely with his human or secular security circle and reserve discussion of his superhuman or putative security circle for the last two chapters.

The members of ego's human security circle themselves have no corporate identity. They are merely those persons with whom he has safe relationships and towards whom he should observe stringent rules governing marriage, diet and political obligation. The structure of the human security circle is a clear example of what Fortes (1970: 102) has called 'a kinship polity': it is based largely on kinship, descent and affinity, but also on special relationships created by common economic interests and residence, exchange, trade and initiation. I now define the forms of these relationships.

Kinship

The term for ego's kindred — all persons with whom he has or acknowledges genealogical relationships through every possible link both on his father's and on his mother's side — is *apunō*. In biological — although, as will appear, rather less in social — terms, the kindred is clearly bilateral. Kinship terminology (for male ego see Figure 3) is basically of the Iroquois type with a few modifications (cf. Scheffler 1971: 239). FZ and MB wife are equated with 'mother', while both FZ husband and MZ husband have a special term *asai,* and are treated almost as affines.

These terminological variations are of no great significance for the argument I present. Yet there are three rules of kinship usage that are vital for understanding certain processes within Garia social structure. First, siblings of the same sex address each other as 'brother' *(awai/amayai),* while those of the opposite sex address each other as 'sister' *(ugi).* Second, children of cross-cousins *(epei)* of the same sex address each other as 'sibling': as 'brother' *(awai/amayai)* or 'sister' *(ugi).* Third, children of cross-cousins *(epei)* of the opposite sex address each other as 'cross-cousins'. In all three cases, classificatory relationships are transmitted to subsequent generations by exactly the same principles as above. The three rules are important for both abstract structural form and land tenure. In the context of structural form, because

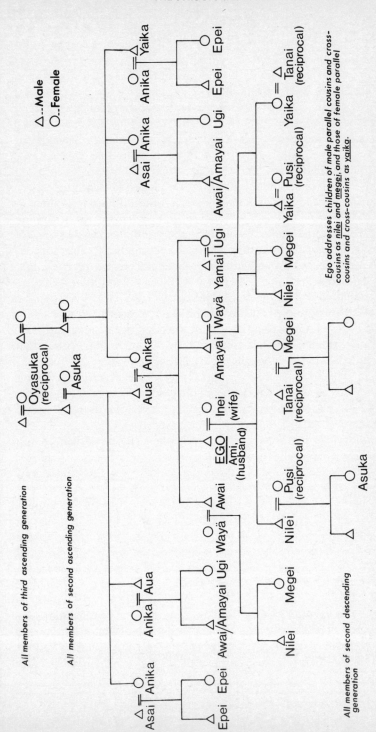

Figure 3 Kinship terminology

Garia society is intrinsically individualistic and flexible, and because the members of ego's security circle are invariably dispersed, he cannot reckon important relationships merely by referring to a group structure. Although he is helped by the system of descent names I have yet to describe, he must rely initially on what I shall call his personal kinship computer. He bases every relationship, especially when he is unclear about genealogical links, on the terms of address his own and the other party's forebears used towards each other. In the context of land tenure the second rule especially is important when ego acquires permanent usufructuary rights from outside the line of patrilineal inheritance.

It is difficult to determine precisely how many persons ego incorporates in his total social and biological kindred. As it is not a defined local group, he may include individuals in it or exclude them from it to suit his own convenience. For his social kindred — those members with whom he shares positive or effective relationships — the surest test is to count the personnel attending his funeral. I recorded several cases with about 300 present. Yet this number would not account for additional people — about 100 to 150 — with whom ego recognized tenuous genealogical ties but who may have felt no obligation to attend. This would expand his total biological as against his social kindred to 400 or even 450. Yet this also can be affected by his social status: as a leader or big man, he would be more likely than an ordinary person to be acknowledged by genealogically distant relatives. Obviously this would alter the proportion of his social as against his purely biological kin. The position can be made clearer by considering important subdivisions within ego's total kindred: patrilateral and matrilateral kin, or patrikin and matrikin; and different degrees and grades of consanguineal relationships.

Patrikin and *matrikin* are persons with whom ego has or claims to have genealogical ties, on the one hand through his father (including FZ children, etc.) and on the other through his mother (including MB children, MZ children, etc.). In everyday conversation Garia distinguish these two general categories as *auamana* (father's people) and *yaikamana* (mother's brother's people), although they say that, for strict accuracy, they should be broken down into subcategories: *awai/amayaimana* (brother people), *ugimana* (sister people), *epeimana* (cross-cousin people) and so forth. This endorses the essential individualism and cognatic character of Garia society despite the bias towards patriliny and patrilaterality.

Degrees and grades of kinship. Within the total kindred ego distinguishes six degrees of relationship: true or immediate *(meru,* Pidgin *tiru);* close *(tō-muloni,* Pidgin *kilostu);* quite close *(tōmuloni aiyaka,* Pidgin *kilostu liklik);* quite distant *(etauloni aiyaka,* Pidgin *longwei liklik);* distant *(etauloni,* Pidgin *longwei);* and very distant *(etauloni meru,* Pidgin *longwei tumas).* Beyond the last degree are unrelated persons *(apu pasi* or *etau'apu,* Pidgin *narapela man tiru).*

In theory Garia reckon degrees of kinship genealogically but after a certain stage find accuracy impossible. Their recordable genealogies are shallow, spanning normally no more than five generations: ego, his F, FF, S and SS. Moreover, the personal names of members of the second ascending generation and above are forbidden *(ese'u,* Pidgin *tambu)* to him: he should never mention them, although he may recall outstanding individuals by nicknames. Thus ego's parents teach him personal names from their own fathers' generation and perhaps nicknames from that of their fathers' fathers but rarely from above that level. Indeed, most names tend to disappear at the level of the third ascending generation, after which genealogical knowledge is bound to be less accurate. Yet, as will be seen, especially where land rights are involved, ego may remember or claim relationships with certain people through marriages in the third, fourth and perhaps fifth ascending generation, even though he does not know the true names or the nicknames of those who contracted them. This is paralleled by beliefs about the spirits of the dead. I discuss the whole topic later.

Despite genealogical inaccuracies and even legerdemain above the second ascending generation, in close discussion, informants gave me the following definitions of degrees of kinship:

1. *True* or *immediate:* all ego's and his mother's traceable agnates; his FZ children and MZ children; and, in special circumstances, all cognates linked to him by marriages in the second ascending generation.

2. *Close:* all cognates linked to ego by marriages in the second ascending generation, although, in special circumstances, those so linked from the level of the third may be included.

3. *Quite close:* all cognates whom ego claims through marriages in the third and, ideally, fourth ascending generations, in which genealogical ties are remembered, even though relevant personal names have been lost.

4. *Quite distant:* all persons whom ego presumes as cognates through marriages in the fifth and perhaps fourth ascending generations.

5 and 6. *Distant* and *very distant* cannot be tabulated even by the foregoing lax standards. They account for persons with whom ego acknowledges vestigial kinship ties through marriages above the fifth or fourth ascending generation.

These definitions are essentially academic. As they shade over into each other, nobody could use them in everyday situations without time-consuming debate. In general conversation Garia habitually refer to two broader grades of kinship: the *close* and the *distant*. The *close grade* incorporates those degrees designated as *true* or *immediate*, *close* and *quite close* (up to the third and, ideally, fourth ascending generations), and the *distant grade* those designated as *quite distant*, *distant* and *very distant* (beyond the fourth or third ascending generation) (see Figure 4).

Ego regards kinsmen of the close grade as the core of his security circle and must observe towards them the rules of behaviour to which I have already alluded. He may not marry among them or eat pigs, dogs, fowls and casso-

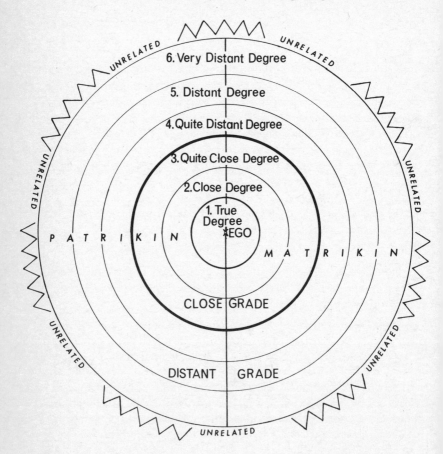

Figure 4 The total kindred

waries they have raised. He must treat those among them he addresses as 'mother's brother' with the greatest respect, never using their personal names, and those he classifies as matrilateral 'cross-cousins' with considerable deference, eschewing their personal names as often as he can. He must avoid all serious physical and psychological violence towards kinsmen of the close grade, never killing them with weapons or sorcery, and never shaming them in any way. In return, he should expect only support and co-operation from them, and never suspect them of plotting his own death by any means. Should he ever have to retaliate against them, he should never go beyond fist- or stick-fighting and mild wounding (especially with a multipronged arrow) or weak sorcery (designed to cause illness but not death).

Ego does not regard kinsmen of the distant grade as members of his security circle unless, for reasons of self-interest, he incorporates some of them in ways I have yet to describe. He is not expected to observe towards them the foregoing rules of behaviour and counts them as little different from totally unrelated persons: he may intermarry with them, eat their livestock, treat them without deference, and kill and shame them at will. At the frontier of the close grade of the kindred, there is a barrier beyond which relationships, unless artificially reinforced, are valueless. It is here that suspicion creeps in and serious quarrels are most likely to erupt.

In the foregoing account there are two obvious points. First, unlike a unilineal descent group, a kindred exists only in relation to a true sibling set. Patrilateral parallel cousins are differentiated by their respective matrikin, matrilateral parallel cousins by their respective patrikin, and so forth. Second, viewed chronologically, relationships within the kindred change every generation. For his son, ego's own *true* or *immediate, close* and *quite close* kin become respectively *close, quite close* and *quite distant*. In each generation, kinship ties are lost and have to be replaced. I discuss this process in greater detail in later contexts.

Descent

That the social, as against the purely biological, kindred is not fully bilateral (cf. Freeman 1961) can be seen in the context of the descent system which, while endorsing the cognatic ties ego inherits from both his father and his mother, ultimately has the manifest agnatic and patrilateral bias I have mentioned. Ego's kindred is divided into a number of cognatic stocks *(nō)*, whose members are generally dispersed throughout several bush god domains and each of which has what I have already described as its own descent name, in some cases derived from a bush god and in others from a special experience.

Ego's membership in a cognatic stock differs from that in a unilineal descent group in that he may trace it through both male and female links, and through either his father or his mother. A stock cannot be exclusive. Ego claims rights to as many descent names or membership in as many stocks as he can recall (cf. Fox 1967: 150; Fortes 1970: 268 passim). Ideally, he should have exact knowledge of eight descent names up to the third ascending generation (specific to his F, FM, FFM, FMM, M, MFM, MM and MMM) and at least recognize others in the fourth (specific to his FFFM, FFMM, FMFM, FMMM, MMFM and MMMM), the last frontier of the close grade of his kindred. In fact, genealogical knowledge tends to correlate with social status. Most people can place five, and the best genealogists —

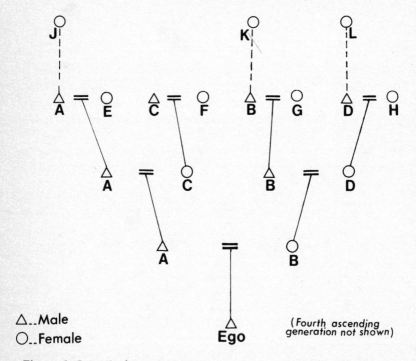

△..Male
○..Female

Ego

(Fourth ascending generation not shown)

Figure 5 Cognatic descent names

A, B, C etc. represent names of cognatic descent groups or stocks. Dotted lines indicate claimed descent through an unknown number of generations. Ideally, ego should remember and claim membership in A, E, C, F, B, G, D and H. In fact, he may not know F, H and possibly G. Yet he may recall vaguely that women of J, K and L came into his genealogy an indeterminate number of generations ago. Should the necessity arise, he may pretend that his relationships with living members of these stocks are still close.

normally big men — six or seven, descent names accurately but are unsure of the others. As mentioned, the pattern varies to suit political interests: ego tends to foster or ignore ties with more remote stocks according to convenience (see Figure 5).

Within the cognatic stock there are two clearly defined categories: the *sawaibopi* and *uibopi*. The *sawaibopi* ('people from males') are those recognized as agnates: in most cases they can trace descent exclusively through males from a known common ancestor. The *uibopi* ('people from females') are the non-agnatic cognates, who trace membership in the stock *at some stage* through females and are, of course, agnates in other stocks. It is essentially in the context of the relationship between *sawaibopi* and *uibopi* that Garia social structure expresses the chameleonic nature to which I have continually referred and which creates considerable terminological problems. To put these problems in clearer perspective I describe *sawaibopi-uibopi* relationships in purely factual terms, in the contexts of both ideal structural form and also everyday situations. I then present the terms by which I define these relationships.

In formal structural terms there are two differences in status between agnates and non-agnatic cognates within a stock. First, relationships between them change every generation. In theory, and very largely in practice, the status of agnates is not affected by the passage of time. They have the perpetual right to use the stock's descent name and, in most cases, use it as their primary appellative. Hence ego always regards his agnates as belonging to the true degree of his kindred. In most cases this poses no problem: because of the shallowness of genealogies, agnates are usually only a set of parallel cousins and their children. Yet, between 1949 and 1953, in at least five cases in northern Garialand precise agnatic links could not be remembered: not all persons claiming the same patrilineal descent name could identify a single, known common ancestor, although they still regarded each other as true agnates. In one case (see Genealogy 4), Nali agnates in Yabapunaku-Eimanaku domain adopted immigrants from Koli and gave them their descent name. I regard these as cases of linked agnates and discuss them in a later context.

The status of non-agnatic cognates in the stock, however, has to be affected by time. It cannot be perpetual as is that of agnates. Relationships between the two categories begin as true but, after each subsequent generation, gradually become more remote. They remain in the close grade of ego's kindred for about four generations, during which non-agnatic cognates may freely use the stock's descent name and are acknowledged as members of the security circles of all other persons claiming the same privilege. Thereafter they weaken as the relevant link marriages pass into the distant grade and are gradually forgotten unless, as already suggested, they are perpetuated for any particular reason.

Second, agnates within the stock enjoy special sociopolitical privileges denied to non-agnatic cognates. They jointly exercise automatic and normally exclusive guardian rights over the land areas (and, in theory, the agricultural ritual spells) bearing its name. Non-agnatic cognates may always ask for temporary rights of access, which, in return for payments of pigs and other valuables to the agnates, they may change fairly quickly into permanent usufructuary rights but not those of guardianship for several generations. In this context and for this period they remain clients of the agnates. I discuss this fully in Chapters 3, 5 and 7.

In everyday affairs the formal difference in status between agnates and non-agnatic cognates within a stock is often ignored. This relates to the Garia concept of 'line' (*kinipu*, Pidgin *lain*), which is cognatic or associational rather than strictly agnatic. Ego's need is to establish as wide a human security circle as he can, so that in tracing a 'line' (or any practical relationship) he uses every available genealogical or associational link. He says of all close patrikin and matrikin: 'We are all one blood (*yaui*), one kindred (*apunō*), and one "line" (*kinipu*)'. He may extend the concept of 'line' to incorporate traditionally important ties based on co-operation rather than genealogy and also recent innovations: he may join the 'line' of a popular village headman, councillor, government officer, missionary, or even anthropologist. In this general context, where they exist, common descent names are most important for programming what I have called ego's kinship computer: they act as mnemonics or signposts for interpersonal kinship ties. Thus a small boy Kiniwa said to me of another lad Miowa: 'He is my "cross-cousin",[1] for we two are Wailagime'. Kiniwa was a Sui agnate (Kutia domain)[2] but his mother's mother's mother, like Miowa himself, was a Wailagime agnate (Munimuninaku and Yabapunaku-Eimanaku domains). His mother and Miowa's father were true cross-cousins. By Iroquois rules, he and Miowa continued this relationship. Yet in this conversation he did not bother to mention his agnatic status in Sui. In the context of his relationship with Miowa only their common Wailagime link was important.

This technique of tracing relationships becomes more important when precise genealogical knowledge is lacking. Labaia [Mosoli][3] of Yabapunaku-Eimanaku domain said of Yuli [Sui] of Kutia domain: 'We are "brothers" — we two are Kebuli'. The relationship stemmed from two women, Naluasi and Uywasi, Kebuli agnates from Ulilainaku domain. Two generations previously, one had married Sui and the other Mosoli. Although nobody could specify the exact link between them, they were regarded as 'sisters', so that Labaia and Yuli could recognize a fraternal bond (see Genealogy 1).

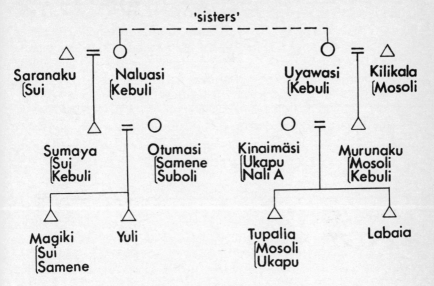

Genealogy 1   Sui-Mosoli link through Kebuli

Naluasi and Uyawasi [Kebuli] were classified as 'sisters'. Thus Sumaya [Sui] and Murunaku [Mosoli] were classified as 'brothers' and, in the context of their relationship to each other, said that they were Kebuli. Likewise, in the next generation, Magiki, Yuli, Tupalia and Labaia were all Kebuli 'brothers'.

The broad equivalence attributed to agnation and cognation in these routine situations was stressed by Labaia: 'If the Mosoli "line" come to me, I am Mosoli; if the Ukapu "line" come to me, I am Ukapu; if the Kebuli "line" come to me, I am Kebuli; and if the Siga "line" come to me I am Siga'. Mosoli and Ukapu were the cognatic stocks of which his father and mother respectively were agnates. He inherited Kebuli from his father's mother and also, through his father, a link with Siga, which he asserted to be close because of his interest in its land, although he could not trace it accurately. It is hardly surprising, therefore, that people juggle descent names and kin ties to their own advantage. When Labaia's wife Mutäriasi ran away to her quite close Ilunō patrikin in Nugu (Mubunaku domain), he shrewdly asked Obenaku [Yaukai] of Yabapunaku-Eimanaku domain, his 'brother' through a Mosoli link, to get her back. On his father's side, Obenaku had a distant cognatic link with Ilunō and, when he arrived in Nugu, he brazenly presented himself as a close 'brother' of Mutäriasi's kinsmen, thereby facilitating negotiations. In this context it is important to note the phenomenon of dual relationships. As cognatic stocks intermesh and kindreds intersect, ego must belong to security circles of many different people. Thus he may be related to some people through both his father and his mother at the same time, being able to call them, for instance, either 'brother' or 'cross-cousin' as he feels appropriate. Especially in cases of not very close relationships, this gives him added scope for manipulation. The importance of this emerges later.

The problem, therefore, is to find terms for social categories that are never discrete. Ego's social identity is invariably elusive. For a start, he is an agnate in one cognatic stock and a non-agnatic cognate in many others. In the language of modern politics he can wear any one of many hats. On the one hand, as an individual agnate or non-agnatic cognate he can be relatively free-ranging, constrained only by interpersonal kinship ties. On the other, as an agnate within a cognatic stock, he belongs to a body that can express itself as a mini-collective: the *sawaibopi* in respect of their joint guardian rights over land and ritual secrets bearing their patrilineal descent name, their use of their patrilineal descent name as a primary appellative, and their insistence that relationships between themselves are always of the true degree despite the lack of precise genealogical knowledge. Terminology has to be sufficiently flexible to meet all these contingencies.

The terms I have selected are intended to emphasize ego's roles in two contexts within the cognatic stock: as an individual and as a member of a mini-collective. In the first context, by cognates I mean all members of the stock in the normal sense: those descended exclusively from males (*sawaibopi*) and those descended at some stage from females (*uibopi*). By agnates I mean of course the *sawaibopi*, especially in their capacity as free-ranging individuals, and I designate as primary the cognatic stock in which ego is an agnate. For the *uibopi* I use a relatively new term, which is less clumsy than 'non-agnatic cognates' and which I take from Fortes (1970: 268): enates (Latin *enati*),[4] those born outside the patriline, towards which, despite emphasis on cognation, Garia society still has an obvious bias.

In the second context, that of the mini-collective, I use the term patrilineage as a synonym for agnates. (Where genealogical ties between sets of agnates sharing the same patronym and claiming a common patrilineal origin are unknown, I use the term linked patrilineage.) My use of the term patrilineage is unconventional. First, in most unilineal societies, patrilineages are said to express themselves as corporate groups in many fields of action, and especially through common residence. The *sawaibopi* are corporate only in respect of their guardian rights to land and ritual and, as will be seen, are often residentially dispersed. Yet I do not regard this as a serious obstacle. In many societies the patriclan is regarded as the patrilineage writ large, although its members may be scattered in several different settlements. Why should we require criteria for one of these groups that we ignore for the other?

Second, patrilineages are normally represented as easily separable segments within ego's kindred, themselves capable of internal fission. The *sawaibopi* are embedded — enmeshed — in formally recognized cognatic groups, which effectively prevent this process, a factor that worried Leach (1956). Yet this is by no means out of keeping with the situation in other parts of Papua New Guinea, as Barnes (1962), Langness (1972) and others have indicated (cf. also Lawrence 1971a). Hence I believe that the term patrilineage is applicable to the *sawaibopi* in respect of their corporate guardian rights over land and ritual, on which they insist most jealously. I illustrate ego's positions as cognate, agnate, enate and member of a patrilineage in Figure 6.[5]

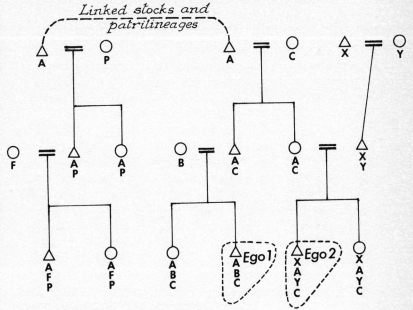

Figure 6 Stock and patrilineage membership

Ego 1 is a cognate in linked stock A (his primary stock), and also in stocks B and C. He is an agnate in A (also his linked patrilineage), and an enate in B and C. He regards both sections of A as equally close to him. Ego 2 is a cognate in X (his primary stock), and also in Y, linked stock A, and C. He is an agnate in X (also his patrilineage), and an enate in C, Y and A.

Finally, the latitude of these definitions accentuates an issue that has been implicit in the argument so far. The close grade of ego's kindred may be conceived in two ways: in terms of free-ranging individualism, as a network of intermeshing cognatic stocks each with a seemingly nominal agnatic kernel; and, in terms of the mini-collective, as a number of patrilineages held together by the bridging enatic links associated with them. It must be regarded not as exclusively only one of these paradigms but as both of them at different times to suit the two contexts I have already specified: ordinary everyday situations on the one hand, and the protection of economic and religious property on the other.

Affinity

Every Garia male aims to marry and even to be polygynous: to have more than one wife is the mark of a leader or big man. The social achievement is matched by calculated economic advantages: additional wives can plant more garden plots, thereby diversifying their husband's food supply, ensuring it against incursions of wild pig and landslides, and enabling him to be prominent in pig exchanges. Most polygynists have two wives, although the ambitious aspire to more. I discuss three aspects of marriage: the social range within which ego may marry; rules of conduct (bride price and respect behaviour) between affines; and the importance of marriage for the structure of the security circle.

Men usually marry in their early twenties and women in their late teens. What is more important, Garia represent those Papua New Guinean peoples who say: 'We marry among those whom we fight' (cf. Berndt 1964; Lawrence 1971a). Provided that she does not belong to his security circle, ego may marry any girl from within or outside the bush god domains in which he lives or has land rights. Ideally she should not come from the close grade of his kindred or have an immediate consanguineal tie with any person with whom he has one of the special relationships to be described. Inevitably, because it is difficult to be precise about the border between the close and distant grades of kinship for the reasons already given, the stated rule is sometimes bent. Even so, in normal situations, ego selects a wife from among people who are at the outset potentially hostile to him and with whom he is likely to have his most serious disputes.

Otherwise, ego is not restricted to any category of kin: he may marry any distant 'sister', 'cross-cousin' and so forth. Yet, on two grounds, he has one preference: for a girl who belongs to the quite distant degree of his kindred and lives within his political region. First, if she comes from just beyond his security circle, her kinsmen may be more likely to remember that his and their forebears once had a close relationship, and so respect their new tie of affinity. Second, if she comes from an area geographically close, his sons' immediate matrikin will not live so far away that they cannot afford them additional economic and political security. If they need to do so, his sons may purchase permanent usufructuary land and ritual rights from their mother's brothers and, of course, always depend on them for support in serious quarrels. Most marriages — certainly first marriages — follow this pattern.

Despite these precautions, particularly in its initial stage, marriage is always an imponderable relationship which has to be reinforced by special rules of conduct, above all two institutions that serve to incorporate ego's affines within his security circle: marriage payments and respect behaviour. This applies equally to both marriages between single spouses and those involving widows and widowers.

Marriage represents a major and prolonged economic burden that a young man cannot shoulder on his own. Not only when his bride first comes to him but also for many years thereafter he has to send his immediate and close affines successive instalments of bride price. When the initial negotiations have been completed, helped by close patrikin and matrikin, he organizes the first payment: a pig, taro, cooked food, clay pots, wooden plates and bowls, dance ornaments and, since the 1930s, money. On the appointed day his father and brothers hand it over in return for the girl, while he absents himself. Her father and brothers then distribute it to her kinsmen to pay off outstanding debts, although they must ensure that a good share goes to her matrikin in recognition of their interest in her in the past and of the fact that, except in special circumstances discussed later, they are equally her husband's affines. In some cases, the first instalment is handed over in two equal parts to save the girl's father having to make an embarrassing distribution.

The acceptance of this initial payment is tantamount to the contract, but does not foreshadow the immediate consummation, of the marriage. For about a year the bride has only marginal relations with her husband, who is supposed still to observe initiatory taboos (see Chapter 7). She lives apart from him, in his mother's house, and may not have prolonged contact with him or even cook his food. At the end of this period the couple start to cohabit. As already indicated, the husband must continue payments to his affines: after the birth of each child, a fowl, cooked food, and one or two clay pots or wooden plates to his wife's parents or brothers, thereby establishing his parental rights; and further instalments of normal bride price, in all about ten pigs, making sure that they are widely distributed throughout his wife's total kindred. Moreover, if he wishes to help his sons acquire permanent usufructuary rights on their mother's (his wife's) brothers' land, he may have to provide or initiate about six more payments of this kind (see Chapter 3).

Affinal respect behaviour begins with betrothal. The bridegroom and his fiancée's kin treat each other with the greatest restraint, expressing their relationship in terms of mutual embarrassment and shame, certainly until the marriage is well established. As noted, the bridegroom does not attend the presentation of the first instalment of his bride price. He avoids close dealings with his affines until he has sent them the second and, when he does at last mix with them, he must never use their personal names, or joke with them or at their expense. He should not share tobacco or betel-nut with them or use their lime containers. He must never eat certain foods that they have cooked, especially pandanus. He should never eat any pig, dog, fowl or cassowary that they have raised. The small payments made after the birth of each child are intended also to cleanse his shame *(maya kolowobu,* Pidgin *wasim sem)* for having impregnated their kinswoman. Above all, he must never humiliate or offend them: to fight or use sorcery against them is unthinkable. They, of course, should behave towards him in the same way.

Rules for second marriages, especially those with widows *(oyo),* on which I concentrate, are more complex, for there is a wider social range of prohibition. The same code as for first marriages still applies: the second husband, like the first, should not belong to the widow's close grade of kindred, whose members become his affines in the usual way. Moreover, there is no sororate or levirate in any sense. Ego should not wed any female affine: either a close relative of his first wife or the widow of any member of his security circle. Ideally, he should marry a widow to whom, and to whose deceased husband, he has no close consanguineal or affinal links.

In a properly contracted second marriage the prospective husband should negotiate through a neutral go-between with the closest kinsmen of the deceased, who now claim full rights over the widow. If they accept him he becomes their secondary affine *(oyopei),* a status associated with the greatest formality. The main content of the new relationship is once again prestation reinforced by extreme deference. Over the next few years ego should send his secondary affines three or four marriage payments and always observe towards them, as well as his new wife's close kin, the respect behaviour I have previously described. In particular, he should avoid meeting his secondary affines until he has sent an instalment of bride price, and he should never plant gardens near theirs — certainly in areas where the first husband worked — while the marriage is still new. Breach of this convention may anger the dead man's ghost, who will cause wild pig or landslides to destroy the culprit's crop. Yet, provided that he observes the code, he may eventually meet his secondary affines with some confidence and even plant his gardens near theirs.

Some second marriages, however, do not proceed along these lines. The new husband may elope with the widow to the anger of the first husband's kin, who may do nothing to retrieve her but are expected to resort to sorcery. The couple lead a precarious existence in remote bush hamlets until the second husband can persuade his kin to help him assemble bride wealth and send it to the first husband's closest relatives. The dead man's brothers' reaction depends on the new husband's standing. If he is a big man with a reputation for sorcery, they will comply with a good grace. Otherwise they will prevaricate until they see advantage in ending the quarrel. Yet, as in the case of first marriages, once the first payment has been accepted, the new relationship is progressively established. Thereafter the couple have to reckon only with the ghost of the first husband if they plant their gardens too close to his land. They have to deal with this issue according to events as they occur, as will be seen later.

As is implicit in the above discussion, Garia practices endorse the usual interpretation of marriage payments and respect behaviour: that marriage payments help create a reciprocal relationship between persons previously hostile or ambivalent towards one another (husband and wife's kin, second husband and first husband's kin), so that the two parties are now mutually obliged; and that respect behaviour forces affines to treat each other carefully and avoid conduct that could disrupt the marriage. Garia recognize that in all marriages the crucial moment is the acceptance of the first instalment of bride price. If this takes place and subsequent payments are maintained, the recipients (a first wife's or a first husband's kin) praise the husband and relax in his company. Although they still avoid personal names, middle-aged affines often become warmly attached to one another, planting gardens together, and even sharing tobacco and betel-nut. Yet affinal respect is never entirely eradicated and continues into the next generation: especially if he wishes to purchase usufructuary land rights from them, ego must defer to his mother's brothers and matrilateral cross-cousins in ways I discuss in Chapter 3.

With his marriage or marriages on a sound, if formal, basis, ego includes both his primary and his secondary affines in his security circle. Nevertheless, especially if he is a polygynist, he is bound to weigh against the additional safety they afford him the economic and social burden they can impose. He has to send them regular instalments of bride price, making sure that they all get a share, and he can never completely unbend in their presence. As, technically, they include all the close grade kinsmen (both patrilateral and matrilateral) of his wives and their previous husbands, they may represent a large sector of a small population. One informant, about to marry a widow, listed for me in confidence forty-one persons whom he should soon treat as secondary affines. Yet there is an obvious means of escape from the embarrassment this may impose: the dual relationships to which I have already referred and because of which, when offered a choice of personal ties, the individual may select the one he finds more convenient for any particular situation. A husband is thus able to shed a number of his nominal affines on the grounds that, through other links, they are already his close kin. Neither he nor they wish to change steady, easy-going relationships into uncomfortable affinal bonds. For example, Umugigi [Yaukai] of Yabapunaku-Eimanaku domain married Nunulime [Keisibu] of Äliliwanaku. There are two linked sections of Keisibu agnates (patrilineage): that of Oi'asa and that of Kopenau-Muguliba (see Genealogy 8). Nunulime belonged to the Oi'asa section, so that Umugigi had to treat its members and close enates as affines. But, unlike the Oi'asa section, the Kopenau-Muguliba section of Keisibu claimed a close enatic link to Yaukai. Umugigi had grown up with its members, whom he addressed as 'father', 'brother' and 'son'. He could not have married one of their girls, and he did not wish to behave towards them as if they were strict affines. Hence he reduced respect behaviour towards them to a minimum, avoiding personal names as often as he could, but addressing them as 'father', 'brother' and 'son', planting gardens with them and joining them in all normal activities.

Special relationships

In this section, I can do no more than describe the nature of the special relationships which ego may either inherit or create and which extend the range of his security circle. I discuss their cultural content in later contexts.

Bush brothers (*sanawa'omei*) are persons with whom ego has common interests in land, although the precise form of the relationship varies between northern and southern Garialand because of differences in the patterns of holdings, which I analyse in Chapter 3. In either case, he treats bush brothers as the equivalent of kinsmen of the close grade on the principle that 'one bush is like one blood' (*kilen saum kilen yaui sie*). He should observe towards them exactly the same rules of behaviour, avoiding intermarriage, eating livestock, and serious feuding, and supporting them whenever he can.

Although inclusion within a bush god domain in itself has no political significance, close common residence and agricultural co-operation may create new, even if transient, relationships. As already said, the population of even a small hamlet may be socially heterogeneous and contain persons not interrelated in any way. Ego should treat as close kin all those distantly related or unrelated individuals living in his hamlet or, after the 1920s, named village ward. (This does not include temporary inhabitants of other wards.) He calls them *weise'omei* ('hamlet brothers'), does not eat their livestock, and helps them when in trouble. In most cases the tie lasts only while the parties live together — perhaps only one or two years, after which they may move to different settlements. Hence it is unlikely to impose a ban on intermarriage. By the same token, ego has comparable, but even less formal, relationships with distantly related or unrelated members of his garden teams, which I discuss on pp. 84-5 below.

Exchange partners (*sawaya* and *nalaya*) are persons to whom ego has sent and from whom he has received domestic pigs, food and valuables. I describe the significance of the Garia terms in Chapter 5. What is immediately important is that ego deliberately creates these partnerships sometimes with close kin but as often as he can with distant kin and unrelated persons to gain political advantage. His aim is to reinforce and extend his security circle by including in it especially influential big men. He should not marry the immediate kin of his partners and, should they wish to perpetuate the tie, his sons should observe the same restriction.

Trade partners (*amai*) are those individuals with whom ego exchanges the artefacts, and who form part of the network of interpersonal links to Usino, the Naru, Bogati and Madang, which I described in Chapter 1.[6] In settlements near his own, ego's partners may be close kinsmen or bush brothers but farther afield they are not related to him. He includes these men in his security circle: although he is not forbidden to intermarry with them or eat their livestock he is bound always to support them in any crisis. He inherits partnerships from his father but may always create new ones. In the past he met partners in areas very remote from his own, with whom he had only secondary relationships, only if he were prepared to make the dangerous journey outside his true political region and had enough contacts along the route to protect and feed him. With modern administration this situation no longer obtains.

Initiatory relationships are created when boys are introduced to the Male Cult between late childhood and marriage (see Chapter 7). The terms of address are: *mali'omei*—those who wear the bark-girdle (*mali*) for the first time together; *sagomei*—those who have their penes incised and are trained in sorcery together by the same expert; *esiapei*—a reciprocal term between initiands and those who train them in sorcery, incise their penes, and dress them in bark-girdles for the first time; and *nawe'omei* — those who eat a certain type of ritually prepared food together. As initiands are recruited from a wide neighbourhood, a boy may go through the ceremonies with both related and unrelated persons. Moreover, with the possible exception of the Nalisägege,[7] ritual experts (*esiapei*) should not be immediate kin to initiands and, if their services are highly regarded, they may initiate many boys with whom they have no prior connexion. Thus, where initiatory relationships do not correspond with and strengthen already existing ties, new persons (ritual experts and fellow initiates) enter ego's security circle. These bonds preclude intermarriage with immediate kin, eating livestock, the use of personal names (except when absolutely necessary) and conflict of any kind. They enjoin the strongest mutual support.

Summary: a Model of Garia Society

So far I have concentrated on the parts of Garia society. In the next two stages of my argument I attempt to show, first, how they are articulated as a model and, second, how this model functions. Of the two structural features I have discussed, the bush god domain is politically unimportant: it merely places ego territorially, indicating where he has land rights and is therefore likely to live at different times. Indeed, political obligation and action are the function of the other feature, the ego-centred security circle, whose members are normally dispersed throughout a number of bush god domains. I now consider the security circle's internal structure and the distribution of its members.

Although it can be described synchronically, the structure of the security circle must not be regarded as static. It must be examined also diachronically. Viewed synchronically, it consists of the three general categories I have defined — close kinsmen, affines, and persons in special relationships — but, viewed diachronically, it has certain genealogical processes that are repeated in the field of social action and are echoed also in religious belief. For the purposes of this analysis, I concentrate on the kindred, the close grade of which accounts for a large part of ego's security circle.

It is easier to tabulate the members of the close grade of ego's kindred in terms of the second of the two conceptions of it offered previously: as a number of patrilineages held together by the bridging enatic links associated with them. Ideally — or at their widest formally recognized range — patrikin and matrikin of the close grade consist of:

1. *Patrikin:* ego's own patrilineage and members of other patrilineages enatically linked to it to the level of the fourth ascending generation — Z children, FZ descendants, FFZ descendants, FFFZ descendants and FFFFZ descendants; patrilineages to which ego is enatically linked through his father up to the level of the fourth ascending generation —those of FM, FFM, FFFM, FMM, FFMM, FMFM and FMMM; and persons who share with him enatic links to patrilineages on his father's side up to the level of the fourth ascending generation.

2. *Matrikin:* patrilineages to which ego is enatically linked through his mother up to the level of the fourth ascending generation — M, MFM, MM, MMFM and MMMM — and persons who share with him enatic links to these patrilineages.

As noted, the actual pattern is never so full or exact because people are vague about enatic ties in the fourth ascending generation — especially to their FFMM, FMFM, FMMM, MMFM and MMMM patrilineages. Of ego's affines, it is necessary only to repeat that they should come from outside this structure — from the distant grade, and preferably the quite distant degree, of his kindred.

A diachronic analysis of ego's security circle, especially of the close grade of his kindred and affines, emphasizes its essentially ephemeral nature. As I have argued, it has no corporate identity, for it exists in relation to him and his siblings alone. This can be seen by reconsidering briefly relationships between agnates and enates — or the patrilineage and the enates linked to it through women — within the cognatic stock over several generations, in both ideal and actual terms.

In ideal terms, although the patrilineage (agnates) always remains the kernel of the security circles of ego and his patrilineal descendants, with each new generation there is a change in the enatic and affinal links of its members: the patrilineages enatically and affinally linked to them and those to which they are so linked. Thus, because the relationship between a patrilineage (agnates) and its enates starts as immediate but then becomes progressively close, quite close, and then quite distant (unless it is rehabilitated for special purposes), in each generation, several descent names and corresponding enatic ties in the fourth ascending generation disappear from ego's son's security circle. For example, the descendants of ego's FFFFZ and the patrilineages of his FFMM, FMFM and FMMM (plus other persons sharing enatic links to them) move into the distant grade of his son's kindred, leaving a gap in its close grade. But, if marriages have been contracted at the correct social range, this is filled by ego's matrikin, who become part of his son's patrikin, although they in turn leave another gap that has to be filled by his affines, who become his son's matrikin (cf. Brown, D. J. J. 1980). The process is one of descent names continually passing into, through and out of the close grade of the kindred. Finally, although bush brotherhood and trade relationships, which fathers normally transmit to their sons, should be as permanent as agnatic ties, exchange partnerships (unless deliberately perpetuated in the next generation) and initiatory relationships last only for the lifetime of the individuals concerned (see Figure 7).[8]

In actual terms this process is less regular than the foregoing theoretical analysis suggests, because of the lack of precise genealogical knowledge at the borderline between the two grades of the kindred. For example, in Genealogy 2, Watutu [Sogumu] of Iwaiwanaku domain, one of the best local genealogists, could place accurately six descent names up to the fourth ascending generation. In circumstances I describe later, he could name a sev-

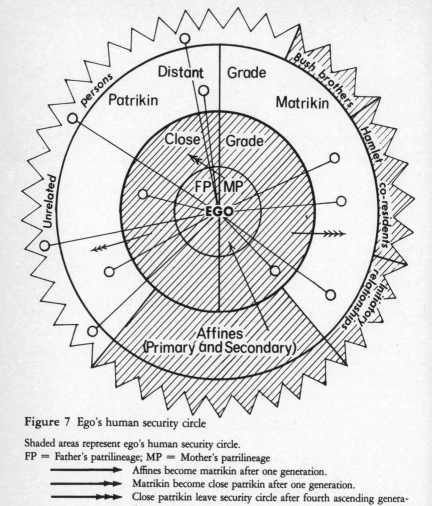

Figure 7 Ego's human security circle

Shaded areas represent ego's human security circle.

FP = Father's patrilineage; MP = Mother's patrilineage

————————▶ Affines become matrikin after one generation.

————————▶▶ Matrikin become close patrikin after one generation.

————————▶▶▶ Close patrikin leave security circle after fourth ascending generation.

————————▶▶▶▶ Close matrikin leave security circle after fourth ascending generation.

————————O Ego's exchange and trade partners.

enth, Oyesinō, at the level of the fifth. In each case, his memory was kept firm by his rights to land and ritual formulae bearing these seven descent names. Yet his parallel cousins Äbalia and Wawaku, who were men of little account, had far less genealogical expertise. In the next generation Labi and Naguni had begun to forget their link with Oyesinō and regard those with Asina and Tulua as somewhat remote.

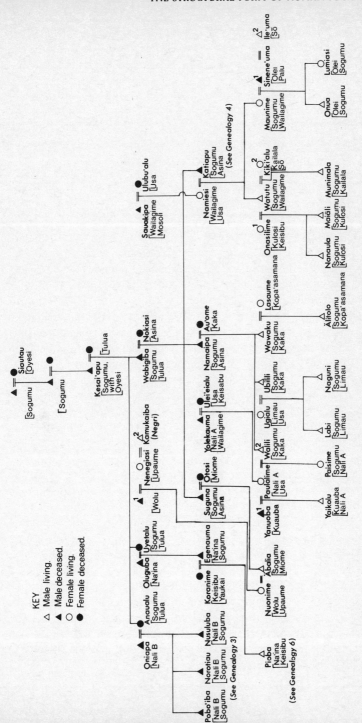

Genealogy 2 Sogumu agnates (patrilineage)

Finally, the members of ego's security circle are geographically dispersed throughout his political region, which, as will be seen, may cover a large part of Garialand. Hence the total human or secular society is, in effect, a mesh of intersecting security circles, each centred on a different nuclear figure. They link bush group to bush group, settlement to settlement, and person to person, not only throughout Garialand but also, because of intermarriage, across the Girawa, Sopu, Kopoka and Yapa borders. Indeed, Garia living near these borders have closer relationships with Girawa, Sopu, Kopoka and Yapa than with people at the centre of their own territory.

A comparison between Genealogy 2 and Map 2 (p. 35) gives a sound impression of the general situation. Between 1949 and 1953 Sogumu agnates claimed kinsmen (Sogumu enates and members of other stocks in which they were themselves enates), affines and bush brothers in the following bush god domains: Iwaiwanaku (through Sogumu, Tulua, Kaka and Limau); Yabapunaku-Eimanaku (through Asina, Nali, Naina, Oyesinō, Limau, Kulosi, Wailagime and Mosoli); Orinaku (through Wolu and Upaume); Ulilainaku (through Oyesinō and Kopa'asamana); Munimuninaku (through Miome, Usa, Wailagime, Sō and Kuauba); Yaulilinaku (through Olei); Aliliwanaku (through Keisibu); and Malainaku, Siliwanaku, Pukusakunaku and Kamai'asa (through Limau). By the end of 1980 they had used their Limau link to strengthen their position in Malainaku and Kamai'asa. With these connexions they could individually and potentially exert influence through all central and south-western Garialand, and towards, but not beyond, its northern border. By the same token, the inhabitants of Munimuninaku and Totogulunaku domains could exert influence from northern and central Garialand into Girawaland, while those of Koli, Mubu and Iborau regarded southern Sopu and Kopoka territory as part of their political arena. I collected also two examples of abnormal dispersal of kinship and affinal ties: in one case, Onumala [Kailala] of Yabapunaku-Eimanaku, who normally lived in or near Iwaiwa village in central Garialand, had effective links as far away as Amasua in Girawaland; and, in the other, Taiyomu of Ibinoru on the Garia-Girawa border had effective links with Kutulu in Sopu country.

From now on my task is to inject cultural content into the largely abstract model of Garia society I have so far presented: its dynamics or the ways in which it operates. To do this, in the following chapters I demonstrate how ego's geographically dispersed relationships correlate with the principles of land tenure and the pattern of local organization, and how he manipulates them, especially through the pig exchange, to consolidate and eventually expand his human security circle. The analysis of this process is essential not only to complete the account of social structure but also to initiate the examination of the traditional system of sociopolitical control.

3

The Principles of
Land Tenure

My earlier assertion that the irregularity of Garia local organization derives from the interplay between the structure of the security circle, land tenure, and the influence of big men should now be at least partly intelligible. Ego has a wide range of geographically dispersed kinsmen with whom he can identify, whose descent names he may use, and in whose settlements he may live provided that he can guarantee his own food supply. Certainly in social terms, periodic migration is no problem for him. I now complete my argument by analysing the principles of land tenure, which make it economically feasible as well. Yet there is no single pattern in this process throughout the whole of Garialand: the society is so idiosyncratic that it would be possible to give a separate answer for each of its twenty-five bush god domains. To simplify the account, I delineate two broad areas: the north, with nineteen domains and about two thousand people; and the south, with six domains and about six hundred people (see Map 3). In both areas the ideal structure of the security circle is a constant that everywhere conforms to the model described in Chapter 2, but land tenure is a variable and functions in somewhat different ways. Hence we are dealing not with a rigid system but with a set of common social principles that can express themselves in a variety of forms.

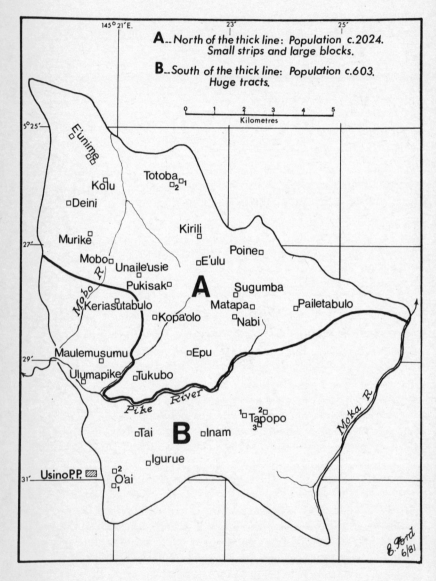

Map 3 Landholding in Garialand

In this chapter I treat land tenure as a separate issue: the rules for usufruct (cultivation, arboriculture, hunting and fishing), inheritance, acquisition and alienation; and the role of leaders in the formation of garden teams. The variations in the exercise of land rights between the north and the south create different emphases on certain crucial relationships within the security circle. I continue the analysis in Chapter 4: as foreshadowed above, the system of landholding gives ego an extensive choice of settlements near his interests. Especially in the north, settlement populations are bound to consist of heterogeneous aggregations of kin, bush brothers, affines and even non-kin. They are often impermanent because, after a given period, individuals invariably move elsewhere to clear other garden sites. This undermines the residential unity of all kin categories, especially agnates (the patrilineage). In the south, settlement populations are somewhat more stable, although local big men can cause periodic migration when they try to increase their followings by persuading kinsmen from remote areas to join them. Finally, this analysis sheds light on two related problems: different conceptions of bush brotherhood in northern and southern Garialand and the degree of interpersonal political allegiance between the inhabitants of a bush god domain.

The General Features of Land Tenure[1]

I have already drawn attention to Garialand's rugged terrain: little of it is flat, little of it is grassland, and most of it is covered with virgin jungle *(urumo)* punctuated with patches of secondary growth *(saum)*. Certainly in the people's own view (cf. p. 16), there are few differences in the quality of the soil throughout the whole area: mountain emigrants moved towards the Ramu in the 1950s not for better but for more land. Informants continually stressed their preference for sloping garden sites which, as already indicated, preserved their taro from wet feet. To have moved too far on to the valley floor would have been agriculturally detrimental.

Except for useless cliff faces, all Garialand is said to be owned. Each of the small strips, larger blocks and huge tracts into which the whole territory is divided not only bears the name of a cognatic stock but also has its human proprietor or proprietors. The system of tenure is complex because of the nature and sources of claimed rights which result, especially in the north, in an irregular distribution of individual holdings. But before I discuss these issues in the two areas I have delineated, I make a brief comment about the general features of Garia land tenure.

The rules of land tenure, to the technical aspects of which I alluded in Chapter 2, clearly reflect and buttress the general framework of Garia society:

both its broad cognatic structure and yet its distinct patrilineal and patrilateral bias. All members of a cognatic stock have the opportunity to exercise some kinds of rights over the holdings bearing its name, but the nature of these rights varies, eventually to the advantage of the agnates. There are two basic categories of rights: *permanent* rights of personal usufruct (as defined above) and collective guardianship; and *temporary* rights of personal usufruct. On any holding, permanent personal usufructuary rights are inherited by male agnates but also may be acquired by male enates (especially sisters' sons), who may then transmit them to their patrilineal descendants *in perpetuo*. Guardian rights are normally the exclusive prerogative of the patrilineage (or male agnates within the cognatic stock). In addition, any enate within a stock may acquire temporary cultivation rights on any parcel bearing its name merely by winning the permission of the proprietor(s).

It is differences in the size of holdings that promote variations in the patterns of land rights between the north and the south. In the north the mountain sides are divided into series of narrow strips of between 18 and 27 metres wide — and sometimes into blocks up to ten times as large — by about 100 metres long, while in the south the whole area is marked out into huge tracts. Strips, blocks and tracts normally consist of patches of both virgin jungle (used for hunting, fishing and collecting) and secondary growth (potential garden sites). The boundaries of these holdings are indicated, in the case of strips and blocks, by planted cordylines *(oai,* Pidgin *tanket)* and, in that of huge tracts, by recognized natural phenomena, such as creeks, rivers and mountain ridges. In northern Garialand strips and blocks bearing a particular descent name are never a continuous whole but are scattered throughout a general locality (as previously noted, up to six bush god domains) and interdigitated with similar holdings bearing other descent names. By way of contrast, in the southern domains of Koli, Mubu and Iborau, with minimal exceptions, each huge tract represents all the land associated with a particular cognatic stock. In northern Malainaku, Pukusakunaku and Kamai'asa, there are small dispersed strips each with a specific descent name, but in the south of these domains the situation is different in each case. Southern Malainaku is just one large tract with which its three cognatic stocks (Yoiyasi, Au and Limau) are jointly associated. In southern Pukusakunaku there are several huge tracts each with a separate descent name. In southern Kamai'asa there are four such tracts, three associated individually with Kamai-Tugu, Mami and Nepele stocks, and one jointly with Yoiyasi, Au and Limau (whose main base is Malainaku). Because of these differences in the size of named holdings, it is hardly surprising that, although in both areas guardian rights are exercised collectively by the patrilineage (male agnates), usufructuary rights are normally held individually in the north but communally in the south.[2] I now examine in greater detail these general features of land tenure in the following contexts: permanent rights; temporary rights; and the composition and leadership of garden teams.

Permanent Land Rights

As I have stressed, permanent land rights fall into two categories: usufruct and guardianship. I deal with each category separately for northern and southern Garialand. In this context I cover only secular rights and leave corresponding agricultural ritual rights for Chapter 7.

Permanent usufructuary rights in northern Garialand

In northern Garialand ego may claim two kinds of permanent usufructuary rights: those he inherits from his father on land bearing the name of the cognatic stock in which he is an agnate — what I now call his patrilineage land; and those he and his patrilineal forebears have acquired on land bearing the names of stocks in which he is and they were enates — what I now call land of patrilineages to which he is enatically linked. I discuss these usufructuary rights in two broad contexts: rights of cultivation and arboriculture, on the one hand, and those of hunting, fishing and collecting, on the other.

Ego's rights of cultivation and arboriculture on his patrilineage land. Every adult male has permanent rights to plant crops and food-bearing trees (banana, pandanus, breadfruit, galip, betel-nut and nowadays coconut) on a number of strips or blocks of his patrilineage land. As I have said, these rights tend to be vested in individuals — although, in some cases, they may be held jointly by true brothers or even patriparallel cousins — and are transmitted patrilineally. An only son inherits all the rights his father held on patrilineage land. Where ego has more than one son, he divides his holdings and food-trees equally between them. The only suggestion of primogeniture is that, should ego die 'intestate', his eldest son should see to the distribution and hold in trust the shares of any of his brothers too young to exploit them. Parity in cultivation rights generally poses no problem but parity in rights to food-trees may be more difficult to achieve, so that, where inequalities occur, those who have fewer trees on the strips they inherit are granted rights on their brothers' holdings. Except where they are held jointly, the above rights vested in each son are personal and absolute: even if ego wants to plant a strip belonging to his true brother, he must observe the formality of obtaining permission.

Rights of cultivation and arboriculture held in common are relatively infrequent in northern Garialand and occur mainly when a man dies 'intestate' and his sons agree not to divide his patrilineage holdings in their own generation. They and their sons use the strips and the already planted food-trees jointly, although any tree that one of the brothers or one of their sons subsequently plants is technically his sole property unless he agrees to joint proprietorship. Large blocks are occasionally held communally by agnates, although they too may be subdivided into strips, the rights to which are vested in individuals — in some cases, as result of a process I describe later, enates of the stock whose name the land bears.

If a man has no sons, his fellow agnates act as a secondary medium of inheritance. His true brothers and their sons take over his patrilineage land and trees. Daughters rarely inherit permanent rights of cultivation and arboriculture because they are regarded as their husbands' responsibility. But where a man has no sons and few agnatic kin, he may seek their permission to bequeath some of his patrilineage strips to a daughter, who should pass the rights to her sons. Where a woman is the last survivor of her patrilineage, she inherits rights to all strips not previously alienated to enates within the stock, unless her father has already made other provision (see p. 72 below). When the last member of a patrilineage (male or female) dies 'intestate', interested enates within the relevant stock may subdivide his or her personal strips among themselves, even if they do not have permanent rights on other strips bearing its descent name. They must not interfere with other enates who already enjoy such rights (see p. 72 below).

Ego's rights to hunt, fish and collect on his patrilineage land.[3] As noted, hunting and fishing are not important in northern Garialand, although collecting wild food-stuffs and cutting firewood and timber are perennial and essential tasks. It is difficult to define precisely the rule for all these pursuits. The people recognize certain conventions but, with two exceptions (shooting birds of paradise and fishing), do not try to enforce them strictly. Ego is, of course, free to shoot all game, take all fish, and collect anything he wants on his own patrilineage land. Yet game may not stand still. Hence, although properly he should stalk only prey he finds on his own strips, he may chase it on to, and shoot it on, the land of another man provided he has good relations with him and tells him what he has done. It is irrelevant whether or not the other man's strip lies in the bush god domain in which the shooter is currently living, but clearly it is relevant whether or not the two men belong to the same security circle. Ego would not take unwarranted liberties with an unrelated and hence potentially hostile person. As long as he observes these niceties, and sees to a reasonable distribution of meat and of the plumage of ordinary birds, he can always count on a fair degree of give and take. Most landholders waive their rights over small game but expect a good portion of any wild pig shot on their strips.

Birds of paradise, however, are heavily protected because of their rarity and value as dance ornaments. Ego has full rights to all birds of paradise that he or anybody else may shoot on his patrilineage strips, although — certainly if he has enough plumes for his own use — he may not always insist on them. He may allow anyone he likes to shoot birds on his patrilineage strips: fellow agnates, other immediate kin, or even quite close and quite distant kin with whom he wishes to curry favour. In other cases — such as quite close kinsmen who are less important to him — he may ask that they give him the first birds they shoot on his land, after which they may hunt without restraint as long as they tell him about their kills. The same rules broadly apply to fishing, although a man is less likely to stalk a fish into his neighbour's section of a river.[4]

Ego's rights on land of patrilineages to which he is enatically linked. In northern Garialand ego may, in theory, purchase and transmit to his sons permanent usufructuary rights over land bearing the name of any stock in which he is an enate, although in most cases he acquires them from that in which his true mother's brother is an agnate — that is, on his true mother's brother's patrilineage land. To explain the process, I examine: first, the motivations for these acquisitions; second, the stages by which they are made; and third, how they are fitted into the general pattern of cultivation, arboriculture, collecting, hunting and fishing.

As all members of a cognatic stock may always exercise temporary rights over land bearing its name by obtaining permission to plant it from those in whom the permanent usufructuary rights are vested, an individual's drive to expand the holdings on which he has permanent rights might seem unwarranted. Provided he has good relations with the landholder, he is never refused and would rarely be asked to pay rent. Hence he should feel secure. Yet there are three interdependent reasons, economic and sociopolitical, why he should try to purchase permanent usufructuary rights.

First, because of the relatively great density of population and the continual process of alienation of rights I am now about to describe, some northern Garia are short of land. The temporary solution of their immediate problems by borrowing or leasing garden sites is not wholly satisfactory in the long run. Such persons have perpetual dependent status: like those who have no pigs, they are 'poor' or of no account (*sarugu,* Pidgin *rabis).* This is intolerable in a society in which the individual lacks the regular protection of a corporate group and must see to his own interests. It represents the greatest handicap if he aspires to leadership: such a person must be able to lend rather than have to borrow land. Thus, the augmentation of permanent usufructuary rights is a special, although not exclusive, characteristic of the politically ambitious. Second, although ego may have many patrilineage strips, it is unlikely that they are so widely distributed that for many years at a stretch they will be situated on sites where big men with whom he wishes to work intend to cut bush. Third, he may see political advantage for himself and his sons in being linked not only by kinship but also by common economic interests to a big man in a cognatic stock in which he and they are only enates.

The process of acquiring permanent usufructuary rights from outside the patrilineage may begin, in a very real sense, when ego hands over the first instalment of bride price. Very often it is difficult to distinguish payments for a marriage from those for land rights. Especially if he wants economic and political advancement for his sons, he should decide early in his marriage whether he intends merely to compensate through normal remittances his affines for his wife and the children she bears him or whether, in addition, his purpose is to augment his sons' landholdings by purchasing for them permanent usufructuary rights on his wife's (their mother's) patrilineage land. In the latter case, he must send the additional remuneration (up to six pigs) already mentioned. Should he die prematurely, his sons must shoulder these responsibilities: certainly payments for their mother's bride price but also, should they share their father's aspirations, those securing rights to their maternal uncle's land. This explains the general assertion that ego should send the first pig he raises to his true mother's brothers, and his behaviour towards his true matrikin: the strict respect he owes his maternal uncles and his marked deference towards his matrilateral cross-cousins, whereby he avoids using their personal names and thus causing them embarrassment. He treats all these kinsmen as if they were *de facto* affines. I discuss this in Chapter 5.

Once accepted, these additional payments are usually regarded as final but, just as a father supplements bride price with small birth payments for his children, in the same way the beneficiary and his sons may send further pigs to the patrilineal heirs of the original benefactor (the maternal uncle) to cement their good will and hence their own claims. Yet, in some cases, maternal uncles may not insist on full payment, especially if they are convinced of their nephews' devotion and co-operation and if their sisters' husbands have paid their bride price regularly. Moreover, ego is not bound to purchase these rights only from his mother's brother, who may be short of land. He may have to turn to his mother's mother's patrilineage or even to those to which he is enatically linked through his father. In such transactions, unless there are special considerations, the purchase price is bound to be higher because the contracting parties are less closely related.

The usufructuary rights which sisters' sons acquire in this way and the precise nature of which I set out below can be exercised in either of two ways. On the one hand, occasionally a mother's brother may invite his nephew to renounce agnatic status in his father's primary cognatic stock and adopt it in his own, enjoying the same rights as himself and the other agnates. He will then hand over a number of strips on which he has exclusive usufructuary rights or, if his patrilineage is small and holds its strips in common, give him equal joint rights. On the other hand, the procedure which is more common in the north and, as will be seen, distinguishes the north clearly from the south, is for the sister's son to retain his natal agnatic status and be given usufructuary rights by his mother's brother on an agreed set of strips.

In this context there are still four important variables: the number of persons who purchase these rights; the amount of land alienated; the long-term future of alienated land; and the bush brother relationship. In the first place, not everybody acquires permanent usufructuary rights from maternal uncles or other kinsmen. A survey of some sixty landholders in Somau and Iwaiwa villages in northern Garialand in 1949-50 showed that in about two-thirds of the cases their forebears had acquired such rights, while in the current generation about half had at least begun to do so. As already indicated, those who had acquired most land in this way either had immediate forebears who were, or were themselves trying to become, leaders or at least men of some consequence.

In the second place, the amount of land alienated and the purchase price demanded in any transaction varies according to the law of supply and demand. The normal payment of six pigs may be sufficient for anything from three to twenty strips according to the number of holdings available and the number of persons competing for them.

In the third place, in contrast to other systems of land tenure in Melanesia in which titles to holdings can be transferred from the unilineal descent line to enates — for example, Wogeo (Hogbin 1967: 23-4) — in northern Garialand acquired usufructuary rights should remain with the sister's son and his direct patrilineal heirs for as long as they wish to exercise them. They are inherited by his sons — and, failing them, his true brothers and their sons — in the same way as his patrilineage strips. The principle is that whoever inherits and exercises the acquired rights should be enatically linked to the original donor patrilineage — an enate of the cognatic stock of which it is the agnatic kernel. Only if the beneficiary's patrilineal heirs become extinct or renounce their claims should the original donor patrilineage resume rights to the land in question. I discuss this issue further in the context of guardian rights.

In the fourth place, the periodic acquisition of permanent usufructuary rights from maternal uncles in northern Garialand determines the local distribution of a man's holdings and bush brothers. Ego regards as bush brothers those persons who have many strips interdigitated with his own, regardless of whether he and they are agnates or enates of the stocks whose names the holdings bear. As his strips are scattered by the process of inheritance and acquisition, he can generally claim bush brothers wherever he has permanent usufructuary rights — throughout several bush god domains in his political region. Clearly, this augments his security circle both socially and geographically.

The usufructuary rights which ego acquires from a maternal uncle or any other kinsman and transmits to his patrilineal heirs are the same as those he inherits on his patrilineage strips, and again are best described separately. Those for cultivation, arboriculture and collecting pose no problems: they are identical with those he enjoys on his patrilineage strips. He may plant, take materials from, and lease or lend acquired land at will. Nobody questions his rights in these contexts. But his rights to hunt and fish are subject to some restriction.

Ego has an immediate right to hunt game (birds, marsupials and wild pig) on his acquired strips. He should stalk only prey he finds on his own land and, if it eludes him, pursue it only on to that of persons with whom he has close ties. He is free to eat what he kills, although it is regarded as an act of courtesy to send occasional gifts of meat, especially wild pig, to the original owners of the land or their patrilineal descendants. But birds of paradise and fish are once again under heavy protection, which emphasizes the residual rights of the donor patilineage. Ego is expected to present the first bird of paradise he shoots on an acquired strip to the person who sold it to him — his maternal uncle, matrilateral cross-cousin, or other relative. Should he keep it for himself, he must allow his uncle or cousin to use it as a dance ornament on demand, and hand over the second one he kills. Fishing rights follow the same pattern. Yet after he has observed these preliminaries, ego and his patrilineal heirs have full rights to all birds of paradise they shoot and fish they take on these strips. Nevertheless it would be pointless to treat these precepts too legalistically. Ego's relationships with all his close kinsmen are based on continual gift exchange: he pays off old debts by presents of fish caught and loans of dance head-dresses as occasion requires. Even when he has honoured an obligation in full, he may yet send his benefactor an additional gift to ensure that there can be no question of his bona fides. As in the case of marriage payments, such is the convergence of activities in this flexible society, it is often impossible to fix any act of prestation in a single rigid category. It may meet several obligations to one person or to several persons at the same time.

Garialand, looking south from Iwaiwa, 1968

Clearing a garden site, Somau-Iwaiwa area, 1949

Dance leader, 1950

After a pig exchange in Somau Village, 1950

Guardian rights in northern Garialand

Although usufructuary rights to land bearing the name of any cognatic stock are shared between its agnates, who inherit them automatically, and its enates, who can inherit them only after an act of purchase, there is yet, as I have foreshadowed, a further category of rights, which are vested exclusively in its male agnates in their capacity as a patrilineage, unless for special reasons they wish to extend them to a favoured male enate. These are rights of guardianship *(ogem yaguwobu,* Pidgin *bosim hapgiraun),* which cover two fields: disputes over any strip or block bearing the stock's descent name, whether the usufructuary rights be vested in an agnate or an enate; and the transfer of usufructuary rights. Some informants claimed also that bush brothers should be consulted in these matters.

When he deals with members of his own security circle, ego treats the formal rules of land tenure with a good deal of latitude: he is always prepared to modify or waive his strict rights. Yet should outsiders infringe his title by planting, hunting, fishing or collecting on his land without permission, he is bound to protect his own interests. This is a normal Melanesian reaction. Even so, he is not free to take retaliatory action as an individual. As agnate or enate, he must refer such a dispute to the members of the patrilineage (the agnates of the cognatic stock) whose name the land bears: *they* must debate it, possibly in consultation with their bush brothers, and reach a decision. If an agnate brings a case, only the patrilineage (and possibly bush brothers) should attend and speak. If the plaintiff is an enate, the members of the patrilineage (again possibly in consultation with bush brothers) take charge of the proceedings. He and other enatic landholders may attend the hearing, although they should not speak unless specific questions are put to them.

Restrictions on the alienation of usufructuary rights are more labyrinthine. I discuss them, first, in the context of ego's patrilineage holdings and, second, in that of those he has acquired or inherited as an enate. Thus, if he wishes to transfer usufructuary rights on some of his patrilineage strips to his immediate sister's sons, there is no problem. At most, he informs his fellow agnates of his intention, which they never oppose because the kinship tie is so close. He is free to distribute as he pleases all payments he receives from his true nephews, although he always sees that his fellow agnates get proper shares. Yet beyond this range of kinship, guardian rights are strictly enforced. Should ego wish to transfer rights on his patrilineage strips to an enate outside the immediate degree of kinship (as to a FZDS, who is classified as a ZS), he must justify his case to his fellow agnates (and possibly bush brothers), who may insist that the beneficiary make additional payments (one to three more pigs, again according to the law of supply and demand), partly to acknowledge the greater distance of the relationship between the parties involved and partly to stress the residual rights of the guardian patrilineage.

Again, if ego wishes to bequeath usufructuary rights on some of his patrilineage strips to a daughter for the benefit of her sons, although he may demand no payment beyond the bride price, he should of course inform his fellow agnates of his intention. If he is the last surviving male of his patrilineage, he may distribute as he wishes those parcels of its land still in his possession. Should his only heirs be daughters, they may exercise the patrilineage's guardian rights with advice and support from those male enates who hold some of its strips. In the same way, as I have already made clear, when the agnates (male and female) are totally extinct, interested enates may distribute those strips not already privately held among themselves and assume the role of guardians.

In the case of holdings which ego has acquired or inherited through enatic links, there is rigid restriction against further alienation for several generations. During this period enatic landholders may not change the name of these strips from that of the donor patrilineage (or cognatic stock in which the donor was an agnate) to that of their own and must defer to the donor (guardian) patrilineage in all cases of the further transfer of usufructuary rights. As noted, although ego's sons and brothers' sons may inherit his acquired strips, his patriparallel cousins may not do so if they are not enates of the relevant cognatic stock. By the same token, should he wish to sell usufructuary rights on his acquired strips to his own sister's son or other relative (especially one who is not an enate of the stock in question), he must obtain the agreement of the whole guardian patrilineage (and possibly its bush brothers), which may demand a higher purchase price.

Nevertheless, the guardianship of the donor patrilineage is not eternal but should continue for about four generations after the initial transfer of usufructuary rights. Thereafter, at the level of the fifth descending generation, the direct patrilineal heirs of the original beneficiary may change the name of the acquired strips to that of their own patrilineage, which now assumes full guardian rights as defined. The previous relationship between the ex-guardians and ex-clients may be recalled for a further generation or so but, as we have seen, the memory of it becomes vague. Except in special circumstances, it is of no further significance for the land in question and no longer belongs to the security circles of the parties concerned. The process is a restatement in terms of land rights of that described in Chapter 2 (p. 41): just as ego continues to recognize interpersonal ties through marriages up to two generations after the loss of personal names in the second or third ascending generation, in the same way he still acknowledges the guardian rights of a donor patrilineage for the same period, even though he cannot recall the individuals responsible for the original transaction. Indeed, as I have suggested, acknowledgement of guardian rights in spite of genealogical ignorance helps preserve the memory of enatic links between specific patrilineages for one or two generations. In a word, guardian rights cease to be recognized at the same time as enatic relationships become almost totally obscure and disappear from ego's security circle. Significantly, as I have mentioned in the context of purely genealogical relationships, the process is paralleled and validated by beliefs about the spirits of the dead which I discuss in Chapter 7.

Once again, the foregoing analysis should not be accepted as an inflexible rule: that a patrilineage's period of guardianship always comes to an abrupt end in the fifth descending generation. Just as there is often overlap in the reckoning of degrees of relationship because of lack of precise genealogical knowledge, even so the change in guardianship often takes place unobtrusively, accelerated or delayed by chance events. When personal names disappear quickly, it may be rapid but, when those of the third ascending generation and above linger on, it may be slow. Thus certain land strips in Yabapunaku-Eimanaku and Ulilainaku domains labelled, in 1949-50, Sogumu (the patrilineage whose members held them jointly) had, in 1952-53, to be renamed Oyesinō, whose members were said to have sold them to the FFFF of Walili and his generation. In 1949 it seemed reasonable to call them Sogumu. Yet, after 1950, Walili, who had been for many years a plantation foreman and was a respected genealogist, persuaded his fellow agnates to restore the name Oyesinō because he could remember the nickname (Siautau) of the woman whose marriage had initiated the transfer of the strips to Sogumu. In 1975, when Walili's generation was extinct, the name Sogumu was restored (see Genealogy 2).

Permanent rights of usufruct in southern Garialand

In comparison with the north, the geographical distribution of landholdings in southern Garialand is fairly regular. Except in marginal areas, bush god domains are divided into huge tracts each bearing the name of and, in most cases, representing the total estate associated with, a cognatic stock. The pattern of landholding in the south correlates with the lack of population: the area is about as large as northern Garialand but has markedly fewer inhabitants. In view of this it is hardly surprising that there is far less emphasis on individual title and correspondingly greater emphasis on communal rights in the south than in the north. Nevertheless, the underlying principles of land tenure are the same. Permanent usufructuary rights are inherited patrilineally and, although the process is less common than in the north, can be purchased from maternal uncles. Enates may exercise temporary usufructuary rights by obtaining permission to plant land bearing their stock's name. Guardian rights are vested exclusively in male agnates (possibly in consultation with bush brothers). Yet, as is by now obvious, these common principles have to be expressed in patterns of behaviour somewhat different from those in the north.

Ego's rights of cultivation, arboriculture, hunting, fishing and collecting on his patrilineage land. Except in northern Kamai'asa, Malainaku and Pukusakunaku, which are subdivided into small strips and in which the land tenure system described for northern Garialand functions, permanent usufructuary rights on the huge tracts in the six southern bush god domains are almost entirely vested not in individuals but communally in the male members of the patrilineages — the agnates within the cognatic stocks — whose names the land bears. Individual agnates have no personal rights to any parcel of land on their named tract: they have joint rights to plant crops and food trees, and to hunt, fish and collect anywhere on it after reaching consensus among themselves. Similarly, enates have to obtain the joint permission of the patrilineage to exercise temporary usufructuary rights. Nevertheless, the pattern is not absolutely fixed. It obtains as I have outlined it in Koli, Mubu, Iborau, southern Pukusakunaku and on those tracts in southern Kamai'asa held by Kamai-Tugu, Mami and Nepele patrilineages. But, as already noted, southern Malainaku and one part of southern Kamai'asa are two single tracts which lack internal patrilineage divisions and over which the three patrilineages, Yoiyasi, Au and Limau, exercise permanent communal usufructuary rights.

Ego's rights of cultivation, arboriculture, hunting, fishing, and collecting on land of patrilineages to which he is enatically linked. Although southerners recognize the process of purchasing permanent usufructuary rights from a maternal uncle or other close kinsman, with so much available land per head of population it is hardly surprising that they follow a system different from that in the north. The practice of acquiring individual usufructuary rights on a number of dispersed strips which the beneficiary's patrilineal heirs eventually absorb into their collective estate by assuming full guardian rights is unknown in southern Kamai'asa, Malainaku and Pukusakunaku, and remembered in Iborau, Mubu and Koli only in a few cases which informants claimed to be unusual. For instance, a man of Konei patrilineage in Mubu domain helped his Se'u matrikin in battle. His maternal uncle rewarded him by helping him find a suitable wife and giving him usufructuary rights on a section of Se'u land.

Hence the preferred southern usage is the one infrequent in the north. The mother's brother or his son invites a nephew or cross-cousin eager to purchase usufructuary rights to adopt agnatic status (*sawaibopi sisi'ebu*) in his own primary cognatic stock — that is, become a full member of his own patrilineage. Subject to the agreement of the other members, the beneficiary may plant, hunt, fish and collect at will, at most acknowledging his adoptive status by giving his mother's brother or matrilateral cross-cousins the first bird of paradise he shoots and the first fish he catches within this new estate. Thereafter he and his sons should be accorded the same status as the original agnates.

Once again, the terms on which ego can change his agnatic status in this way vary according to the law of supply and demand. A patrilineage with few men and ample land will always offer easy terms, a considerable inducement to young men in relatively populous northern Garialand who have matrikin in the south. This places the southern area at least firmly in the context of much recent Papua New Guinean ethnography, in which leaders 'buy' men for land rights. Their aim is to increase their followings irrespective of considerations of unilineal descent, for a strong hard-working enate is as good as any agnate. Moreover in Garialand the absorption of sisters' sons and cross-cousins into a patrilineage does not, in the long run, create irregularities in kinship terminology in what still presents itself to outsiders in this context as a unilineal descent group. Because of the Iroquois rule set out on p. 38, the sons of ego and his male matrilateral cross-cousins address each other as 'brother' (cf. Lawrence 1973).

In these circumstances ego's land interests have to be concentrated rather than dispersed. In the main, they are no more than his communal patrilineage tract. This influences his definition of his bush brothers. In contrast to the north, like his land interests, his bush brothers cannot be scattered but have to be people near his own patrilineage tract. They are those persons whose patrilineage tracts are adjacent to his own, either within his own domain or just outside its borders.

Guardian rights in southern Garialand

In southern Garialand the emphasis on communal usufructuary rights is so strong that guardianship is by no means as important as a diacritical sign of a patrilineage's identity as in the north. Guardianship is merely one aspect of the joint rights that male agnates exercise over their tract and extend to sisters' sons and other enates whom they absorb. The only exceptions are the few claimed cases of the transfer of individual rights to sisters' sons in Iborau,

Mubu and Koli, about which I obtained little hard information and which I am therefore forced to ignore.

Yet one question remains: How far does adoption of agnatic status in another cognatic stock force a man to renounce membership in his natal patrilineage, and the usufructuary and guardian rights that go with it? In 1949-50 informants stated a strict rule: that after adoption into his mother's brother's patrilineage, ego should forfeit the status and benefits he would normally have inherited from his father. In fact, actual examples that I collected between 1949 and 1980 suggest that, while expounding it in principle, individuals invariably interpreted it to their best advantage. Thus, in northern Garialand, the brothers Saiku and Wakamua [Mamu], whose land in the northern tip of Pukusakunaku domain was insubstantial, accepted agnatic status in Ukapu (Kutia domain), their father's mother's primary cognatic stock. As Saiku was a rising big man and their own numbers were dwindling, Ukapu agnates welcomed them. But the brothers did not renounce their natal status in Mamu for the good reason that they were its last male agnates. Sasauba claimed dual agnatic status in Kamai and Ulawa stocks on the same basis.

I was able to trace one case, however, from 1944 until 1980. As it involved individuals in both northern and southern Garialand it is of some interest. Within Nali linked patrilineage[5] (Yabapunaku-Eimanaku domain) members of Nali B, whose forebears were Salasi immigrants from Kolese in Koli, were always short of land, although members of Nali A, who adopted them, had been as generous as they could (see Genealogy 3). Before the Japanese invasion the two brothers Muyäli and Imoguli lived in Iwaiwa but, after 1942, with no patrol officers to insist that they stayed in their pre-war villages, they became increasingly interested in the holdings of Au, their mother's brother's patrilineage, in Malainaku, Pukusakunaku and Kamai'asa domains. They went to Kopa'olo to join their matrilateral cross-cousin Pubule'uma [Au], who with some of his neighbours had already established gardens in southern Malainaku and Pukusakunaku, and was also planting his Au holdings at Sielina in northern Malainaku, not far from Iwaiwa. They hid there with him during the Shaggy Ridge campaign in 1944. With the restoration of Australian rule and official villages, Muyäli and Imoguli returned to Iwaiwa, and Pubule'uma to Kopa'olo. Yet the lure of Au land was very great: a huge estate with few men to supervise it. During the next five years the two brothers sent Pubule'uma six pigs with food and valuables to purchase land rights. At that time they intended to continue living in Iwaiwa, retain Nali agnatic status and acquire some Au strips in northern Malainaku, where they were planting gardens in 1950 when I left the field.

When I returned to Garialand two years later Muyäli was dead and Imo-

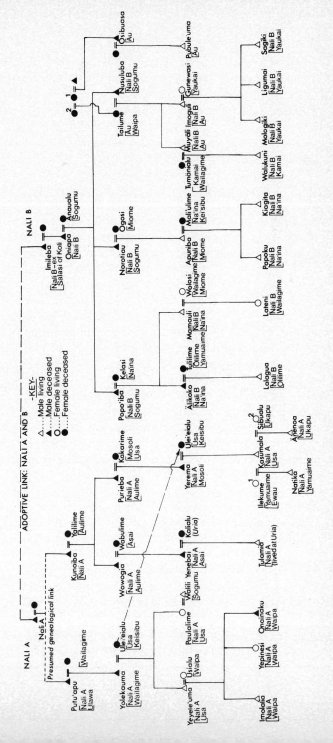

Genealogy 3 Nali A and B linked agnates (patrilineage)

guli had changed his plans. Pubule'uma had persuaded him to accept agnatic status in Au stock for himself and his sons, and for Muyäli's son Walukuni should he wish it in the future. Hence Imoguli and his sons acquired not only personal rights to small holdings around Sielina but also communal rights over the huge Yoiyasi-Au-Limau estate in southern Malainaku and Kamai'-asa. I narrate the later stages of this history in Chapter 4. What is important here is Imoguli's and his sons' eventual decisions about their status as Nali agnates.

In contrast to Saiku, Wakamua and Sasauba, Imoguli initially upheld stated convention. By 1952 he had publicly renounced Nali agnatic status for himself and his sons, with whom he had emigrated to Maulemusumu in southern Malainaku. He left Walukuni in Iwaiwa to supervise the Nali and Sogumu strips that he and Muyäli had held in the past. But, in 1953, their numbers reduced by a series of deaths, the Nali B survivors prevailed on Imoguli to resume his former agnatic status at least until the younger generation could produce a big man to take his place. As a result Imoguli and his sons could now claim dual agnatic status, in both Nali and Au. This agreement was reached in the mid-1950s and has never been rescinded. After the opening of Usino Patrol Post in the 1960s Walukuni moved to the Pike, where he died in 1972. Although they were all now firmly entrenched in their Au estate, neither he nor Imoguli and his sons ever finally renounced their original Nali agnatic status. During the 1970s, some ten years after Imoguli's death, his sons openly asserted, without any objection from other Nali agnates, that they could return to Iwaiwa and take up their guardian and usufructuary rights again at any time they pleased.

This is once again typical of the Garia — indeed, of many Melanesian peoples — who state a convention as if it were a fixed rule only to interpret it to meet a specific contingency. There is no opposition provided nobody's personal interests are threatened. I suggest that there are two important variables here. First, just as in northern Garialand changes of land names may not always occur with the precision suggested by informants, in the same way a sister's son adopted by his maternal uncle may not renounce his natal agnatic status immediately but rather try to exploit his dual ties for as long as he can. This may continue for several generations until his patrilineal heirs forget their original identity and cleave to the one he purchased. Already in the 1970s, despite their statements already quoted, it was clear that the economic tie to the Nali and Sogumu land around Iwaiwa was becoming less important to Imoguli's sons, especially as they were by now well established in Malainaku and could not be challenged there. Second, in a cognatic society the amount of unilineal indoctrination that parents give their children is bound to vary. Among the Garia some men care less about patrilineal sentiment than others. Thus Imoguli, my shrewdest informant, was always conscious of, and impressed on his sons, their immigrant origin. His status as a Nali agnate did not rate with him much more highly than his enatic status in other stocks. Ubilili, however, was an aggressive Sogumu agnate, who once strongly reproved me for suggesting that Alitolo, the son of his brother Wawaku (see Genealogy 2), might change his agnatic status as he had spent so much of his life at Uria in Ulilainaku domain. 'No', he replied, 'he is a child of Sogumu'. I did not take the matter further. Clearly, he transmitted this attitude to his own sons Labi and Naguni: they lived in Malainaku for nearly a decade before even considering the strong and flattering invitation to adopt agnatic status there. In August 1978 they eventually accepted, although it took a further two years for them to overcome the resistance of other Sogumu agnates still in the Iwaiwa area and make their decision public. I describe this incident in greater detail in Chapter 4.

Temporary Rights to Land

A salient feature of Garia agriculture is that only bachelors, old people and men of no account plant just one garden strip every year. Especially if he has status or ambition, ego must prepare up to five or six plots annually to cover his basic socioeconomic needs: apart from his family's domestic consumption, he must meet the demands of pig exchanges and other ceremonies, for which, either as principal or helper, he is expected to contribute considerable amounts of food; and he must insure against incursions of wild pig and, particularly in the wet season, landslides, which may destroy whole gardens at a stroke. Obviously he needs extensive land resources. In northern Garialand, because of the prevailing system of inheritance and acquisition, his holdings may be dispersed throughout several bush god domains. Nevertheless, in any one year, he may find that only a few of his personal strips can be incorporated in the garden sites chosen. Big men may not wish to clear land in every area where he has permanent rights; or, even if he himself is important, he may not be able to assemble the requisite teams of workers around some of his own plots. He must then either plant his own strips in small gardens with a few other workers, which brings little prestige and is never satisfactory because of the lack of labour, or borrow or rent land in gardens in which he can join larger teams, even though he must cast himself in a dependent role. In the south, because of both the greater abundance of land and the corresponding lack of population, even the biggest men are driven to compete for personal followings. Hence, in any one year, ego may be forced to turn to land bearing the names of stocks in which he is but an enate without permanent usufructuary rights, because no sizeable teams are scheduled to work on his patrilineage tract. In view of this, clearly throughout all Garialand temporary cultivation rights are bound to be important.

Ego may seek temporary cultivation rights from most members of his security circle: kinsmen of the close grade such as fellow agnates, members of stocks in which he is an enate, persons enatically linked to himself (for example, Z children, FZ children and so forth), and those with whom he shares common enatic links (MZ children, etc.); bush brothers, wherever they may reside; and, when his marriage is safely established, his primary affines. (For reasons already specified, he would be slow to approach his secondary affines: kinsmen of the previous husband of any widow he has married.) Unless there are special circumstances, his request is never refused, especially in cases where, as in southern Garialand, garden leaders may be so short of labour that they openly solicit workers. These temporary rights are limited to cultivation: they allow ego to plant crops but not food-trees and do not extend to hunting, fishing and collecting. They cover only that part of the strip, block or tract taken up by his garden plot and last only for the eighteen months during which it is under cultivation. They end as soon as he has eaten out his crops and at once revert to the lessor(s) or lender(s).

The transaction may be a lease or a free loan according to the formal ties and general relations between landholder and dependant. Normally, ego does not ask rent from, or offer it to, most members of his security circle, although, if he is using their land, he at least suggests it to his wife's kin (his primary affines) until he is certain of them. He may, of course, volunteer it also to any member of his security circle whose favour and support in other contexts are important to him. Otherwise, he regards rent as due to or from only persons on the fringe of or beyond his security circle — distant kinsmen and unrelated persons — unless there are special considerations. There is an additional sanction, which I discuss in Chapters 7 and 8: respect for the spirits of the dead, who are said to protect their living descendants' interests and punish people infringing their land rights. A dependant will always pay rent if he thinks that his relationship with the landholder is so distant and tenuous that he could incur ghostly wrath by not doing so (see p. 237). Rent is paid before the end of the dry season: enough cooked pork, game or fish with vegetables to provide a full meal for the landholder and his nuclear family. This is a final payment: the landholder cannot expect any share of the crops grown on the plot he has leased. Finally, when ego leases land on which he has usufructuary rights only as an enate, the guardian patrilineage does not demand any share of the rent.

It should be clear from my account that, even in northern Garialand, where some people have permanent usufructuary rights on only a limited

Table 2 Sogumu agnates: permanent and temporary usufructuary land rights, 1949-53

Agnate	Land interests: descent names	Bush god domain	Type of rights
Äbalia	patrikin: Sogumu, Tulua	Iwaiwanaku	permanent
	Asina (Kailala)*	Yabapunaku-Eimanaku	permanent
	Oyesinō†	Yabapunaku-Eimanaku	permanent
	Oyesinō†	Ulilainaku	permanent
	matrikin: Miome	Munimuninaku	temporary
	affines: Wolu, Upaume	Orinaku	temporary
Walili	patrikin: Sogumu, Tulua	Iwaiwanaku	permanent
	Asina (Kailala)*	Yabapunaku-Eimanaku	permanent
	Oyesinō†	Yabapunaku-Eimanaku	permanent
	Oyesinō†	Ulilainaku	permanent
	matrikin: Kaka	Iwaiwanaku	permanent
	affines: Nali A	Yabapunaku-Eimanaku	temporary
	Usa, Wailagime	Munimuninaku	temporary
	Keisibu	Äliliwanaku	temporary
Ubilili	patrikin: Sogumu, Tulua	Iwaiwanaku	permanent
	Asina (Kailala)*	Yabapunaku-Eimanaku	permanent
	Oyesinō†	Yabapunaku-Eimanaku	permanent
	Oyesinō†	Ulilainaku	permanent
	matrikin: Kaka	Iwaiwanaku	permanent
	affines: Limau	Iwaiwanaku, Malainaku, Pukusakunaku, Yabapunaku-Eimanaku, Siliwanaku, Kamai'asa	temporary
	Usa	Munimuninaku	temporary
Wawaku	patrikin: Sogumu, Tulua	Iwaiwanaku	permanent
	Asina (Kailala)*	Yabapunaku-Eimanaku	permanent
	Oyesinō†	Yabapunaku-Eimanaku	permanent
	Oyesinō†	Ulilainaku	permanent
	matrikin: Kaka	Iwaiwanaku	permanent
	affines: Kopa'asamana	Ulilainaku	temporary
Watutu	patrikin: Sogumu, Tulua	Iwaiwanaku	permanent
	Asina (Kailala)*	Yabapunaku-Eimanaku	permanent
	Oyesinō†	Yabapunaku-Eimanaku	permanent
	Oyesinō†	Ulilainaku	permanent
	matrikin: Wailagime, Usa	Munimuninaku	permanent
	Mosoli	Yabapunaku-Eimanaku	permanent
	affines: Kulosi	Yabapunaku-Eimanaku	temporary
	Keisibu	Äliliwanaku	temporary
	Kailala	Yabapunaku-Eimanaku	permanent*
	Sō	Munimuninaku	temporary

(continued)

Table 2 — *continued*

Agnate	Land interests: descent names	Bush god domain	Type of rights
{ Labi	patrikin: Sogumu, Tulua, Kaka	Iwaiwanaku	permanent
{ Naguni	Asina (Kailala)*	Yabapunaku-Eimanaku	permanent
	Sogumu (ex-Oyesinō)†	Yabapunaku-Eimanaku	permanent
	Sogumu (ex-Oyesinō)†	Ulilainaku	permanent
	matrikin: Limau	Iwaiwanaku, Malainaku, Pukusakunaku, Yabapunaku-Eimanaku, Siliwanaku, Kamai'asa	temporary
	Usa	Munimuninaku	temporary
Älitolo	patrikin: Sogumu, Tulua, Kaka	Iwaiwanaku	permanent
	Asina (Kailala)*	Yabapunaku-Eimanaku	permanent
	Sogumu (ex-Oyesinō)†	Yabapunaku-Eimanaku	permanent
	Sogumu (ex-Oyesinō)†	Ulilainaku	permanent
	matrikin: Kopa'asamana	Ulilainaku	temporary
{ Nanaula	patrikin: Sogumu, Tulua	Iwaiwanaku	permanent
	Asina (Kailala)*	Yabapunaku-Eimanaku	permanent
{ Maiäli	Sogumu		
	(ex-Oyesinō)†	Yabapunaku-Eimanaku	permanent
	Sogumu (ex-Oyesinō)†	Ulilainaku	permanent
	Mosoli	Yabapunaku-Eimanaku	permanent
	Wailagime, Usa	Munimuninaku	permanent
	matrikin: Kulosi	Yabapunaku-Eimanaku	temporary
	Keisibu	Äliliwanaku	temporary
Munimala	patrikin: Sogumu, Tulua	Iwaiwanaku	permanent
	Asina (Kailala)*	Yabapunaku-Eimanaku	permanent
	Sogumu (ex-Oyesinō)†	Yabapunaku-Eimanaku	permanent
	Sogumu (ex-Oyesinō)†	Ulilainaku	permanent
	Mosoli	Yabapunaku-Eimanaku	permanent
	Wailagime, Usa	Munimuninaku	permanent
	matrikin: Kailala*	Yabapunaku-Eimanaku	permanent
	Sō	Munimuninaku	temporary

Notes to Table 2

*Asina cognatic stock takes its name from Asinasi, a Kailala woman from whom its members claim descent. Asina and Kailala stocks are now genealogically separate but all land associated with Asina is called Kailala. Hence Watutu, Asina by his FM, broke no rule by marrying Kikialu [Kailala]. Yet, through his enatic status in Asina, he had permanent usufructuary rights on Kailala land, which he transmitted to Munimala, who had an additional claim to it through his mother Kikialu. She also had been given permanent usufructuary rights on Kailala strips by her father. With Watutu, she held them in trust for Munimala (see Table 4). Moreover, Watutu was purchasing additional rights on Kailala land for Munimala.

†As noted on p. 73, Oyesinō strips in Yabapunaku-Eimanaku and Ulilainaku domains purchased by Sogumu agnates several generations ago retained their original name in Walili's generation but had been renamed Sogumu in that of Labi and Naguni. I have tried to indicate this in the table.

number of strips, everybody can find enough garden sites each year for his needs, some on his own, and others on borrowed or rented, holdings. It is impossible to tabulate the situation precisely but I attempt to illustrate the range of possibilities in Table 2 (see also Genealogy 2). Between 1949 and 1953 Sogumu agnates claimed permanent and temporary usufructuary rights in ten bush god domains in northern and southern Garialand: permanent usufructuary rights, which granted them potential status as lessors or lenders, in Iwawanaku, Yabapunaku-Eimanaku, Ulilainaku and Munimuninaku through Sogumu, Tulua, Kaka, Asina (Kailala), Mosoli, Oyesinō (later Sogumu), Wailagime and Usa; and temporary usufructuary rights, which allowed them only dependent status, in Munimuninaku, Orinaku, Yabapunaku-Eimanaku, Äliliwanaku, Malainaku, Iwaiwanaku, Pukusakunaku, Siliwanaku, Kamai'asa and Ulilainaku through Miome, Wailagime, Usa, Sō, Upaume, Wolu, Nali, Kulosi, Keisibu, Limau and Kopa'asamana. In addition, they could solicit temporary rights also from persons enatically related to themselves — as, for example, agnates in Nali B and Na'ina (see Genealogies 3 and 7). By the end of 1980, as I have already noted and shall elaborate in Chapter 4, they had established communal permanent rights in Malainaku and Kamai'asa domains.[6] Finally, especially in northern Garialand, it is only in the context of the dispersal of usufructuary rights that it is possible to understand the formation of garden teams and the part played by leaders in the process.

The Leadership and Composition of Garden Teams

Throughout all Garialand the composition of garden teams has no strict pattern: people follow their individual interests. In the north, because of the fragmentation and dispersal of ego's land interests, and his need to plant up to six strips in different gardens every year, it is inevitable that their teams are socially as irregular as I shall show the populations of hamlets and village wards to be. Even in the south, where ego's interests are concentrated rather than fragmented and dispersed, the same pattern tends to emerge. In both areas the catalysts are always the garden leaders: men flock to them because of their personal reputations. Hence it is best to begin the analysis of this issue by examining a garden leader's popularly recognized qualifications and the way in which he brings his team together, and then consider the implications of his *modus operandi* for northern and southern Garialand respectively.

An established garden leader is generally a middle-aged man, experienced in co-ordinating his fellow workers' physical activities, especially in the case of adolescents, who have to be shown how to solve technical problems in tree-felling and fence-building. Yet, beyond this, he must have a 'great name' (*kokai wenum,* Pidgin *biknaen/naen antap),* which he derives from proven success and his religious knowledge: mastery of the mythology and, more particularly, the ritual that harnesses the power of the relevant deities and ghosts to his most important enterprises and brings them to fruition. (I analyse this in detail in Chapters 7 and 8.) He achieves such a reputation only after years of apprenticeship, experimentation and effort. As a novice, helped by his closest kin, he supervises a garden of perhaps three strips. If it prospers, he will graduate to gardens of some ten or fifteen strips. At the pinnacle of his fame, he accepts responsibility for gardens of about thirty strips each, covering areas of approximately 550 by 100 metres. With credit of this kind, he has no problem in assembling a team. As noted in Chapter 1, he may seek out a few associates or merely announce that he intends to cut bush in a specific area where he has usufructuary rights. Within a few days many co-workers announce their interest in him and form up as a team.

In these circumstances, the membership of garden teams is bound to be heterogeneous. Ego will join a team because he has permanent or can acquire temporary rights on the site being cleared. But, especially in the north, his land interests are so scattered that it is unlikely that he can work always with specific categories of kin. Agnates rarely work together in the same garden and generally join different teams. This may be true also of the family, both nuclear and compound: husband, wife/wives, and adolescent children may plant on separate sites because they cannot find enough adjacent plots to accommodate them all together. Once again, this is a protection against loss from landslides and marauding wild pig. Hence ego is not always related to all or even most other members of his garden teams. If he has borrowed or rented a strip, he may have no formal tie with the garden leader. Indeed, many garden leaders welcome distant kinsmen and even unrelated persons to their teams: such persons not only increase their followings but are also clear evidence of their great prestige. This has two important results. First, ego extends his human security circle by associating for eighteen months (from first clearing until the end of harvesting) with distant kin and non-kin, whom he calls *saina'omei* (Pidgin *wanwok*,[7] 'work brothers'), in up to six gardens. Because of common economic interests, he must have safe relationships with them in the same way as with his unrelated co-residents in a hamlet or village ward *(weise'omei)*. Unless there are reasons against it, these relationships end when the garden teams disintegrate. Second, it may be difficult for leaders to co-ordinate the activities of people who have to share their time between different gardens. A man may sometimes concentrate on one site at the expense of another, which will therefore fall behind schedule: he may trade on a close kinship tie and pay more attention to an unrelated leader in the hope of currying favour. In this situation a neglected leader's most powerful sanction is to withdraw from the offender the main benefit he can bestow, agricultural ritual.

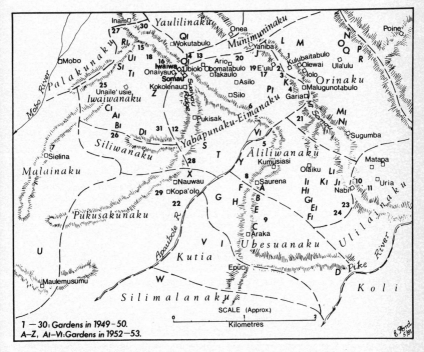

Map 4 Scatter of hamlets and gardens — Somau-Iwaiwa locality

Table 3 Gardens worked by Sogumu agnates and their families: 1949-50 and
1952-53

Agnates and their families	Gardens (bush god domains)	
	1949-50	1952-53
Family 1		
Äbalia	17 (Yabapunaku-Eimanaku)	in prison, Madang
No'anime (wife)	19 (Yabapunaku-Eimanaku)	at Negri, Girawaland
Family 2		
Walili	15, 18, 27 (all in Iwaiwanaku)	O1, *R1 (both in Iwaiwanaku)
Paulalime (wife)	17, 20 (both in Yabapunaku-Eimanaku)	B1 (Iwaiwanaku)
Family 3		
Ubilili	12 (Yabapunaku-Eimanaku)	U (Malainaku)
Ugialu (wife)	12 (Yabapunaku-Eimanaku)	B1 (Iwaiwanaku)
Labi	12 (Yabapunaku-Eimanaku)	U (Malainaku), B1 (Iwaiwanaku), O1* (Iwaiwanaku)
Naguni	in hospital, Madang	O1* (Iwaiwanaku)
Family 4		
Wawaku	at Uria (Ulilainaku)	at Uria (Ulilainaku)
Lasaume (wife)	at Uria (Ulilainaku)	at Uria (Ulilainaku)
Älitolo	at Uria (Ulilainaku)	at Uria (Ulilainaku)
Family 5		
Watutu	6 (Yabapunaku-Eimanaku), 13 [3 strips] (Munimuninaku), 19 (Yabapunaku-Eimanaku)	K (Yabapunaku-Eimanaku), O1* [2 strips] (Iwaiwanaku and Munimuninaku)
Onasilime (1st wife)	19 (Yabapunaku-Eimanaku)	J (Yabapunaku-Eimanaku), W (Silimalanaku), O1* (Iwaiwanaku)
Kikialu (2nd wife)	20 (Yabapunaku-Eimanaku)	O1* (Munimuninaku)
Namiesi (mother)	6 (Yabapunaku-Eimanaku) 13 (Munimuninaku), 19 (Yabapunaku-Eimanaku)	O1* (Munimuninaku)

*Garden O1 lay on the border between Iwaiwanaku and Munimuninaku domains.

In southern Garialand — certainly in Koli, Mubu and Iborau domains —
the situation is less random. Land tracts are so large that ego is more often
able to plant together with his agnates, the persons with whom he shares

Table 4 Gardens of Sogumu agnates and their families, 1949-50 and 1952-53: sources of personal rights

Personal names	Garden	Year	Land name and personal rights
Family 1			
Ábalia	17	1949-50	Oyesinō: own acquired strip
No'anime (wife)	19	1949-50	Oyesinō: husband's own acquired strip
Family 2			
Walili	15	1949-50	Kaka: acquired from MB
	18	1949-50	Sogumu: own patrilineage strip
	27	1949-50	Kaka: acquired from MB
	O1	1952-53	Sogumu: own patrilineage strip
	R1	1952-53	Tulua: own strip, acquired by FF
Paulalime (wife)	17	1949-50	Nali: lent by brother
	20	1949-50	Oyesinō: husband's own acquired strip
	B1	1952-53	Limau: lent by daughter's husband
Family 3			
Ubilili	12	1949-50	Na'ina: lent by close 'brother'
	U	1952-53	Limau-Au-Yoiyasi: lent by wife's kin
Ugialu (wife)	12	1949-50	Na'ina: see Ubilili above
	B1	1952-53	Limau: lent by brother
Labi	12	1949-50	Na'ina: see Ubilili above
	U	1952-53	Limau-Au-Yoiyasi: lent by MB
	B1	1952-53	Limau: lent by MB
	O1	1952-53	Sogumu: father's own patrilineage strip
Naguni	U	1952-53	Laimau-Au-Yoiyasi: lent by MB
Family 4			
Wawaku			During 1949-50 and 1952-53 they
Lasaume (wife)			lived at Uria in Ulilainaku domain,
Álitolo			planting Wawaku's own Oyesinō and Lasaume's father's Kopa'asamana land
Family 5			
Watutu	6	1949-50	Mosoli: acquired by Wailagime from matrikin and then transferred to Watutu with special agreement of Mosoli
	13a	1949-50	Usa: 3 strips acquired from MM patrilineage
	13b	1949-50	
	13c	1949-50	
	19	1949-50	Kailala: bequeathed to Kikialu [Kailala] (second wife) by her father
	K	1952-53	Kailala: bequeathed to Kikialu [Kailala] (second wife) by her father

(continued)

Table 4 — *continued*

Personal names	Garden	Year	Land name and personal rights
Family 5 — contd			
Watutu	O1	1952-53	Tulua: own strip, acquired by FF
	O1	1952-53	Wailagime: lent by cross-cousins
Onasilime	19	1949-50	Kulosi: lent by FB
(first wife)	J	1952-53	Kulosi: lent by FB
	W	1952-53	Togolu: borrowed through close 'father' Labaia [Mosoli], who had enatic ties to Togolu
	O1	1952-53	Tulua: husband's own strip, acquired by his FF
Kikialu	20	1949-50	Kailala: own strip, bequeathed by father
(2nd wife)			
	O1	1952-53	Wailagime: lent by husband's cross-cousins
Namiesi (mother)	6	1949-50	Mosoli: lent by brother, whose father acquired it from his MB
	13	1949-50	Usa: acquired by Watutu from MM patrilineage
	19	1949-50	Kailala: bequeathed to Kikialu [Kailala] by her father; Kikialu lent it to her husband's mother
	O1	1952-53	Wailagime: lent by her brother's children, Watutu's cross-cousins

permanent usufructuary rights. Even so, particularly for ambitious garden leaders, as I have already indicated, competition for labour may be so keen that, to meet the demand for large teams, ego may find himself, in some years at least, planting land of stocks in which he is an enate or of which he is an affine. A typical garden team consists of a band of agnates supplemented by enates and affines, the pattern being annually repeated although individual roles are changed as gardeners move from one tract to another. This is very true of southern Malainaku and Pukusakunaku domains, which have been reoccupied only during the last two and a half decades. Indigenous patrilineages on their own have been too small to provide garden teams capable of exploiting the big estates to their full potential. They have had to attract enates either as adopted agnates or as dependants, and they have had to be prepared to work on each other's land in alternate years.

This general situation is illustrated by Tables 3 and 4, and Map 4 (see also Genealogy 2). Table 3 sets out the gardens worked by Sogumu agnates and their families in 1949-50 and 1952-53. Table 4 lists their rights on the strips they worked. Map 4 shows the distribution of gardens in the Somau-Iwaiwa area at that time, which is fairly typical for all northern Garialand, and also southern Malainaku and Pukusakunaku domains. The analysis is most relevant for the next two chapters. As I have continually stressed, the system of land tenure I have described is a prime determinant of local organization, the details of which I present in Chapter 4. Yet, beyond this, the interlocking rights vested in agnates and enates within the same cognatic stock are of vital importance for the study of social control, which I take up in Chapter 5.

4

Land Tenure and
Local Organization

I have now presented the bulk of the evidence necessary to support my recurrent assertion about Garia local organization: that it has to be irregular and cannot correlate with any single feature of social structure. It has to be understood initially in the interchange between the ego-centred security circle and land tenure (especially the geographical distribution of personal holdings), although shifting allegiances to leaders or big men also exert a strong influence. In this situation, patriliny is not of overriding importance. In abstract structural terms, agnates *(sawaibopi)* are clearly distinguished from enates *(uibopi)* within the cognatic stock and, in land tenure, they are accorded special privileges and responsibilities in their collective capacity as a guardian patrilineage. Yet this does not determine where people live: patriliny does not provide a framework for settled local groups with clear political functions and, as already noted, is never granted primacy over enation in most everyday affairs. In fact, the stress on enation contributes to local instability on two counts. On the one hand, enatic ties very often compete with agnatic loyalties and enable the individual to acquire land rights from sources outside the patriline. On the other, they make possible a good deal of geographical mobility on the part of both whole families and individual males, although women are normally tied to their parents before, and their husbands after, marriage. There is a further relevant factor, which I have not stressed so far: the very strong division, not to say antagonism, between the sexes, which I summarize here but discuss in detail in Chapter 7.

Traditionally, the Garia family is not tightly knit. Its life is rarely intimate or close. This is apparent in normal male attitudes towards women and in residential patterns. Men dominate women, whom they regard as inherently dangerous. Men alone should eat betel-nut. They should not spend long hours in the company of women of child-bearing age if they value their health. Between adolescence and marriage a youth is forbidden to associate with — and certainly to take cooked food from — such women lest he become ill or, at the very least, ritually impotent. Only established married men may take such liberties, and even they are circumspect until late middle or even old age. In gardens and at other work sites men and women may labour side by side but, during rest periods, invariably sit, smoke and take snacks apart. Even if they engage in good-natured badinage, it is usually at a distance.

As already noted, a marriage begins in a tentative way. Even after the first marriage payment has been made, the bride and bridegroom are enjoined to live apart for about a year. When they consummate their marriage, they still do not live together in the European sense. The husband builds separate dwellings for his wife and himself (*uiata* and *yana* respectively), although he may continue to sleep in the men's clubhouse. He visits his wife briefly at night for sexual union.[1] Young children sleep with their mothers, girls continuing to do so until marriage. Adolescent sons, however, break away from their parents to sleep in the clubhouse, where they will be safe from female contamination. Indeed, at this time, they may leave their parents' settlements for either of two reasons. First, their inclination now is to see the world: they rove from settlement to settlement where they have close kin who will provide for them. Second, especially if their fathers' land resources are small, they will move in on those kinsmen most likely to help them out — for instance, winning favour with mothers' brothers by planting their land, swelling their followings and labour lines, and generally seeing to their welfare.

Hence, because of the social division between the sexes, family life is bound to be unstable, and conflicting kinship loyalties and economic interests encourage a boy to be migratory. In this he is helped by another obvious technological factor: the paucity of material possessions and the simplicity of architecture. He can carry virtually everything he owns or needs in a haversack or netbag and, if he does not choose to sleep in a clubhouse, he can erect a dwelling with at most one or two helpers. This migratory pattern may persist until well after his marriage. A man may not give it up until late middle age, and I have recorded examples of even elderly couples still on the move. Adult males, no less than adolescents, change settlements for comparable reasons. They have dispersed land interests which they wish to utilize. Also, as I have already indicated, leadership is a significant factor: people are attracted to different settlements by the presence of particularly influential and successful big men. Yet ego does not owe allegiance to only one leader at any one time: because of the dispersal of his economic interests, he is bound to work under several garden leaders in any single year. Moreover, big men wax and wane, and new ones take their place. Ordinary people like to be in or near a settlement with a big man with whom they can identify, provided this does not conflict with other considerations.

Nevertheless, for obvious reasons, local organization is bound to be more kaleidoscopic in northern than in southern Garialand. In the north ego's personal holdings are more fragmented and more widely dispersed than in the south, so that he has to be residentially flexible to exploit them satisfactorily until old age normally makes him more sedentary. In his prime, not only does he move from settlement to settlement over a period of years but also, in any one year, he may maintain and commute between houses in different settlements. Hence it is inevitable that settlement populations have no standard pattern. Hamlets contain irregular human aggregations: ego may find a random selection of 'brothers', 'parallel cousins', 'cross-cousins', 'fathers', 'maternal uncles', bush brothers, close and distant relatives, and even totally unrelated persons, together with their wives and unmarried daughters, wherever he is living at any one time. Such aggregations are rarely stable, for people join and leave them as they change garden sites and leaders. Agnates may be residentially separated for considerable periods, occasionally because of quarrels but more often because of their dispersed land interests, which may cause even true fathers and sons, and true brothers, to live apart. Finally, ego is not restricted to only one bush god domain. He may live in any domain in which he has permanent usufructuary rights, as either agnate or enate, or in which he has acquired only temporary cultivation rights. In short, the composition of northern settlements is based on the same principles and takes the same form as that of garden teams.

In three southern domains—Koli, Mubu and Iborau—local organization is more stable because the land named after a specific cognatic stock is generally a huge tract administered communally by its agnates or patrilineage. Traditionally, people lived in hamlets near their garden interests, so that agnates tended to live on their own land. Before 1942 the Australian Administration had concentrated the populations of the three domains in two villages: that of Koli in Tapopo, and those of Mubu and Iborau in

Igurue. These two settlements appear to have held together until the middle or late 1960s. Although agnates did not form residential clusters, many more whole patrilineages were found in these two villages than elsewhere in Garialand. Even so, this did not eliminate temporary migration. Individuals planted gardens with kinsmen other than agnates, even in neighbouring domains, and were thus required to live away from their normal homes. It is impossible, of course, to discuss Kamai'asa as it is now virtually uninhabited, but the situation in southern Malainaku and Pukusakunaku is essentially idiosyncratic because of their recent history. As indicated in Chapters 1 and 3, these areas were virtually unoccupied for more than two decades after the establishment of Australian administration and were resettled only during the 1950s. The problem of the leaders was to attract followers, a population to man what had become essentially a new frontier. As suggested, the pattern that has emerged is, in miniature, not unlike that now recognized as typical of many other parts of Papua New Guinea: settlements consisting of bands of agnates with clusters of enates and affines attached to them in various forms of dependence. Sets of agnates or local patrilineages within cognatic stocks — particularly those with few members, ambitious leaders, and hence a need for manpower — have attracted to themselves sisters' sons, patrilateral cross-cousins, any other available kinsmen, and even affines. Some of these people have purchased agnatic status, while others, who have opted for dependence, are either long- or short-term residents, or commuters, granted temporary cultivation rights.

Although the structure of the security circle is a constant throughout Garialand, my argument so far endorses my earlier comment on this subject: 'Local organization and land tenure can be regarded as linked variables, for any change in the one necessitates a corresponding change in the other' (Lawrence 1955: 44; 1967: 133).[2] Yet these linked variables are far more complex than I realized at the time. As I have suggested, local organization is capable of many permutations, which I can explain most easily by retracing in greater detail the history of migration which I sketched in Chapters 1 and 3. In the broad situation I observed and reconstructed, traditionally the people lived in dispersed hamlets (of fewer than fifty people each). After about 1925 they were concentrated in fourteen villages that survived the Japanese invasion, the fighting in 1944 and, to a large extent, the cargoist disturbances of 1947. In 1949 they were still more or less grouped in or around these official villages, although some persons were beginning to build and live in hamlets near their gardens, appearing in the villages only for visits by Administration officers or representatives of the Lutheran Mission. After 1950, with the relaxation of Administration pressures for consolidation, the villages began to atrophy as the people reverted to a more traditional form of local organization. By the late 1960s the pattern had become one of smaller villages or larger hamlets, with two subsequent exceptions. First, Mobo village was established west of Iwaiwa on the bank of the river from which it took its name. Second, Uria village, whose people had been dispersed in Matapa, Nabi, and hamlets near its original site, was reformed. Certainly in northern Garialand the return to traditional local organization has not led to stability. Migration and commuting are still common, and settlements rise in importance and then disappear. I present the account in three stages: the general picture I could see during my early field work; the history of specific settlements until about 1980; and the migrations of members of four sample patrilineages (see Maps 1, 4, 5, 6, 7, 8 and 9). I conclude the chapter with a summary of the main features of the Garia secular social order.

Sample Garia Settlements: 1949-50

In 1949-50 I studied the following villages: Somau and Iwaiwa, which were adjacent and consisted largely of persons with permanent usufructuary rights in Yabapunaku-Eimanaku, Äliliwanaku, Siliwanaku, Kutia, Iwaiwanaku, Malainaku and Kamai'asa domains; Pukisak, with those who had land rights in Pukusakunaku and Malainaku; Inam, with those who had rights in Palak-unaku; Onea, with those who had rights in Yaulilinaku; Yaniba and Kirili, with those who had rights in Munimuninaku; and Uria, with those who had rights in Orinaku and Ulilainaku. At that time the three villages of Somau, Iwaiwa and Pukisak inhabited a Y-shaped ridge complex focusing on Ubiolo, the then site of the Administration rest house. Architecturally and socially these Administration villages were merely hamlets writ large. I substantiate this by describing, first, Iwaiwa (Iwaiwanaku and Yabapunaku-Eimanaku domains), with an official population of 131 in 1949-50, and, second, a number of local hamlets that had hived off from several of the above villages.

Iwaiwa

Iwaiwa was a typical Administration village of the post-war period. It had seven wards: Ulabuaiyau, Pobulowau, Mamainesiau, Aubanuku, Änepoli-tabulo, Onai (uninhabited) and Yagili'ese'u. These wards were originally named bush sites at which hamlets were periodically established and then deserted. It had four men's clubs: Mamainesiau (1), Aubanuku (1) and Yagili'ese'u (2). Dwellings were both stilt houses, to suit Administration regulations, and traditional men's and women's houses attached to them, enabling married men and women to observe their rule of sleeping apart (see Map 5 and Table 5).

I list the principal patrilineages that were represented in Iwaiwa: Nali A and B, Yaukai, Kulosi, Na'ina and Kailala of Yabapunaku-Eimanaku domain; Sogumu, Uliamuni, Kaka and Tulua of Iwaiwanaku; Sulu and Usa of Munimuninaku; Pusuku of Yaulilinaku; Mawe'u'asamana of Palaku-naku; and Yoiyasi and Limau, identified with Iwaiwanaku, Malainaku, Ya-bapunaku-Eimanaku, Kamai'asa, Siliwanaku and Pukusakunaku. This general survey endorses the view that the bush god domain is unimportant in both political and local organization. The border between Iwaiwanaku and Yabapunaku-Eimanaku domains bisects the village. It is clear that, even allowing for administrative interest in village size rather than traditional so-cial categories, the people felt no obligation to live in domains primarily associated with their patrilineage land but chose residence to suit themselves. Of the above fifteen patrilineages, only two (Uliamuni and Yoiyasi) had all their male members registered in the village book. The others were dispersed. Thus, although all males of Nali B and some of Nali A lived in Iwaiwa, other Nali A males were in Uria or commuted between Kumusiasi and Araka. Yet, after 1950, Nali B also had split. Again, in 1949, Uliamuni, Yoiyasi and Nali B agnates did not form residential groups but were distributed through-out the village. True brothers might build close to each other but at a distance from their patriparallel cousins: for Nali B, Muyäli and his true brother Imoguli had houses directly opposite each other in Ulabuaiyau but some fifty metres away from that of their parallel cousin Apuniba in Mamainesiau (see Genealogy 3). Small patrilineages might not have even this degree of solidar-ity. For Yaukai (properly of Yabapunaku-Eimanaku), Usauba lived near his Tulua 'cross-cousins' in Yagili'ese'u, his patriparallel cousin Obenaku with his Uliamuni matrikin in Aubanuku, and his true younger brother Umugigi with his Keisibu affines in Somau village (Yabapunaku-Eimanaku domain). Finally, many inhabitants were continually migratory, commuting between Iwaiwa and various bush hamlets near their gardens.

I now describe three examples of hamlets at this time: Olaiku, E'ulu and Kulubaitabulo.

Olaiku

In 1949-50 there were thirty inhabitants of Olaiku hamlet in Äliliwanaku domain. This population consisted of members of the Kopenau-Muguliba section of Keisibu linked patrilineage (see Genealogy 8), together with their Siga and Karua bush brothers (also of Äliliwanaku), some Sui agnates (from

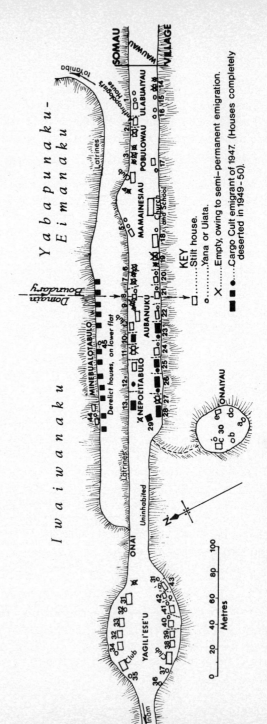

Map 5 Sketch map of house sites in Iwaiwa Village, 1949–50

Table 5 Householders in Iwaiwa, 1949-50

Householder	Patrilineage	Domain
1 Imoguli	Nali B	Yabapunaku-Eimanaku
2 Pesesa	Sulu	Munimuninaku
3 Pieku	Kulosi	Yabapunaku-Eimanaku
4 Taiguku	Kulosi	Yabapunaku-Eimanaku
5 Mogulu	Kaka	Iwaiwanaku
6 Waguta	Kulosi	Yabapunaku-Eimanaku
7 Nuoloku	Uliamuni	Iwaiwanaku
8 Ubilili	Sogumu	Iwaiwanaku
9 Abalia	Sogumu	Iwaiwanaku
10 Tomba	Sō	Munimuninaku
11 Mutiti	Uliamuni	Iwaiwanaku
12 Siki'apu	Asina	Yabapunaku-Eimanaku
13 Awoba	Maweu'asamana	Palakunaku
14 Onumala	Kailala	Yabapunaku-Eimanaku
15 Agiasi	Memuli	Palakunaku
16 Muyäli	Nali B	Yabapunaku-Eimanaku
17 Lalagua	Nali B	Yabapunaku-Eimanaku
18 Apuniba	Nali B	Yabapunaku-Eimanaku
19 Watutu	Sogumu	Iwaiwanaku
20 Yeyele'uma	Nali A	Yabapunaku-Eimanaku
21 Yorua	Pusuku	Yaulilinaku
22 Walili	Sogumu	Iwaiwanaku
23 Lagiki	Usa	Munimuninaku
24 Obenaku	Yaukai	Yabapunaku-Eimanaku
25 Ile'uma	Kina	Yaulilinaku
26 Tura	Sō	Munimuninaku
27 Mataraiba	Uliamuni	Iwaiwanaku
28 Kikipua	Sō	Munimuninaku
29 Payo	—	—
30a Pioba	Na'ina	Yabapunaku-Eimanaku
30b Taigilime	?	?
30c Tualime	Tulua	Iwaiwanaku
30d Usialu	Waipa	Siliwanaku
30e Yeyele'uma	Nali A	Yabapunaku-Eimanaku
31 Ilomala	Yoiyasi	Malainaku (see below)
32 E'uloku	Limau	Malainaku (see below)
33 Kukupia	Limau	Malainaku (see below)
34 Latiti	Uliamuni	Iwaiwanaku
35 Tebusi	Tulua	Iwaiwanaku
36 Manawalu	Tulua	Iwaiwanaku

(continued)

Table 5 — *continued*

Householder		Patrilineage	Domain
37	Kapapua	Keisibu	Ăliliwanaku
38	Kopulolime	Aliko	Kutia
39	Uluma	Usa	Munimuninaku
40	Kutumaiba	Tulua	Iwaiwanaku
41	Usauba	Yaukai	Yabapunaku-Eimanaku
42	Abulai'apu	Limau	Malainaku (see below)
43	Konoiba	Yoiyasi	Malainaku (see below)
44	Mutiti	Uliamuni	Iwaiwanaku
45	Nuoloku	Uliamuni	Iwaiwanaku

Householders 2, 10, 13, 23, 25, 26, 28 and 39 were 1947 cargo cult immigrants who had so far not returned home.

Householder 5 was the village evangelist, living near the church and away from his land in Iwaiwanaku domain.

Householders 7 and 11, true brothers, had alternative house sites (44 and 45) just north of Iwaiwa, where they preferred to live.

Householder 21 was a permanent immigrant: a Mission helper.

Householder 29: pre-war coastal evangelist who never returned.

Householders 30b-30e: Pioba's wife and three occasional residents — Yeyele'uma and his wife, and Mogulu's wife, who helped care for Pioba.

Householders 31, 32, 33, 42 and 43, all being Yoiyasi and Limau, had land rights also in Iwaiwanaku, Yabapunaku-Eimanaku, Pukusakunaku, Siliwanaku and Kamai'asa.

Kutia domain), who were also Keisibu enates, and Karoli, an adopted immigrant from the Rai Coast. The other Keisibu agnates were dispersed, partly because of land shortage and partly because of feud. The descendants of Kopenau's true brother Muguliba lived at Yagili'ese'u (Iwaiwa) near Tau land, which they had acquired. The Oi'asa section (an elderly man, and four parallel cousins and their children) was divided between Kumusiasi, Saurena and Wauwau (Somau village). Its members identified closely with other patrikin, especially with Mosoli agnates in Yabapunaku-Eimanaku domain, from whom they had acquired land. Otherwise two junior members of the Kopenau-Muguliba section ignored the enmities of the past and lived with Oi'asa representatives at Kumusiasi and Saurena. I recount the history of this situation in Chapter 6.

E'ulu and Kulubaitabulo

Although these two hamlets were respectively in Yabapunaku-Eimanaku and Orinaku domains, I discuss them jointly because their inhabitants had very close ties. They illustrate once again that identification with a bush god domain is largely irrelevant in settlement composition, even though, with the exception of two males (Kimolia in Iwaiwa and Ausilapu in Nugu), the two hamlets, albeit several kilometres apart, contained all male Kulosi agnates. Before describing how the two hamlets were established, I detail the inhabitants of each in Tables 6 and 7 (see also Genealogy 4).

Table 6 Inhabitants of E'ulu (Yabapunaku-Eimanaku domain), 1949-50

House 1: *Yana* — Pieku [Kulosi] of Yabapunaku-Eimanaku domain

House 2: *Uiata* — Pieku's wife Yobulime [Sogumu] of Iwaiwanaku domain and three small children, Kuguta (son), Selualime (daughter) and Ibaia (son).

House 3: *Yana* — Iwaiwanaku [Uliamuni] of Iwaiwanaku domain, Pieku's bush brother, a bachelor

House 4: *Uiata* — Yobulime's widowed mother Namiesi [Wailagime] of Munimuninaku and Yabapunaku-Eimanaku domains

House 5: *Uiata* — Onasilime [Kulosi], daughter of Pieku's true elder brother Enibuli and first wife of Watutu [Sogumu] of Iwaiwanaku domain, with her two small sons Nanaula and Maiäli.

House 6: *Yana* — once inhabited by Pieku's true elder brother Waguta, who had emigrated to Kulubaitabulo in Orinaku domain. It was occasionally used by Waguta's true son Taiguku, who commuted from Kulubaitabulo.

E'ulu had eleven inhabitants: Pieku's own elementary family minus his adolescent son Kimolia, who lived in Iwaiwa; a bachelor; an elderly widow; a married woman temporarily separated from her husband, with her two small children; and an occasional commuting male.

All these people officially lived in Iwaiwa, in whose village book they were registered. They slept in E'ulu mainly when they were preparing gardens in the vicinity. Iwaiwanaku is not listed as a householder in Table 5: as a bachelor, he slept in the Aubanuku clubhouse, together with other unmarried men, whenever he was in Iwaiwa.

Onasilime (House 5) was living temporarily with agnatic kin until her husband Watutu, recently returned from European employment, could build her a house at Wokutabulo just north of Iwaiwa village in Iwaiwanaku domain (see Map 4).

Table 7 Inhabitants of Kulubaitabulo (Orinaku domain), 1949-50

House 1: Clubhouse occupied by: Taiguku, Ilobibi and Patuma [Kulosi], and Onumala [Kailala], all of Yabapunaku-Eimanaku domain; Ulani and Pale [Kimanu] of Orinaku domain; and Uapu [Oyesinō] of Ulilainaku domain

House 2: *Uiata* — Uapu's wife Nalaialu [?] of Yaulilinaku domain and her four children, Pobotili (son), Naruna (son), Yaureba (son) and Nuranime (daughter)

House 3: *Uiata* — Patuma's wife Kebaniasi [Tei] of Orinaku domain and her daughter Uiyoyosi

House 4: *Uiata* — Onumala's wife Mobialu [Sakura] of Unoba domain, and her son and daughter, Togia and Unagime

House 5: *Uiata* — Waguta's half-sister and Ulani's mother Uninime [Kulosi] of Yabapunaku-Eimanaku domain and her adolescent daughter Aulime. Her husband To'ila [Kimanu] of Orinaku domain was dead

House 6: *Yana* — Waguta [Kulosi] of Yabapunaku-Eimanaku domain

House 7: *Uiata* — Waguta's wife Kililime [Keisibu] of Äliliwanaku domain

House 8: *Uiata* — Taiguku's wife Punaume [Wolu] of Orinaku domain

House 9:   Derelict.

The hamlet had a population of twenty-two, with five elementary families and males of four patrilineages from three bush god domains, the boundaries of which converged in the general vicinity of the settlement. Most of the inhabitants were linked by ties of kinship, affinity and bush brotherhood.

All these people officially lived in either Iwaiwa or Uria village, where their names were registered. They slept in Kulubaitabulo mainly when they were preparing gardens nearby.

The three hamlets described were typical of northern Garialand between 1949 and 1953 in that they had no uniform composition. People lived in them because of security circle relationships, land interests in the area, and the attraction of big men. E'ulu and Kulubaitabulo bear this out very clearly. Pieku and Iwaiwanaku lived in E'ulu initially because they had land strips (Kulosi and Uliamuni) interdigitated along that part of the border between Iwaiwanaku and Yabapunaku-Eimanaku. Iwaiwanaku, a bachelor of no consequence, was happy to attach himself to Pieku, who was by now a big man. Pieku was glad to have a helper at hand. The other inhabitants were his permanent or temporary dependants.

Kulubaitabulo was the more interesting of the two settlements largely because of Waguta's role in establishing it in early 1949. Kulosi was a large and most influential patrilineage with two big men apart from Pieku: Waguta was highly regarded throughout northern Garialand and Taiguku was beginning to make a name for himself. Wealth in land enhanced their self-assurance, as was apparent in their periodic disrespect for marriage rules.

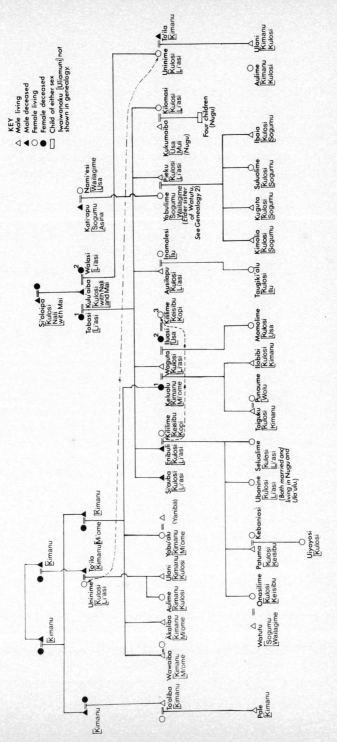

Genealogy 4 Kulosi and Kimanu agnates (patrilineages)

They had intermarried with Kimanu of Orinaku domain, although some people asserted that the two patrilineages had enough interdigitated land strips to be bush brothers. Kuluaiba had married two Liasi women, the second of whom was his affine, technically forbidden to him. Recently his son Waguta (then at E'ulu) had married the widow of his own true brother Enibuli — in complete defiance of accepted usage — on the excuse that she needed protection and the supposition that the dead man's ghost would not molest him as they had been very close during his lifetime. Yet, when wild pig ravaged his gardens around E'ulu, he acknowledged his fault and took his wife to Kulubaitabulo, which had been uninhabited since the cargo disturbances of 1947 and where he had rights on Mai land. Mai agnates were now extinct, and Kulosi and Kimanu claimed to be the only surviving enates. Hence they assumed both usufructuary and guardian rights over this new estate. Waguta used these holdings, without further trouble from feral pigs, while Pieku planted Kulosi and Nali strips (the latter acquired from his FFMB) around E'ulu. Their sons commuted between the two settlements.

Waguta's reputation as a garden leader soon attracted other residents to Kulubaitabulo. The Kulosi and Kimanu agnates had a common interest in Mai land. Indeed, Kimanu agnates were no strangers to the hamlet: Ulani's father To'ila had lived there in the past, and his widowed mother Uninime had now returned. Uapu [Oyesinō] had no ties with Kulosi but was a bush brother of Kimanu agnates. Onumala [Kailala] claimed bush brotherhood with both Kulosi and Kimanu agnates, and found the hamlet a convenient staging post between his gardens near Somau-Iwaiwa and those he planted with his MZS near Amasua in Girawaland (cf. p. 60 above). There were five other transients not listed in Table 6: To'aliba and Äkaliba [Kimanu], who lived normally in Uria and Ula'ulu, Ausilapu [Kulosi], who lived normally in Nugu, and two other men [Li'asi and Miome] from Yaniba. All these men planted strips in gardens around Kulubaitabulo supervised by Waguta as well as others in those nearer their normal places of residence. For several years, therefore, the hamlet was an important socioeconomic link between the main Garia settlements of Somau, Iwaiwa, Yaniba, Uria and Nugu, and — through Onumala — between them and the Girawa village of Amasua.

The History of Settlements until August 1980

I now trace the broad pattern of Garia settlement formation from about 1942[3] until 1980 against the background of the cases I have given. Again I deal, first, with the northern area together with southern Malainaku and Pukusakunaku domains, in which I did the bulk of my field research, and,

Slaughtering a pig, 1972

Rising big man addresses moot, 1952

A moot, 1952: close relatives shake hands

A football match at Uria, 1949

second and more briefly, with Koli, Mubu and Iborau. I ignore Kamai'asa for want of information.

My description of Iwaiwa village and two of its associated hamlets, E'ulu and Kulubaitabulo, substantiates my previous claim that the northern Garia, while preferring their traditional system of small settlement local organization, did not resent the new one imposed by the Australian Administration as long as it did not remove them too far from their land interests — a factor ignored by the cargo cultists in 1947. During 1949-50 — in fact, for several years thereafter — villages and their surrounding hamlets maintained a genuine symbiosis: people moved easily from one to the other to meet different requirements, those of Administration work on the one hand, and those of traditional socioeconomic life, especially agriculture, on the other.

Yet, even in 1949 — and certainly after 1950 — the pattern was beginning to break up as the people realized that the Administration was no longer enforcing its pre-war policy of concentrating them in large villages. By mid-1949, although they maintained their villages architecturally against Administration patrols and Mission visits, they were spending progressively more of their time in their bush hamlets. The new settlements were rarely stable for long: in the way I have demonstrated, populations fluctuated because of shifting garden interests and loyalties to big men, and petty disputes. Near Iwaiwa, in Iwaiwanaku domain, Pioba [Na'ina] had already established Onaiyau, although his interests were largely in Yabapunaku-Eimanaku, and Watutu [Sogumu] (see Table 6) was founding Wokutabulo. Near Somau, in Yabapunaku-Eimanaku domain, Kokopula [Wailagime] had left Yaniba for Takaulo (not far from E'ulu), where he had some patrilineage strips, and was joined by his close 'son' Tupalia [Mosoli] and his family (see Genealogy 9). The settlement disappeared after Kokopula's death in 1953. South of Somau and near Olaiku, in Äliliwanaku domain, two new hamlets Saurena (population 3) and Kumusiasi (10) formed round Munia, leader of the Oi'asa section of Keisibu patrilineage, which, as noted, was estranged from the Kopenau-Muguliba section (see Genealogy 8). He attracted some, but not all, Oi'asa section agnates together with the two junior descendants of Kopenau who had no interest in their forebears' dispute. Other Oi'asa section agnates (Wila, Liwei, and their children) remained in Wauwau (Somau village), while Muguliba's agnatic descendants lived, as noted, in Yagili'ese'u (Iwaiwa). Munia was joined by Kasumala [Nali A], who already had, and Apuniba [Nali B], who was at that time acquiring, unsufructuary rights to Muli land near Araka and Epu. Kasumala was a frequent resident of Kumusiasi, while Apuniba used it as a staging post because he was *Tultul* of Iwaiwa, where he had to spend much of his time (see Genealogy 3).

At the southern end of Mount Somau, in Yabapunaku-Eimanaku domain, eight people formed Malugunotabulo on Siga land. Paradoxically, its central figure was Lugia, an eight-year-old and orphaned Siga agnate who had inherited considerable landholdings in the area. He was under the care of a true cross-cousin (Poianiba) and quite close 'father' Labaia [Mosoli], who had Siga interests in his own right and whose true brother Tupalia was in Takaulo with Kokopula. Labaia was also a close 'brother' of Poianiba. Nearby, also in Yabapunaku-Eimanaku domain, was Garia hamlet (12). As Siga land lay also in Äliliwanaku, the inhabitants of both these settlements planted gardens in that domain as well.

Between 1950 and 1953 Garia population movements became more obvious. In October 1952 there were at least thirteen new hamlets in the area bounded by Araka, Uria, Yaniba, Iwaiwa and Somau. I present details only for the most important. Late in 1950, with Administration approval, partly because of divergent land interests and partly because of a dysentery epidemic, Uria (158) split into two settlements — Matapa (51) and Nabi (34) — the rest of the people moving to hamlets elsewhere. Onaiyau disappeared when Pioba emigrated to Tai near Igurue in Mubu domain. E'ulu doubled its size to twenty-three, while Kulubaitabulo was halved to eleven, some of its inhabitants joining emigrants from Uria and Ula'ulu at Iolo (24) nearby. Olaiku dropped from thirty to twenty-four, while Kumusiasi expanded from ten to thirty-four, its most significant immigrants being the remaining Oi'asa agnates of Keisibu from Wauwau (Somau). Araka slipped from twenty-three to seventeen, even though Apuniba [Nali B], no longer *Tultul* of Iwaiwa, and his two sons had settled there (see Genealogy 3).

As I have said, the most interesting development at that time was the reoccupation of southern Malainaku and Pukusakunaku by their original inhabitants, who had been concentrated at Nauwau and Kopa'olo south of Somau and Iwaiwa before 1942, dispersed by the fighting in 1944, regrouped after the Allied recapture of Madang, and then concentrated once again as Pukisak village (81) along Suaiyau Ridge near Ubiolo by the cargoists in 1947. After 1950 they began to move down towards the Pike.

The central figures in this migration were the two leaders I have already introduced: Pubule'uma [Au] of Malainaku and his patrilateral cross-cousin Imoguli [Nali B] of Yabapunaku-Eimanaku, who, by 1952, had decided to accept agnatic status in Au cognatic stock. The combination of these two men was formidable. Pubule'uma was a traditional big man of very great renown but he lacked modern skills, especially fluency in Pidgin and, therefore, the ability to deal with the Australian Administration and the development programme it was just beginning to introduce. Imoguli had these qualifications as well as traditional skills: he had been to Mission schools; he had worked for Europeans; he spoke excellent Pidgin; he was clearly a man of intellect who enjoyed cordial relations with visiting Administration officials; and he was widely respected for his ability as a political negotiator and for his mastery of religious knowledge, the importance of which I discuss in Chapters 7 and 8. In addition, he could help solve Pubule'uma's most pressing need, manpower, by bringing him, apart from himself, his three sons and, potentially, his brother's son Walukuni, who was for several years a continual visitor to, and eventually a permanent resident of, the Pike area. He could attract also other members of his security circle.

In 1951 Pubule'uma and Imoguli led the inhabitants of Suaiyau Ridge and Kopa'olo to the new village of Maulemusumu[4] (111) in southern Malainaku, where they remained until the early 1960s. They attracted some other dependants, such as Ubilili [Sogumu], a close 'brother' of Imoguli and an affine of Limau (see Genealogies 2 and 3). Ubilili died in 1952, but his second son Naguni settled permanently in Maulemusumu. His elder son Labi remained in Iwaiwa to supervise his father's Sogumu holdings. About 1960, Labi went to work in Lae for ten years. When he returned in 1971 he settled with Naguni in the new big hamlet of Ugalimuku by the Pike, which had replaced Maulemusumu. He brought in additional kinsmen such as his Kaka 'brother' Neiku from Iwaiwa.

Maulemusumu lasted until the establishment of Usino Patrol Post in 1963, by which time Pubule'uma was dead and Imoguli, who survived him by two years, could no longer hold the village together. Thereafter it split into three hamlets: Isi'oku (27) and Ulumapike (38) in Pukusakunaku, and Ugalimuku (35) in Malainaku. These three settlements were still there in 1972 although, by 1975, Ulumapike was deserted, its inhabitants opting about equally for either Isioku or Ugalimuku. Also, Ugalimuku was moved away from the Pike to avoid flooding during the wet season. The populations of these settlements were as irregular as those in northern Garialand, from which many of their inhabitants were recruited. In 1972 Pubule'uma's son Yolili [Au] and Imoguli's brother's son Walukuni [Au adopted] lived in Ulumapike in Pukusakunaku, although most of their land interests were in Malainaku. Walukuni kept a second house in Ugalimuku. Again, Imolalia [Nali A] (Genealogy 3) commuted between Suaiyau Ridge, where his widowed mother then lived, and the Pike, where he claimed rights to Ulapu land in Pukusakunaku through his matrikin. He did not sleep in Isi'oku or Ulumapike, as might have been expected, but in Ugalimuku (Malainaku) because of his Nali tie with Imoguli's sons. His garden interests were still sufficiently close. Even the desertion of Ulumapike did not lead to the consolidation of Ugalimuku and Isi'oku: although their composition broadly followed that of local garden teams—agnatic bands augmented by enates and affines from elsewhere—by no means all the male agnates of a cognatic stock (a whole patrilineage) were always living in either settlement. Thus, in May 1975, Yolili [Au] and Imoguli's eldest son Mologiki [Au adopted] had moved north from Ugalimuku to Keriasutabulo, on the border between the small strip and huge tract complexes in Malainaku domain. They left the southern tract to their younger brothers in Ugalimuku to supervise.

After 1950 this general process repeated itself continually throughout northern and southern Garialand. In the north it was particularly marked. Somau and Iwaiwa dropped from 99 and 131 in 1949-50 to 78 and 130 in 1952-53, and 46 and 76 in 1965, respectively. In 1965 E'ulu was deserted: Kulosi agnates and their clients, led by Waguta's son Taiguku, had moved to Ario, which had a population of 32. Kulubaitabulo also was deserted but there were 18 people in nearby Iolo. Olaiku's population fell to 18 and that of Kumusiasi to 7, while Epu (near Araka), uninhabited between 1949 and 1953, had become a thriving village of 53 persons under the leadership of Kasumala [Nali A]. He attracted people from his own domain (Yabapu-naku-Eimanaku), from which he was now a permanent emigrant, and also from Kutia, Ubesuanaku and Aliliwanaku. Like himself, they claimed land rights in the area through enatic ties. Although Poine, Nugu, Onea, E'unime, Kolu and Inam were still largely intact, Totoba, Yaniba and Kirili, like Uria, had each split into several settlements.

In 1972 the distribution had changed again. Somau and Iwaiwa were no longer villages in the technical sense: Somau now had 29 inhabitants (21 in Wauwau and 8 in Ubi'olo), and Iwaiwa 24 (21 in Aubanuku and 3 in Yagili'ese'u). They were no more than clusters of geographically adjacent hamlets. On Suaiyau Ridge the only settlement was Kokolenau with two persons. Ario had been deserted in 1971, while E'ulu was resettled with a population of 23 and Asilo, a new hamlet nearby, had 26 inhabitants. Iolo now had 23, Olaiku 13 and Epu only 31, although Araka and Kumusiasi were re-established with about five people each. Uria, split into a number of settlements for about twenty years, came together again around a new Administration medical aid post with a population of about 140, while the inhabitants of Onea, Yaniba, Kirili and Inam moved down to the riverain village of Mobo, which had 68 people in 1972. Subsequently this number was gradually augmented by immigrants from Kolu and E'unime although, by August 1980, the village showed signs of disintegrating: 7 people had returned to Onea, 17 to Yaniba and about 10 to Kirili, because they had moved too far away from their habitual garden sites. In 1972 Totoba no longer existed but settlements around Nugu were still intact despite the serious earthquake in 1970. In 1975 Somau village had entirely disappeared except for 6 people at Ubiolo, although Kokolenau on Suaiyau Ridge (two persons in 1972) had expanded considerably. In 1975 Iwaiwa's population had grown to 30, although it was entirely concentrated at Yagili'ese'u, which, as noted, in 1972 had only three people. Again, despite its population of 23 in 1972, E'ulu was once again deserted by August 1978. Taiguku [Kulosi] re-established Kulubaitabulo, which had been uninhabited for over a decade, although his sons moved to Yagili'ese'u in Iwaiwa, Ubiolo in Somau and Od near Madang. E'ulu was still deserted in May 1979.

Of the six domains in southern Garialand I have already given the figures for, and described the general pattern in, southern Malainaku and Pukusak-unaku during the first two decades after their resettlement in the 1950s. (As noted, I ignore Kamai'asa because of its lack of population.) Mubu, Iborau and Koli (Igurue and Tapopo villages) appear to have been relatively stable until the establishment of Usino Airstrip and Patrol Post in the early 1960s. In 1965 Igurue was still intact, although Tapopo had split into two, each group remaining in Koli but living near its own patrilineage tracts. In 1975 there were still only two Koli settlements, although Igurue was now dispersed: two groups remained in Mubu, while another settled at Waburu in Iborau, where its members claimed their land.[5]

The figures in Table 8 do not cover all Garialand or represent all my census material, which is too complex to present. They are a general sample intended to summarize my foregoing account of village and hamlet formation in the northern and south-western areas between 1949 and 1980. Clearly, in the aggregate, settlement composition seems unpredictable, even capricious. It is only from the point of view of the individual that it is possible to appreciate the inherent logic of local organization. As I have stressed, ego's movements are dictated by his personal economic and social interests. Settlements are not 'continuing units' in the sense posited by Leach (1956). Certainly, named hamlet sites are permanent in that they are always there. Especially if big men show the necessary interest — as in the cases of Olaiku, E'ulu, Kulubaitabulo and Epu — they may be occupied for long periods or intermittently reoccupied after having been abandoned for several years, even though their personnel continually change. Yet there are no strong attachments to these sites: there is no unwavering conviction that they must be occupied. Ego's attitude is utilitarian. He will inhabit a site only if it is to his advantage to do so: if it enables him to exploit his landholdings; if a reasonable number of its inhabitants belong to his security circle; and particularly if it has a leader on whose protection he can rely. To recapitulate, the crucial feature of northern and south-western Garia society is not a system of territorial groups but the nexus between land rights, security circle bonds, and ties to big men. The same argument applies, to a lesser degree, to the southern domains of Koli, Mubu

Table 8 Sample Garia settlements: population figures, 1949-72

Settlement	1949-50	1952-53	1965	1972
Araka	23	17	0	c.5
Ario	0	0	32	0
Asilo	0	0	0	26
Epu	0	0	53	31
E'ulu	11	23	0	23
Inam	85	86	c.86	9
Iolo	0	24	18	23
Isioku	0	0	c.27	27
Iwaiwa	131	130	76	24
Kirili	37	38	0	0
Kulubaitabulo	22	11	0	23
Kumusiasi	10	34	7	c.5
Matapa	0	51	c.51	0
Maulemusumu	0	111	0	0
Mobo	0	0	0	68
Nabi	0	34	c.34	0
Olaiku	30	24	18	13
Onea	34	18	c.18	0
Pukisak	81	0	0	0
Saurena	3	0	0	0
Somau	99	78	46	29
Ugalimuku	0	0	c.35	35
Ulumapike	0	0	c.38	38
Uria	158	0	0	c.140
Yaniba	56	69	c.69	27

and Iborau. To illustrate the logic of the process from the individual's point of view, I now detail the migrations of the male members of four patrilineages (sets of agnates), especially since 1949.

Migration of Members of Four Sample Patrilineages

Of the four cases I have chosen, I begin with Sogumu and show how its members' movements have correlated with their access to land through either permanent or temporary usufructuary rights as previously recorded, and with their allegiance to specific big men. I then present Kulosi, Mosoli and Nali in less detail, although I demonstrate that their situations are comparable.

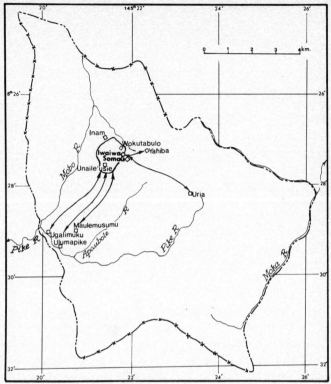

Map 6 Migrations of Sogumu agnates

Sogumu (Genealogy 2, Tables 2, 3 and 4, and Map 6)

During the last three decades Sogumu agnates have had to be migratory because of the dispersion of their personal holdings. Named Sogumu strips are few — a fact attributed to heavy alienation in the past — and concentrated largely in Iwaiwanaku domain, although there are outliers in Yabapunaku-Eimanaku and Ulilainaku.[6] As a result, past and present generations have acquired unsufructuary rights to additional strips from matrikin and transmitted them to their patrilineal heirs. Until recently their acquired holdings have been in central Garialand: Iwaiwanaku, Yabapunaku-Eimanaku, Ulilainaku, Äliliwanaku and Munimuninaku through affinal and enatic ties. Since 1980, however, they have acquired permanent usufructuary rights in Malainaku and Kamai'asa domains.

Before 1925 Sogumu agnates seem to have lived mainly in Iwaiwanaku and Yabapunaku-Eimanaku domains. After the establishment of modern administration, from 1927 until 1942, Walili worked as a highly respected foreman (Pidgin *bosboi*) at Dylup Plantation north of Madang. Ubilili trained in the Madang Native Hospital to become Medical *Tultul* of Iwaiwa. Watutu spent some of this time away in indenture but, like Walili, came home soon after the Japanese invasion. Äbalia and Wawaku did not go away. At this time, they all regarded Iwaiwa as their home and lived there until the Shaggy Ridge operations, when they scattered in the bush. Thereafter they and their children rarely lived together. In 1949 Walili and Ubilili, with their families, were in Iwaiwa. Watutu, once again just back from European employment, was setting himself up at Wokutabulo, north of Iwaiwa. Äbalia and his wife lived in Yaniba (Munimuninaku domain), planting his own Oyesi and his maternal uncle's Miome land, until he went to prison and she to Negri (Girawaland) in 1950-51 (see Chapter 6). Wawaku was in Uria (Ulilainaku domain), farming his inherited Oyesinō and his affines' Kopa'asamana holdings. In 1950 he and his family returned to Iwaiwa to plant Sogumu strips but a year later were back in Uria, where he and his wife died. His son Älitolo went to Administration school and has never come home: in May 1979 he was a clerk at the Mount Hagen Airfield. Walili and his wife died in Iwaiwa in the 1950s.

After 1950 the most important Sogumu agnates were Ubilili, Watutu, and their sons. In 1950 Ubilili, who had been ill, moved to Unaile'usie, south of Iwaiwa. A year later he accepted an invitation from his 'brother' Imoguli {Nali B-Au} to emigrate with his younger son Naguni to Maulemusumu in southern Malainaku, where, as an affine, he had access to the joint Yoiyasi-Au-Limau estate. Before Ubilili's death in 1952 his elder son Labi planted a garden with him in Malainaku but thereafter lived in Iwaiwa until the early 1960s, when he went to work in Lae for about ten years. Meanwhile Watutu, *Tultul* of Iwaiwa in 1950 and *Luluai* in 1952, brought his family from Wokutabulo to live permanently in the village. At that time he was a strong supporter of the District Office's abortive project to build the motor road from Madang to Bundi. Despite his disappointment in this venture, together with Saramuri, *Luluai* of Usino, he used his influence to establish the airstrip and patrol post at Usino before he died in 1965. Äbalia, released from prison, died in Iwaiwa about the same time.

The future now lay with Ubilili's and Watutu's sons. Labi, who returned from Lae about 1971, settled in Ugalimuku (Malainaku). Naguni, who had lived in Ulumapike (Pukusakunaku), at once joined him there. As I have already indicated, they initially declined Imoguli's sons' overture to adopt agnatic status in Limau, their mother's primary cognatic stock. In August 1978, when Ilimaipa {Au} died and left Malainaku domain short of adult males, they agreed to accept it — on the understanding that they should not forfeit their natal agnatic status in Sogumu — and they provided the custom-ary pigs for the funeral as a down-payment. Yet, by May 1979, they had met with serious opposition from Watutu's sons, who had left secondary school in Madang, were now living at Asilo near E'ulu, and did not wish to see the loyalties of their big men (even though they were living virtually permanently in Malainaku) divided in this way. It was only in June or July 1980 that they overcame these objections and were able to formalize their decision.

Kulosi (Genealogy 4 And Map 7)

Until 1949 Kulosi agnates were relatively localized because of their ample holdings in Yabapunaku-Eimanaku and Iwaiwanaku domains. With the exception of Ausilapu, who chose to live in Nugu (Mubunaku domain) with his Ilunō affines, they were all in Iwaiwa until the Shaggy Ridge campaign in

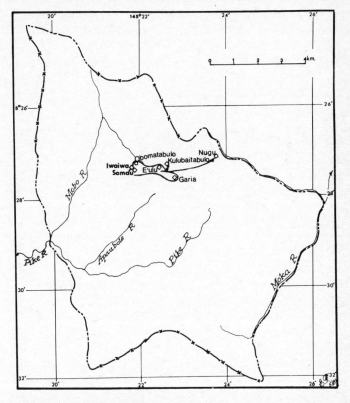

Map 7 Migrations of Kulosi agnates

1944, when they hid in the bush around E'ulu. By 1947 Ausilapu was back in Nugu, while the others had regrouped in Iwaiwa. Two years later they were dispersed: Pieku, Kuguta, Ibaia, Selualime and Onasilime in E'ulu; Kimolia in Iwaiwa; and Waguta, Ilobibi, Patuma, Taiguku (who commuted to E'ulu), Uiyoyosi, Uninime, and occasionally Ausilapu (who commuted from Nugu) in Kulubaitabulo. In 1952 the position was much the same, although Kimolia, Kuguta and Ilobibi, now adolescents, regularly commuted between Iwaiwa, E'ulu, Kulubaitabulo and Iolo. In 1965, although Ausilapu was still alive in Nugu, Waguta and Pieku were dead. Taiguku, now a big man, had brought together most of his fellow agnates and their dependants at Ario near Somau village, where they used Kulosi rather than Mai land: Ilobibi, Kuguta, Kimolia (and their wives and children) and several enates and bush brothers. Patuma was away in European employment. In 1972 Kulosi agnates were once again dispersed. They abandoned Ario: Taiguku and Ilobibi returned to E'ulu; Kuguta and Ibaia went to Asilo; and Kimolia went to Obomatabulo north of Aubanuku. At this time they were once more using Mai land in Orinaku domain, so that Taiguku, Ilobibi, Kuguta and Ibaia spent a good deal of their time in Kulubaitabulo. By August 1978 they had entirely vacated E'ulu, Asilo and Obomatabulo. Taiguku lived in Kulubaitabulo, while the others were distributed between Yagili'ese'u (Iwaiwa), Ubiolo (Somau) and Od (Madang). There was no change in May 1979.

Mosoli (Genealogies 5 and 8, and Map 8)

The two linked sections of Mosoli are most properly associated with Yabapunaku-Eimanaku domain, which contains most of its named land strips, although there are outliers in Äliliwanaku. Yet Mosoli agnates have generally been geographically dispersed. In the 1930s Sonobonaku took his family to live with his Kopi affines at Pailetabulo near Nugu (Mubunaku domain), where he died before 1949, although his son Siopai returned to Somau (Akiau ward) to become its *tultul* before the Japanese invasion. Meanwhile Ibagia and his family were with his affines [Milimili] in Uria (Ulilainaku domain) and then with his Keisibu cross-cousins at Olaiku in Äliliwanaku, where he had some Mosoli strips together with others he had acquired from his matrikin. In 1940 he became *Luluai* of Somau, a position he held until 1952, when he was succeeded by Watutu [Sogumu]. He died soon afterwards. During these twelve years he set up house in the Oitewau ward of Somau, although he did not live there permanently until 1945.

Tupalia and Labaia grew up in a similarly independent atmosphere. Their father Murunaku lived and died on the southern slopes of Mount Somau in

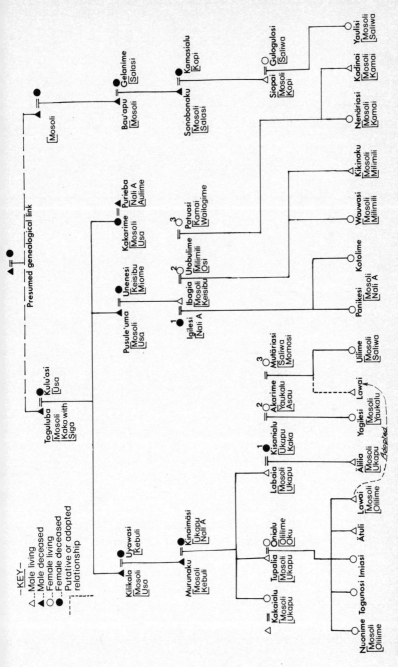

Genealogy 5 Mosoli agnates (patrilineage)

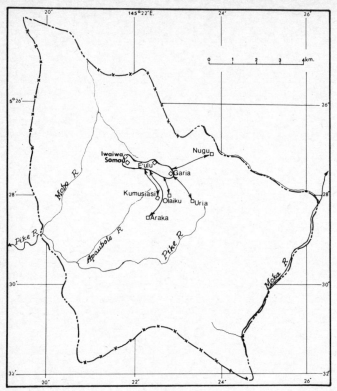

Map 8 Migrations of Mosoli agnates

Yabapunaku-Eimanaku and Äliliwanaku domains, where he had Mosoli and Siga holdings. After adolescence Tupalia lived continually with his father's patrilateral 'cross-cousin' Yerema [Nali A] at Araka and Kumusiasi (Ubesuanaku and Äliliwanaku domains), while Labaia stayed near his father, living in Garia hamlet (Yabapunaku-Eimanaku) under the care of a classificatory 'father' Uimepu [Mai] of Orinaku. He planted Murunaku's Mosoli and Siga land. The two brothers entered European employment in the 1930s, although Labaia became Medical *Tultul* of Somau before the Japanese occupation.

In 1949, after years of dispersal, all Mosoli agnates were concentrated in Somau village, although not as a single residential group: Tupalia and Siopai in Akiau ward, Ibagia in Oitewau, and Labaia in Yomestabulo. The younger children were with their parents, but Kadinai and Älilia slept in the clubhouses in Oitewau and Usitabulo respectively. This pattern lasted more or less until 1953, except that in 1950 Tupalia moved to Takaulo to look after his close 'father' Kokopula [Wailagime]. By 1965 Ibagia and Kadinai were dead, and Siopai and Kikinaku in European employment. Tupalia and Labaia, with their unmarried children, had moved to Ubiolo in Somau. They remained together until late 1974 or early 1975, when Tupalia left for Silo hamlet east of Somau village, on the border of Yabapunaku-Eimanaku and Äliliwanaku domains. Labaia died at Ubiolo in 1976. During this time Ätuli was working at Usino Patrol Post, Älilia was at Asilo and Lawai was said to be working in Lae.

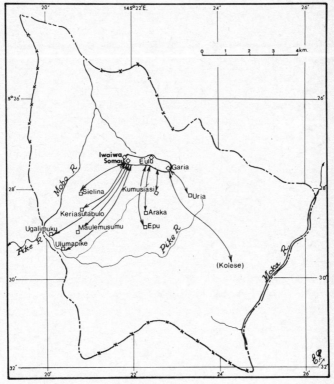

Map 9 Migrations of Nali agnates

Nali (Genealogy 3 and Map 9)

The three Nali agnatic sections — the patrilineal descendants of Putu'apu and Kunoiba putatively linked as Nali A, and those of Imileba adopted as Nali B — were properly associated with Yabapunaku-Eimanaku domain but were always dispersed. By 1949 Nali A agnates had little social cohesion.

Tulamia lived obscurely on his mother's land in Uria. The others had been estranged before the war when Yerema abducted Ulei'eialu, the wife of his patrilineage 'father' Yolekauma, an ageing nonentity, whom he threatened to kill. As a big man he ignored general opinion, and nothing at all was done. The two men's sons, Yeyele'uma and Kasumala, did not perpetuate the quarrel but never lived together and rarely co-operated. Yolekauma remained under the protection of his Wailagime and Ulawa kin, and near his own land, in Iwaiwa, where his son Yeyele'uma became a close associate of the Lutheran Mission until his death about 1964. Yerema moved to Araka and Kumusiasi, where he died in the 1940s. His son Kasumala was in European employment until 1942 and served as a scout with the Australian Army thereafter. In 1949 he was listed as a resident of Somau, but spent most of his time between Kumusiasi and Araka. As noted, in the 1960s he became the leader of Epu, which he built into an important settlement. But by August 1972 he was an ill man and his followers were melting away. He died at Kumusiasi in April or May 1975.

Until 1950 Nali B agnates showed a degree of solidarity. They liked each other, tended to live in the same settlement, and co-operated whenever they could. Yet economic considerations forced them to be periodically migratory and eventually to scatter. As immigrants from Koli domain, they were always short of land. By 1940 they had some Nali and Sogumu strips but otherwise had to depend on the goodwill of kinsmen, bush brothers and affines to lend or lease them garden sites. But, as they were now relatively numerous with several established or emerging big men, they did not relish dependent status. It was inevitable that they should turn to different sets of matrikin to increase their holdings.

After 1925 Apuniba and Imoguli were away at Mission school and then on contract labour, but had returned before the Japanese occupation. Together with Älikoko, Mamauli, Muyäli, and their respective families, they lived in Iwaiwa in association with Yeyele'uma [Nali A]. They were now respected men: Apuniba was *Tultul* of Iwaiwa and Imoguli a rising big man. All Nali B agnates seem to have remained in Iwaiwa until 1943 when, under the circumstances I have described, the people began to move out to bush hamlets. During the Shaggy Ridge operations of 1944 they all fled — Älikoko, Mamauli, Lalagua, Apuniba and their families to Araka (Ubesuanaku domain), where they had an interest in Muli land, and Muyäli, Imoguli and their families to Kopa'olo and Si'elina in Malainaku. After the war, they were all regrouped in Iwaiwa but by 1950 they were showing signs of a new and more permanent dispersal. Älikoko and Mamauli had recently died. Apuniba was purchasing rights to Muli land in Ubesuanaku domain from his exchange partner Wowoli (see Chapter 5), while his sons Papoku and Kiagita looked to their own mother's brother, Pioba [Na'ina] of Yabapunaku-Ei-manaku, for help. As noted, Muyäli and Imoguli had purchased rights to Au land, and it was now merely a question of how they would exercise them: as client enates with permanent usufructuary rights to a number of strips in northern Malainaku or as quasi-agnates sharing communal rights to the huge estates in south-western Garialand. Muyäli died in 1951.

By early 1953 the situation was resolved. Lalagua, who had commuted between Iwaiwa and Araka, was dead. Apuniba, no longer *Tultul* of Iwaiwa, was at Araka with his sons Papoku and Kiagita, who also commuted to Iwaiwa to use the Na'ina land they had acquired from their maternal uncle Pioba, then living at Tai near Igurue. Imoguli and his three sons, now tech-nically Au, had emigrated to Maulemusumu in southern Malainaku domain, while Muyäli's son Walukuni remained in Iwaiwa to supervise their Nali and Sogumu strips.

By 1965 Imoguli was dead, and the surviving original Nali B agnates were divided between Iwaiwa and the new Pike settlements, Ugalimuku (Malainaku) and Ulumapike (Pukusakunaku). Apuniba, soon to die, had returned to Iwaiwa, where his sons — Papoku, who became a local govern-ment councillor, and Kiagita, who became a Government mechanic — cared for him. Of those who had adopted Au agnatic status, Mologiki and Ligumai were in Ugalimuku, and Sagiki in European employment in Wau (Morobe Province). Walukuni had finally left Iwaiwa for Ulumapike although he commuted to Ugalimuku. He died in August or September 1972. In 1975 Ligumai was still in Ugalimuku but Mologiki (who died in 1978) had moved north to Keriasutabulo. Papoku commuted between Iwaiwa and Epu, where he used Muli land acquired by his father, although his political duties fre-quently brought him to Usino, so that he used Ugalimuku as a staging post. Kiagita and Sagiki were still away in Madang and Wau.

The surviving Nali A agnates were similarly scattered. After his death Kasumala's sons continued to commute between Epu, Araka and Kumusi-asi, when they were not visiting Madang. Yeyele'uma's widow remained for a while in Iwaiwa but by May 1975 was in Kokolenau on Suaiyau Ridge. Her son Imolalia lived alternately in Iwaiwa and Ugalimuku, planting his Nali strips in Yabapunaku-Eimanaku domain and Ulapu holdings in Pu-kusakunaku, although he preferred to live in Malainaku because of his Nali ties with Mologiki and Ligumai.

Summary: the Main Features of Garia Secular Society

Two things emerge from the analysis: first, Garia social structure clearly does not endorse the common assumption that the corporate human group is ubiquitous and indispensable. Such groups as it comprises are rarely cohesive and have only the most limited collective functions. Second, it is imperative to analyse ties based on genealogy, land titles and bush brotherhood completely separately from those derived from local organization and everyday land use. Those in the former category are, in a sense, free-floating and exist independently of those in the second. They represent a socioeconomic potential on which ego is always free to draw no matter where and with whom he is living and working at any one time. This has important consequences for relationships between those persons associated with a particular bush god domain on the one hand, and between ego and other members of his security circle on the other.

The bush god domain

I return to the issue raised early in Chapter 2: that, although a bush god presides over war, hunting and weather, which Europeans should regard normally as communal interests, the inhabitants of his domain do not always acknowledge social and political obligation towards each other. The crucial factor is the size of landholdings: small strips and large blocks in the north, and huge tracts in the south. This broad difference correlates with the contrasting interpretations of the common principles of land tenure in the two areas: usufructuary rights either inherited patrilineally or acquired by purchase, generally from true matrikin. The implementation of these principles leads, in northern Garialand, to the indiscriminate dispersal of ego's permanent personal holdings and of his bush brothers (persons with whom he has many strips in common) throughout several domains and, in much of southern Garialand, to the concentration of his personal interests on a single communally held tract, the closest neighbours to which he counts as bush brothers.

As I have emphasized, informants continually asserted that they would help and support only those inhabitants of the domains in which they were living who belonged to their personal security circles: close kinsmen, affines, bush brothers and so forth. Of the twenty-five domains, basing their computations on the agnates within the cognatic stocks associated with them, representatives of thirteen denied, while those of twelve asserted, common sociopolitical solidarity on the grounds of interpersonal relationships. I consider this, first, in northern and, second, in southern Garialand.

In northern Garialand loopholes in networks of interpersonal relationships in bush god domains are more likely because of the relative density of population. In this context the obvious ties are those of marriage, kinship and bush brotherhood. The initial central issue is marriage. As I have explained, ego prefers a wife from his own geographical ambience so that her sons may have reasonable access to her brothers' land. Marriages between inhabitants of the same and adjacent domains are equally frequent. Within heavily populated domains it is more likely that some eligible partners do not marry, so that their respective kin remain distant or unrelated, and hence potentially hostile, to each other.

The second issue is the dispersal of ego's landholdings and bush brothers. Ego claims bush brotherhood only with those persons with whom he has many strips interdigitated. He does not claim it with persons with whom he has only a few strips in common or merely because he and they happen to have strips in the same domains. Hence there may be people — especially in populuous domains — whom he cannot seriously regard as bush brothers. It is possible that occasionally he will clear gardens and share hamlets with them, so that he will incorporate them temporarily in his security circle to suit his own advantage. But he may have closer permanent ties with landholders in adjacent domains than in the one in which he normally lives. In border areas he counts as bush brothers all those with whom he has many strips interdigitated irrespective of the domains in which they lie. The same applies to his relationships with persons across the linguistic boundaries which, like those between bush god domains themselves, are not always precise.

Although special relationships can fill gaps in interpersonal networks to some extent, their importance within ego's normal domain is limited. As I explain in Chapter 5, unless there are special circumstances to the contrary, ego prefers to extend his political region by creating exchange partnerships in as many remote domains as he can. The same applies to his trade ties. Even initiatory ties, which tend to be more localized, leave significant fissures. Hence, it is the domains with smaller populations and associated with relatively few cognatic stocks that are likely to achieve political solidarity among their inhabitants through concentration of interpersonal ties. Such northern domains are: Totogulunaku, Unoba, Yaulilinaku, Äliliwanaku, Silimalanaku, Kutia and Ubesuanaku. The other twelve northern domains have larger populations and more cognatic stocks associated with them, so that their internal networks of relationships are more likely to have loopholes. They are: Iwaiwanaku, Munimuninaku, Yabapunaku-Eimanaku, E'uruanaku, Motubanaku, Ininaku, Palakunaku, Orinaku, Siliwanaku, Ulilainaku, Mubunaku and Mamunaku.

In four of the six bush god domains in southern Garialand, with a relatively smaller population, there is a correspondingly greater concentration of interpersonal relationships and political allegiance. I examine this also in the contexts of marriage, kinship and bush brotherhood, although again I ignore Kamai'asa for lack of evidence.[7]

In three of these domains — Koli, Mubu and Iborau — populations are not only small but also relatively isolated and stable. As people prefer to marry as close to home as possible, affinal and kinship networks are more tightly meshed than in the north. As soon as kin ties between inhabitants of a domain become distant, marriages are likely to recur for want of alternative partners, so that gaps are quickly plugged. Moreover, in these domains bush brotherhood is based on ties not between individual landholders but between sets of agnates and adopted enates with communal rights on adjacent tracts. In contrast to northern Garialand, persons whose individual mutual economic involvement is minimal are not automatically excluded from the relationship. Where the other special relationships (based on exchange, trade and initiation) exist within a domain, they reinforce already existing ties. Within these domains the degree of interpersonal political solidarity is bound to be high.

Malainaku and Pukusakunaku domains are different. Those inhabitants with permanent land rights in Malainaku claim complete political solidarity on special grounds. Only three cognatic stocks are associated with the domain: Yoiyasi, Au and Limau. Their agnates exercise joint usufructuary and guardian rights overs its southern area and are therefore bush brothers, who should not intermarry. Pukusakunaku alone among the southern domains does not claim full political solidarity between its regular inhabitants. Agnates within at least two of its stocks — Ulapu and Unigime — are neither close kin nor bush brothers to each other and thus may intermarry, although they have not done so for over four generations. They owe each other no political loyalty.

Nevertheless, in the everyday world, the foregoing discussion of political solidarity within the bush god domain is largely academic for two reasons. First, it is based on the assumption that a domain's regular inhabitants are the agnates within the cognatic stocks associated with it. Yet, except possibly in Koli, Mubu and Iborau, this frequently does not obtain because, as we have seen, populations continually fluctuate. In both the north and the south, enates with either permanent or temporary usufructuary rights may be periodic or even long-term residents of a domain, frequently bringing in their own kin as additional dependants. Thus by 1975 Labi and Naguni [Sogumu], properly of Iwaiwanaku but then living as dependent enates in Malainaku, had sponsored their close 'brother' Neiku [Kaka] of Palakunaku as an additional immigrant. He had kinship ties with few other residents, especially the Au agnates by whom the domain had been re-established. Clearly, his presence weakened the internal network of interpersonal loyalties. This situation is repeated, at some time, in all the twelve domains claiming internal political solidarity. Second, even in those cases where, despite every obstacle, a domain's current inhabitants recognize loyalty among themselves, they probably never express it in practice. From ego's point of view, such persons are no more than a sector of his security circle, which is bound to radiate well beyond the domain and incorporate inhabitants of others nearby. As virtually all disputes occur between relatively close neighbours, it is almost impossible for all the residents of a domain to stand shoulder to shoulder. In any quarrel, either within the same domain or between adjacent domains, some people are bound to be related to both principals, have divided loyalties, and thus observe some degree of neutrality. I discuss this in detail in Chapter 6 and, in Chapter 8, show how it is paralleled in religious belief. In short, the only situation in which common residence on its own imposes political allegiance between otherwise unrelated persons is in the traditional hamlet or modern village ward (*weise*). Yet the hamlet, like the village ward, is not a parish with a fixed territorial boundary or a specific area of land formally attached to it. As my account makes clear, its inhabitants are in large measure individuals who wish to cultivate their holdings in its general vicinity, and the association between them is often so fleeting — it is no more than an epiphenomenon of the lottery of local organization — that it is best regarded as part of ego's security circle, to which I now turn.

The human security circle

It emerged at the end of Chapter 2 that the ultimate reality of Garia social structure was the mesh of intersecting ego-centred security circles that reach out through a number of bush god domains and, in places distant from central Garialand, span the nominal linguistic borders. The structure of the security circle is a constant throughout Garialand, modified only by the different interpretations of land acquisition that I have already described. Ego's security circle exists wherever marriage has established cognatic stocks to which he belongs, wherever he has special relationships, and wherever he has associational ties. The latter are of particular significance. They may be permanent, as in the case of bush brothers, or transient, as in the case of distantly related or unrelated co-gardeners and co-residents in his hamlet or village ward. Yet, if circumstances warrant it, they may be advanced to the equivalent of close kinship bonds. This is the Garia version of a common Melanesian theme: personal association can create quasi-kinship ties. For bush brothers it is formalized in the phrase I have already quoted: *kilen saum kilen yaui sie*, 'one bush is like one blood'. In other cases ego may validate distant relationships as if they were close by placing false emphasis on half-forgotten kinship links. Even so, it should be remembered that his security circle does not account for every inhabitant of his political region, in which there are always certain people completely unconnected with and hence potentially inimical to him.

The security circle stresses the concept of the corporate group no more than does the bush god domain. In northern Garialand the agnates within a cognatic stock express such corporateness when, as a patrilineage, they exercise joint guardian rights over the land and ritual secrets that bear the stock's name. Otherwise, they may rarely live together or unite for common action. In southern Garialand this pattern is less marked. Agnates (the patrilineage) generally exercise permanent joint usufructuary as well as guardian rights over land and ritual bearing the stock's name, and tend to live together more often than in the north. Yet, in normal situations, they are rarely an exclusive group as they are invariably augmented by dependent enates to whom they are bound to grant temporary usufructuary rights. For everyday purposes ego does not rely on them alone for co-operation and support but draws on his security circle at large as a reservoir of help: those members (irrespective of their particular relationships with him) who are at hand and ready to join him in any enterprise such as agriculture and, as I shall show in Chapter 5, pig exchanges. This correlates with a phenomenon which we are gradually coming to accept as normal in Papua New Guinea but which clearly puzzled Leach (1956): the Garia patrilineage within the cognatic stock does not segment in the classically accepted sense. As in other parts of Melanesia, when Garia agnates move away from each other, they do not establish each a new and exclusive unilineal group but attach themselves to cognates and affines elsewhere. Thus, when the Wailagime brothers Kokopula and Polilipa quarrelled, they did not create new agnatic segments but merely settled in separate areas where they had permanent land interests: Kokopula in Takaulo (Yabapunaku-Eimanaku domain), where he had Wailagime and Mosoli strips; and Polilipa in Yaniba (Munimuninaku domain), where he had Wailagime and Usa strips. Each brother established his local political security by associating with Mosoli and Usa kinsmen respectively.

This social process, although frequent in Melanesia generally, is made especially easy in Garia society by ego's recognized right to use multiple descent names. He is not tied only to one descent group (of either parent), as in a single unilineal system, or to those of both parents, as in a double unilineal descent system (cf. Lawrence 1965 and 1973). Although he claims full agnatic status in the primary cognatic stock whose name he inherits patrilineally, he may equally use the names of others in which he is only an enate: those of his FM, FFM, M, MFM, MM, and as far back as he can remember. He is recognized as *belonging* to all these stocks even though, as an enate, he has only limited rights to their property in land and ritual, rather than, as in strictly patrilineal systems, as *having only personal ties* with individual members of specific patrilineal groups. Despite variations in this pattern — relatively greater elasticity and negation of local solidary groups in the north than in the south — his formally recognized membership in multiple cognatic stocks is an essential substitute for the political weakness of the bush god domain, which in itself affords him no real protection. As I have argued, the domain does no more than place him territorially, whereas his rights to use certain descent names establish him politically, defining his interpersonal relationships with other individuals in many domains, especially those with influence and power. Although geographically dispersed, multiple descent ties serve the same function as a single solidary descent group. His problem is to devise means of reinforcing these initially abstract biological or genealogical links with effective economic and cultural content. I discuss this in detail in Chapter 5, in the context of sociopolitical control, although I allude to its importance here in the broad field of land tenure.

As I have consistently argued, Garia land tenure is based on two common principles — inheritance of rights through the patriline and the acquisition of additional rights from outside it, normally from matrikin — which can be expressed in two different ways. In the north the individual usually acquires additional holdings, which his agnatic descendants gradually absorb into their patrilineage's estate. In the south he ideally changes his agnatic status whereby, instead of increasing his personal holdings, he is absorbed as an agnate into another cognatic stock (*sawaibopi sisi'ebu*), acquiring new communal usufructuary and guardian rights. This reverses Meggitt's (1965) argument concerning the availability of land and stress on agnation among the Mae Enga of the Western Highlands of Papua New Guinea and, spelt out literally, presents a structural paradox.

Meggitt's argument is that among the Mae Enga land shortage and the difficulty of acquiring landholdings from sources other than patrilineal inheritance sustains the principle of agnation, inhibiting emigration and accentuating membership in local patriclan-parishes. The Garia, however, emphasize the reverse. Relatively dense population and the consequent pressure on land in the north tends to stress cognation because of the need to acquire rights from outside the patriline. In the south where, by way of contrast, the population is less dense and land is correspondingly in greater supply, the emphasis on patriliny and viripatrilocal residence is somewhat heavier. As I have argued from more general material elsewhere (Lawrence 1971a: 31), land shortage leads a people to endorse their structural ideology, however they may phrase it: single unilineal, double unilineal, or cognatic. Moreover, in the Garia system, there is this inherent paradox. In the south, provided that those who are adopted renounce their natal agnatic status (even though the process may take several generations to complete), the relative

stress on partriliny is maintained often at the expense of genealogical manipulation and the adulteration of patrilineages by the formal incorporation of
sisters' sons. In the north, however, cognation does not have to attract people
to join corporate descent groups, so that it helps preserve the genealogical
purity of the patrilineage. Agnates are not often tempted to change their
status and almost invariably acknowledge their bonds to each other even
though they may be scattered through several bush god domains.

The significance of the foregoing discussion is that strict unilineal integrity
is possible only where there is no competition between local groups in need
of personnel whose adoption has to be validated by genealogical legerdemain.
This is an issue at least implicit in recent studies of other Papua New Guinean
societies. Indeed, even if the answer is a resounding negative, this question
should at least be asked: Do sociopolitical groups in Papua New Guinean
socieities described as solidary have this character *sui generis* or because of the
concentration of interpersonal relationships within them, for which so-called
sui generis solidarity is merely a convenient shorthand term? It is certainly
consistent with comments by at least two anthropologists who have worked
in the eastern Highlands, where analysis in terms of group structure first
became a primary research technique. Brown, P (1971: 119) says that a
Chimbu tribe's 'solidarity is a consequence of common defence, common
pride in ceremonies, and the thick mesh of cognatic and affinal ties between
[its component] clans'. Langness (1972: 926) suggests that the Garia security circle, although perhaps 'an extreme case', 'appears to be' pertinent, at
least to a degree, to other areas of Papua New Guinea, a view which Brown,
P. (1978: 182) herself tacitly endorses specifically for the Highlands. In any
case, the argument for the existence of *sui generis* solidary groups would be
more convincing if it took greater account of the ego-centred kindred, which
often has been ignored. The resolution of this question might shed light on
other controversial aspects of modern Papua New Guinean ethnography. As
I suggest in the Epilogue, the Garia human security circle has its counterparts
in today's urban residential and political patterns, and in what European
observers regard as capricious voting habits in the National Parliament. It
may also be relevant to the resurgence of traditional warfare in the Highlands.

The same considerations are relevant to Freeman's (1961: 200) comment
to which I referred in the Introduction: that *no* cognatic society can be ade-
quately described until we can divide it into fixed territorial groups. Although
I accept the proposition as probably valid in the strictly bilateral society in
which he worked, I reject it in the case of *all* flexible cognatic societies. Thus,
the Iban of Sarawak are organized on the basis of a number of long houses in
which each family has its own compartment. They recognize no system of
descent of any kind. Instead, each child in a family makes a firm decision

either to remain in his/her parent's compartment or to move out into that of his/her spouse's parents. This kind of irrevocable choice clearly can make the inhabitants of the long houses stable groups, although Freeman shows that political ties ramify well outside them. Yet especially in northern Garialand, where ego is continually offered a wide variety of temporary residential choices based on multiple descent names inherited from both his father and his mother, such local stability is most unlikely, if not entirely impossible. In southern Garialand, of course, the situation is perhaps less fluid.

Nevertheless, detailed examination of these kinds of conjecture has no place in a work such as this. Hence I now take the second part of my first question in the Introduction: the problem of Garia sociopolitical control.

5

Sociopolitical Control: Self-regulation in Human Society

As I have foreshadowed, this chapter serves a dual function. Initially, it is concerned with the issue of social order. In previous contexts, while allowing that people at times treated the rules or conventions they enunciated to me with a degree of latitude, I have presented my account of social structure as if they obeyed or respected them, at least in spirit, most if not all of the time. At the outset, this approach is essential because it is impossible to describe the structure of any society in other terms. In fact, however, many individuals invariably break some rules. The social system I have described is an abstraction derived from the principles expounded to me by informants and checked against the behaviour patterns I observed. Social reality is always at best only an approximation to the expressed ideal. I now introduce the forces that tend to narrow the gap between the two. Yet these forces still represent part of the ordinary dynamics or everyday behaviour of Garia society, so that this chapter also concludes my presentation of its structure. In particular, I deal with an important category of relationships, exchange partnerships, to which so far I have been able only to allude. As I have suggested in the Introduction, this kind of duality is inevitable in a stateless society, in which there is no theoretically separate political-legal system as in modern and rudimentary states, and in which sociopolitical control is merely one function of the generalized social structure. This is especially true in a flexible cognatic society.

Social order is an implicit theme also in Garia religion. As I indicated early in Chapter 2 and shall make clearer in my last two chapters, the people regard their total cosmic structure as beyond argument. The gods ordained the economic and sociopolitical system, which the ghosts reduplicate, and thus endorse, in the lands of the dead. Yet divine ordination and ghostly validation alone, although effective sanctions in some fields, are no guarantee of total cosmic harmony, which men also must try to achieve by their own efforts. In the human realm Garia recognize conflict as part of everyday reality, comparing it to a snake that wriggles its way free from a hole in the ground. In the same way, disputes search out interstices between interpersonal security circles and break through them to create disturbances. It is logical, therefore, to consider two sets of forces: those that tend to maintain social order by helping to uphold the rules on which it is said to depend; and those that work to restore it when they have been broken. In the superhuman realm the people have devised comparable processes to regulate relationships between gods, ghosts and men.

I present the argument in the following stages. In this chapter I begin by summarizing the types of behaviour Garia regard as wrong: offences against human beings, on which I now concentrate, and those against gods and spirits of the dead (sacrilege), which I set aside until later. I then stress that other sociopolitical models — a hierarchy of officials vested with defined authority and, as should now be abundantly clear, the segmentary system based on strong, corporate territorial groups — are irrelevant for the Garia. Although, as I contend also in Chapter 8, their leaders have a crucial cosmic role in co-ordinating the activities of human and superhuman beings in major socioeconomic enterprises, they have no authority of a judicial nature. Hence I adopt the alternative approach of analysing the forces of self-regulation, which are embedded in the security circle, generate and sustain a strong sense of moral obligation between its members, and regulate the conduct of disputes, the main theme of Chapter 6. In Chapters 7 and 8 I show that the same approach is equally relevant for understanding the putative relationships between men and deities, and men and spirits of the dead.

Types of Behaviour regarded as Wrong

As in earlier publications (Lawrence 1969 and 1971b) and suggested above, I classify wrong actions as follows:

1. Offences against human beings, which can be subdivided as:
   a) Wrongs of omission or the neglect of social obligations towards members of the security circle — flouting kinship, affinal and other ties.
   b) Wrongs of commission or positive wrong actions against either members of the security circle or persons outside it — theft, trespass, the killing of domestic pigs, marriage with proscribed kin, the abduction of a widow, adultery, serious physical violence, homicide (by physical means or sorcery) and default in a pig exchange.

2. Sacrilege or offences against specific deities and spirits of the dead, who ordained or preside over certain activities. This includes: for both sexes, indulging in coition in or near a garden; for males, breaches of initiatory taboos, knowledge of Male Cult secrets before initiation, and disrupting the performance of esoteric ritual; and for females, any knowledge of the secrets of male initiation.

Further classification, especially in terms of western concepts, is impossible. As I shall argue in Chapter 6, our terms crime and tort—or their anthropological substitutes public and private delicts—are meaningless in Garia society. Even the separation between offences against human beings and sacrilege is not always absolutely strict. In the main, only gods and ghosts are thought to take action against persons who infringe religious rules, while men deal with those who commit secular offences. Yet there is one act of sacrilege which is said to have provoked an immediate human response, and there are two nominally secular offences which cause ghosts to show their displeasure. In the past, men had to put to death any woman who witnessed male initiatory secrets and, as has been seen, spirits of the dead as well as the human beings concerned are held to take vengeance on those who ignore their living kinsmen's land rights or make off with widows without the previous agreement of the first husbands' brothers. I discuss these issues later.

The Problem of Sociopolitical Control in Garia Society

Although my previous assertion that sociopolitical control in a stateless society is merely one function of its generalized structure is now a commonplace, social anthropologists still find this a difficult proposition in the case of flexible cognatic systems. Colson had to face this issue among the Plateau Tonga of Zambia, who may be described most accurately as primarily matrilineal with a very strong cognatic bias. *Mutatis mutandis*, her comments (1953: 199) neatly fit the Garia situation. She records how readers of her account of Tonga society (Colson 1951)

. . . cannot see how controls can function in what seems at first glance to be an essentially unorganized society without clear-cut lines of allegiance to affiliate people to definite local groups. We understand the implications of the organized state with its delegation of authority to instituted leaders. Since the publication of Evans-Pritchard's studies of the Nuer, it has been possible to understand how stateless societies organized on lineage principles operate. But there are other forms of stateless societies, where the lineage system does not appear, and where no large group organized on kinship principles can be mobilized to enforce the rights of its members. Nor do local units relate themselves to each other through any genealogical hierarchy, or any system of perpetual relationships phrased in kinship terms. The Tonga form such a society.

So also, quite obviously, do the Garia. There is no need, in this context, to comment further on the principal features of their social system: its lack of firm territorial groups with the political functions to which Colson refers. But it is necessary to reconsider their leaders, this time in the context of the maintenance and restoration of social order. Although, as I have already indicated, leaders' status and renown derive from not only secular considerations — such as their access to land for their followers and wealth that they can feed into exchanges — but also their mastery of religious knowledge, I concentrate for the moment on their role in secular affairs.

My descriptions of garden teams and settlement formation make it clear that, in the secular realm, leaders are the catalysts of social action. The same point will emerge in pig exchanges and initiation. Big men's decisions set all these activities in motion. They publicize their intentions and are almost automatically followed. They announce that they will clear bush or live in specific areas, that they will celebrate exchanges or Male Cult ceremonies at certain times, and other people — often a motley crew of close and distant kin of varying categories, affines, bush brothers, and even unrelated persons — join their garden or dance teams, or elect to live in their settlements. They are, therefore, microcosms of human society: their ties with their followers are individual and heterogeneous; and they are generalized in that they have to be successful in more than one field before they establish their reputations.

Leaders enjoy considerable influence, power, and even authority (Nadel's [1951: 169] *de facto* and *de jure* command over the actions of others) in the important fields I have listed. Yet their power and authority rest ultimately on popular approval: their positions are not hereditary but derive from democratic competition. They initiate enterprises, and thereby perform services, that the people invariably and intensely desire: food-production, the consolidation and expansion of political relationships, and the preparation of young men for adult life. Furthermore, because of the relative stasis of the socio-economic system—which does not search for new resources or productive techniques — the events they set in motion are essentially routine, dictated by the culture. Thus, although they devote much of their lives to politics, advancing their own and their followers' interests, their role as innovative policy-makers is obviously limited. They have to judge astutely the time to act but their courses of action are already largely laid out for them: they do not have to make decisions to cope with ever-changing circumstances as do politicians and state officials in modern industrialized societies. Conversely, of course, when they fail to provide the services expected of them because of old age, illness, bad luck or bad judgement, their followers soon desert them for luminaries elsewhere. Despite this, while they satisfy popular demand, they perform a necessary role in the maintenance of the social system. As I shall soon argue, the major activities they initiate and carry through represent the most important cultural content of relationships within the security circle and hence are central to the whole process of self-regulation.

Nevertheless, this unquestioned status does not grant leaders what we should call judicial authority, the categorical prerogative to settle disputes by giving binding decisions. Were they to assume such a role, they would lose followers for two reasons. First, there is the problem of rivalry. A leader's effectiveness is restricted to his political region. Yet, even within this range, he does not enjoy sole dominion: he has to compete with other big men. Second, there is the flexible structure of Garia society. As a leader's followers are not a fixed social and territorially bounded group (such as a clan with its own parish) but an irregular aggregation, many of them will attach them-selves also to several other big men in any one year for agriculture, exchanges, and even initiatory ceremonies. They may use these multiple allegiances to put pressure on him. Certainly he can influence or manipulate the conduct of a dispute between them but, should he try to give a binding decision, he would be morally bound to find in favour of his closer kin. The other party, less closely related followers, especially if guiltless, would reject his decision and decamp in anger to another patron, possibly taking with them others frightened of the same treatment. When followers of another leader are in conflict with his own, quite obviously he can exercise no direct power or authority. At most he can use his prestige to influence negotiations with his rival.

In substance, therefore, leaders do not represent a structure of judicial authority akin to that found in modern and rudimentary states: a separate system within the total social order with the specialized function of restoring it. Nevertheless, as I have emphasized, they play a crucial part in the process of self-regulation, which serves to maintain it and to which I now turn.

Self-regulation in Garia Society

The forces of self-regulation (Nadel 1953) are those that sustain ego's relationships with members of his security circle, prompting him and them to co-operate, and to refrain from offending or harming each other seriously. They also tend to moderate quarrels between such persons and to prevent more serious disputes between those who do not belong to the same security circle from getting out of hand. Garia express these forces in terms of moral obligation, which the parties to any relationship should honour by fulfilling expected reciprocal commitments. Yet moral obligation is not *sui generis*: it has to be buttressed and it has to have a source. To understand this problem it is necessary to re-examine the dynamics of the social structure.

The expression of moral obligation

Garia describe the individual who behaves correctly and has a proper sense of moral obligation as *nanunanutua* and *eiyotua*: *kabia asinaku tina* (Pidgin *pesin bilongen gutpela); nanunanu asinaku tina* (Pidgin *emi gat gutpela tingting);* and *eiyo'ina* (Pidgin *emi gat sari)*—'he/she behaves well', 'he/she has proper attitudes,' and 'he/she has concern'. The antithesis is: *kabia o'i tina* (Pidgin *pesin bilongen nogut); nubo nanunanu o'i* (Pidgin *tingting bilongen nogut*); *pu/mamu kabia tina* (Pidgin *emi bihainim pesin bilong pik/ dok); nuba eiyo u'e* (Pidgin *emi nogat sari)*—'he/she behaves badly', 'he/she has wrong attitudes', 'he/she behaves like a pig or a dog', and 'he/she has no concern'. In a word, moral obligation — *nanunanu asinaku* and *eiyo* manifest in *kabia asinaku*—is the prime quality, the *sine qua non*, of the well adjusted person.

This quality cannot be taken for granted but must be instilled into the individual from infancy. As soon as a child can walk and talk, it is taught the elements of kinship terminology and the duties associated with specific relationships. Gradually it learns that co-operation and support are not automatic but have to be earned by correct behaviour. Thus ego recognizes that he can count on the help of only those persons who 'think on' (*nanunanu*) and are concerned (*eiyo*) for him and, to that end, must be wooed. He says of any such potential helper: *nubo nanunanu/eiyo täbule'ine/puluwobule'ine* (Pidgin *mi laik kisim/pulim tingting/sari bilongen*) — 'I intend to get him to "think on" and have concern for me'. This is implicit recognition of the other two aspects of the problem: the sanctions reinforcing, and the source of, moral obligation. It is also replicated in beliefs about deities and spirits of the dead, which I discuss in Chapter 8.

Sanctions reinforcing moral obligation

As in all Melanesian societies, the immediate sanctions for moral obligation are, of course, shame (*maya,* Pidgin *sem*) and its more effective counterpart, local criticism (cf. Malinowski 1926). Garia say that a properly indoctrinated person should at once be ashamed and desire to make amends, should he be guilty, even unintentionally, of a wrong of either omission or commission, or even have merely harboured thoughts of such behaviour. Yet not everybody is so upright, so that many have to be governed by the more powerful constraint of popular opprobrium. As in any small community, nobody can commit a misdemeanour without soon being discovered. The culprit is condemned on the basis of ideal values even by those who have been guilty of the same offence in the past: he or she is mocked, lampooned and abused. In contrast to more extensive western society, which offers a degree of anonymity and a chance of escape, in Garia settlements virtually everyone is known to everyone else. There is no sanctuary, so that voluntary exile or even suicide may be the only release from socially impossible situations. Voluntary exile on coastal plantations was still common in the 1940s.

The source of moral obligation

Shame and public criticism maintain but are not the source of proper behaviour and moral obligation. They are merely shorthand terms for considerations of mutual self-interest, summarized by Maine (1965) and Malinowski (1926) as the rule of reciprocity, and perpetuated by Burridge (1960) as the principle of equivalence. Ego cannot survive as a socioeconomic isolate. He depends on others for everyday co-operation and protection, which he will forfeit if he does not fulfil his obligations to them. If he does not help them prepare new gardens he will find himself without a labour line of his own. If he is lax in his duties at exchanges and initiatory ceremonies, or does not share the gifts of pork he receives, he will be deserted or ignored when he is a principal in one of these undertakings in the future. As I have said, he must create a sense of *nanunanu/eiyo* (Pidgin *tingting/sari*) or moral indebtedness so that others will 'think on' him when the time is ripe. An abstract relationship is merely an empty shell. What matters is the 'food' (*oiye*, Pidgin *kaikai*) or, as we should say, the 'meat' or 'substance' of a practical association — the content that confers advantages on both sides. The threat of withdrawal of these advantages helps prevent wrongs of omission and commission: deviance may offer rewards in the short term but, in the long term, involves the sacrifice of the essentials for living. This is a crucial consideration in a society that even nowadays lacks a true cash economy: co-operation or the exchange of goods and services is still its basic currency.

In this context there are two vital considerations. First, in contrast to the theory of modern industrialized society, moral obligation among the Garia is not even supposed to be universal. In Read's (1955) terms, it is essentially distributive. From ego's point of view, it applies not to all mankind, all Garia, or even all the inhabitants of his political region but only to those persons he counts as members of his security circle: close kin, affines, those in special relationships, and those with whom he has temporary but close practical associations — in a word, persons with whom he has positive and effective ties. Many people whom he sees every day — even inhabitants of bush god domains in which he has land rights — are excluded. I discuss this at the end of this chapter.

Second, as ego restricts his sense of moral obligation to members of his own security circle, it is essential to examine the content as well as the forms of his relationships with them. Taken literally, this could lead to an undifferentiated analysis of all expressions of reciprocity and equivalence, which would have only limited consequence. It does not help evaluate the differential importance of specific relationships in holding the security circle together. This introduces Nadel's (1953) concept of the focal or multivalent activity or institution. For ego, not all activities and institutions are equally advantageous. Some outweigh everyday routine events. They are focal in that other activities or institutions depend on them for their own fulfilment and lapse if they are ignored. They are multivalent in that they have more than one capacity, serving also 'ends or interests other than [those] for which [they were] explicitly or primarily designed'. They are so important that the necessity to perform them ensures conformity among a large number of people in several spheres of life. They enhance the status of the leaders because they are fields in which the latter perform the essential services on which their positions and reputations depend.

Focal or multivalent activities and institutions

In Garia society the main focal or multivalent activity or institution is the giving or exchange of domestic pigs, on which depend correct marriages, the acquisition of land rights from matrikin, and the consequent consolidation of the security circle — each again focal or multivalent in its own way. In greater detail, when ego gives or exchanges pigs, he inevitably buttresses certain ties within his security circle or enlarges it by creating new ones. Conversely, if he does not send out pigs, his security circle is correspondingly weaker. It follows, therefore, that as big men are more often able to organize exchanges, they reap these advantages in greater measure. To illustrate this argument, I describe, first, attitudes towards domestic pigs and, second, the pig exchange itself. Third, I demonstrate how the exchange provides essential content to crucial relationships within the security circle, not only in the short-term or *ad hoc* situation of the ceremony itself but also, in the longer term, between affines and close kinsmen in respect of land rights, and finally between exchange partners.[1]

Attitudes towards domestic pigs

As noted in Chapter 1, there are two categories of pig. Wild pig (*pu pasi*, Pidgin *wailpik*) roam the bush, are subject to no taboos (except as food for youths during initiation), are believed to be bred and herded by the spirits of the dead, who send them to their living relatives to shoot, and are of no concern in the present context. Domestic pigs (*pu* or *weise po pu*, Pidgin *pik bilong peles*) live in human settlements and their environs, are fed by their owners every evening, and are the most prized form of wealth in every exchange. They should not be shot unless they have invaded a garden and are subject to the most stringent taboos. Ego should never eat any pig raised by himself, herself, or any member of his/her security circle (other than exchange partners), for 'a pig's flesh is like a human being's flesh'. To break the taboo is tantamount to an act of cannibalism. Garia explain it thus:

> If I raise a pig, I perform ritual (*osa*) for its growth and feed it. If I raise a son or daughter, I perform ritual (*osa*) for his/her growth and give him/her food. I do not eat my son or daughter. Thus I do not eat my own pig.

By the same token, ego regards pigs raised by his close relatives as associated with his own flesh. Indeed, a common test of the distance or closeness of the relationship between two persons is whether or not they would eat each other's pigs. Thus, for ego to eat domestic pig, his own beast must go in return for another raised by someone outside his security circle: a distant relative or unrelated person. The social identity of his partner is of the greatest significance to him. Yet what is immediately more important is that these considerations qualify concepts of rights over pigs. A man and woman who raise a particular beast are more than its owners in the western sense: they are described as its 'father' and 'mother' (*pu omo/ana*, Pidgin *papa/mama bilong pik*) or 'guardians' (*pu otaba'apu/otaba'ui*, Pidgin *asman/asmeri bilong pik*). But when the time comes for it to be exchanged, the 'father' and 'mother' determine only its final destination. Many members of the security circle of the 'pig's father' now identify themselves with him. They say of the exchange:

Abaiwala procession, 1950

Auwobu: a traditional leader practises his craft, 1950

A child dressed for formal dance, 1950

Sä orumu: apprentices prepare *musa,* 1952

pu elälenigebinuku (Pidgin, *mipela laik salim pik long ol*) — 'we are going to send *them* a pig'. They confidently expect to share the carcass of the animal received in return because of their contributions of food and labour during the exchange. In this they do not deny that the transaction is primarily be-tween two principals but assert that it is not entirely individual or private and they also have rights in it.

These views are formally validated by a myth which recounts the origin of pigs and the pig exchange, and which I now summarize:

> An old man was unhappy because his married daughter never visited him. When he died, his sons moved to another hamlet. His daughter and her husband visited his old settlement, but his ghost chased them away. Event-ually the husband shot and killed the ghost. As the body decomposed,[2] *selu* insects pullulated, of which some turned into wild pig and ran away into the bush, and others became domestic pigs in the settlements. From the latter, the husband and wife gave beasts as presents to other people, telling them that they were going to celebrate dances and exchanges, and that they should collect firewood and taro. The husband and wife roped the pigs' legs, and other people carried the beasts away.

The myth ends with two secret names for the husband and wife, who are the deities of domestic pigs.[3] It is important in two respects. First, it explains the theme I have stressed above: the physical identification between domestic pigs and human beings. Pigs derive ultimately from human flesh, the ghost's rotting body, through the agency of insects, and in this sense are men.[4] Sec-ond, it explains the origin of the pig exchange and establishes it as part of the sociocultural system.

The ceremonial pig exchange

Pig exchanges (*umalu*), as mentioned in Chapter 1, take place from late May until late August, the dry season proper, when there is plenty of food in the gardens and the weather permits large gatherings in the open air. An ex-change begins when two partners (*umalukepu*) decide to celebrate a simulta-neous transaction or when one of them arranges to send out a pig which he expects to be returned only in a few years time. These negotiations concluded, other pairs can join in: a small ceremony with only two partners is uncommon. The situation can be made more complex by the rules governing the eating of domestic pigs. In some cases, people exchange pigs with, or send them to, members of their security circles — such as close kin and affines — who cannot eat them but have to send them on elsewhere in return for others which are not forbidden to them. Obviously, this can set up multiple exchanges with chains of at least three partners and explains the terms of address they subsequently use towards each other: *sawaya,* the originator of a pig, and *nalaya,* a person who passes on one that he has received. Where A and B exchange directly, they use the reciprocal term *sawaya.* Yet when A sends a pig to B, who sends it to C, who kills it, and C then returns a pig to B, who sends it to A, who kills it, then B addresses A as *sawaya* and C addresses B as *nalaya,* while B addresses C as *sawaya* and A addresses B as *nalaya.* The two terms confer equal prestige, and impose exactly the same rights and duties in the ensuing relationship.

Negotiations for these multiple exchanges involve careful diplomacy and ceremony. They begin when one set of principals brings the other *pu enumu* (Pidgin *dewel bilong pik*) — 'souls of the pigs' — mainly a number of betelnuts, one for each beast to be offered. When all principals have endorsed the essential issues — the amount of wealth to be provided by each party, and the date and place of the exchange — those who have received *pu enumu* return it in like measure, thereby sealing the contract. Arrangements vary. In some cases, especially if few partners are involved, the entire exchange may take place in the settlement of its initiator, although participants from elsewhere may spend several nights dancing at home in preparation for the final event. In others, where there are several sets of partners, it may be conducted in more than one settlement, each principal visiting his opposite number on one night and receiving him on the next. Each night, visitors dance in honour of the hosts (and also, as I shall explain in Chapter 8, the spirits of the dead), receiving pigs and food next morning. Inevitably, exchanges of this kind are not closed but may link with others elsewhere.

These details settled, the principals set in motion the work of the exchange. They assemble the pigs they have promised — either their own, or those they can borrow or obtain by calling in old debts — and arrange for the provision of food, especially taro, at least a hundred corms to go with each beast, although a really big man will aim for many more. While they themselves must supply much of this food, they rely on helpers from their security circles for a substantial amount. Again, as dancing, which is one of the festival's most important features, takes the form of a ballet, they have to organize their own teams. At last, on the afternoon before the exchange is due to take place, the visiting principals lead their helpers to their host's settlement and set up a public display of the live pigs, taro, and other wealth they have brought. The dance teams arrive after dark. Except for a brief interlude after midnight, when the hosts provide food and betel-nut, they keep up a continual performance from about 2100 until sunrise (about 0600) next morning. Hosts and their helpers do not dance or eat: nothing must divert them from the work of the exchange and looking after their guests. The dancing finished, the principals hand over their pigs and food to their partners, whose helpers carry them away to be slaughtered, cooked and distributed. I now illustrate this outline with a case example.

The pig exchange at Araka

The pig exchange I now describe took place between 16 and 21 May 1949. It illustrates the complexity of the arrangements and relationships in these festivals in that it involved people from central and southern Garialand: from Somau, Iwaiwa, Inam, Kirili, Yaniba, Onea, Pukisak, Kopa'olo, Araka and Igurue — a considerable section of the population throughout a significant part of its territory. More than six hundred people,[5] over half of them dancers, gathered in Araka on the final night and morning, when ten principals sent out eight pigs in two separate exchanges (1 and 2 in Table 9): one between Iwaiwa, Araka and Igurue; and the other between Somau, Araka and Igurue. A third (Exchange 3 in Table 9, involving two pigs), between Kirili, Araka and Igurue, had to be conducted on the previous day in circumstances I give later. Araka, at that time a small hamlet, was the festival's entrepôt or pivot and hence most important.

Of the principals in Table 9, I watched closely Apuniba [Nali B] and Pieku [Kulosi], both of Yabapunaku-Eimanaku domain and living in or near Iwaiwa. Although both were big men, Apuniba was more prominent: he provided two pigs to Pieku's one. Thus I tabulate full details for Apuniba and refer to those for Pieku only by way of comparison.

The effective work of the exchange began on 16 May, when the principals arranged for their wives and other helpers to collect betel-nut, taro and other food stuffs. I list Apuniba's helpers in Table 10. All adult male Nali B agnates but only one from Nali A participated although, as will be seen, another Nali A agnate (Kasumala) led a dance team in his honour and also carried his pig. Otherwise, apart from two affines and a bush brother, the rest of his supporters were non-agnatic kin. Pieku's helpers showed a similar pattern: all adult male Kulosi agnates except Ausilapu, who lived in Nugu, together with non-agnatic kin, bush brothers and affines in the Iwaiwa area. As soon as sufficient betel-nut and food had been collected, Apuniba and Pieku organized a series of dances in Iwaiwa. Their closest helpers prepared and cooked food for this: for Apuniba, his wife Mauome, Muyäli and Imoguli [Nali B] and their wives, a bush brother's daughter, and a close 'sister's son's' wife. Again, Pieku had a comparable team. Thereafter, the two principals fed the cooks and themselves had a meal for, as hosts for the evening, they could not eat in public.

Table 9 The principals in the Araka exchange

Exchange 1: one pig with taro sent in each case listed

From Iwaiwa	*to Araka*	*to Igurue*
(a) Pieku [Kulosi] (Yabapunaku-Eimanaku domain)	Wowoli and Keisa[6] [Muli] (Ubesuanaku domain)	Oninagu [?] (Mubu domain)
(b) Apuniba [Nali B] (Yabapunaku-Eimanaku domain)	Wowoli and Keisa [Muli] (Ubesuanaku domain)	Ätobai [?] (Mubu domain)
(c) Apuniba [Nali B] (Yabapunaku-Eimanaku domain)	Wowoli and Keisa [Muli] (Ubesuanaku domain)	Anu'aiapu [?] (Mubu domain)

From Igurue	*to Araka*	*to Iwaiwa*
(d) Keisa [Muli] (Ubesuanaku domain)	Wowoli [Muli] (Ubesuanaku domain)	Pieku [Kulosi] (Yabapunaku-Eimanaku domain)
(e) Ätobai [?] (Mubu domain)	Wowoli and Keisa [Muli] (Ubesuanaku domain)	Apuniba [Nali] (Yabapunaku-Eimanaku domain)

From Igurue	*to Araka*	*to Iwaiwa*
(f) Anu'aiapu [?] (Mubu domain)	Wowoli and Keisa [Muli] (Ubesuanaku domain)	*Apuniba [Nali] (Yabapunaku-Eimanaku domain)

*Apuniba sent on pig (f) to Onumaiba [Kaka] (Palakunaku domain) in Inam.

Exchange 2: one pig with taro sent in both cases listed

From Somau	*to Araka*	*to Igurue*
(a) Munia [Keisibu] (Äliliwanaku domain)	Wowoli and Keisa [Muli] (Ubesuanaku domain)	Kinigara [?] (Mubu domain)

From Igurue	*to Araka*	*to Somau*
(b) Kinigara [?] (Mubu domain)	Wowoli and Keisa [Muli] (Ubesuanaku domain)	Munia [Keisibu] (Äliliwanaku domain)

Exchange 3: one pig with taro sent in both cases listed

From Kirili	*to Araka*	*to Igurue*
(a) Ile'uba [Kerulu] (Munimuninaku domain)	Tetele'uma [Komai] (Ubesuanaku domain)	Taloloma [Osi] (Mubu domain)
--------------	*From Araka*	*to Kirili*
	Tetele'uma [Komai] (Ubesuanaku domain)	Ile'uba [Kerulu] (Munimuninaku domain)

Table 10 Those helping Apuniba [Nali B]* of Yabapunaku-Eimanaku domain

Name	Settlement	Agnatic status	Domain	Relationship to Apuniba
Muyäli	Iwaiwa	Nali B	Yabapunaku-Eimanaku	true patriparallel cousin
Imoguli	Iwaiwa	Nali B	Yabapunaku-Eimanaku	true patriparallel cousin
Mamauli	Iwaiwa	Nali B	Yabapunaku-Eimanaku	true patriparallel cousin
Lalagua	Iwaiwa	Nali B	Yabapunaku-Eimanaku	true patriparallel cousin's son
Yeyele'uma	Iwaiwa	Nali A	Yabapunaku-Eimanaku	linked patrilineage 'brother'
Walili	Iwaiwa	Sogumu	Iwaiwanaku	close 'brother'
Ubilili	Iwaiwa	Sogumu	Iwaiwanaku	close 'brother'
Watutu	Wokutabulo	Sogumu	Iwaiwanaku	close 'brother'
Mutiti	Iwaiwa	Uliamuni	Iwaiwanaku	close 'brother'
Matara	Iwaiwa	Uliamuni	Iwaiwanaku	close 'son'
Nu'oloku	Iwaiwa	Uliamuni	Iwaiwanaku	close 'brother'
Obenaku	Iwaiwa	Yaukai	Yabapunaku-. Eimanaku	close 'brother'
Pesesa	Iwaiwa	Sulu	Munimuninaku	bush brother
Mogulu	Iwaiwa	Kaka	Iwaiwanaku	close 'wife's brother'
Pioba	Onaiyau	Na'ina	Yabapunaku-Eimanaku	wife's true half-brother
Labaia	Somau	Mosoli	Yabapunaku-Eimanaku	close 'brother'
Poliloma	Yaniba	Mi'ome	Munimuninaku	close 'son'

*For Nali agnates, see Genealogy 3 and Map 9.

From 16 until 19 May people danced in Iwaiwa from about 2100 until 0600 next morning. A variety of teams took part. On 16 May a Somau group led by Labaia [Mosoli] performed Kanam, while an Iwaiwa group led jointly by Yeyele'uma [Nali A] and Latiti [Uliamuni] brought up Uluai. On 17 May Labaia [Mosoli] and Kasumala [Nali A] jointly led a Somau team in Kaurai, while Iwaiwa brought up Suluma-Mogoku, and Pukisak and Kopa'olo Uluai. People in Kirili, joined by others from Yaniba and Onea, also began to dance on this night.

In Iwaiwa, in the early hours of the morning, the dancers enjoyed a short interlude when they took the light refreshment prepared by Apuniba, Pieku and their helpers: taro, betel-nut and tobacco. During this break on 18 May Apuniba announced that there would be one more night's dancing in the village, after which they should all go to Araka for the final ceremony. He added: 'Wowoli has told me that he wants Uluai — so that when we go to Araka, that is the dance we shall take!' The four hundred men and women from Yabapunaku-Eimanaku, Iwaiwanaku, Äliliwanaku, Pukusakunaku, Malainaku and Palakunaku domains, who had so far performed more than four dances in Iwaiwa, together with others from Munimuninaku and Yaulilinaku who had performed in Kirili, were now to combine as a single team. Yet, at the last moment, the exchange had to be postponed for twenty-four hours because Keisa, who was acting for his father Wowoli but had to commute between Igurue and Araka, could not meet all his commitments on time. Apuniba and Pieku stifled the consequent grumbling by holding yet another dance — a Somau team performing Silali and a joint Iwaiwa-Pukisak-Kopa'olo team performing Uluai — on the night of 19 May.

Meanwhile, on the afternoon of 19 May, Apuniba's and Pieku's helpers caught and trussed their pigs. On the afternoon of 20 May teams of men and women carried them together with the food and betel-nut to Araka. I list Apuniba's carriers in Table 11.

The carriers reached Araka about 1500 after a short rest during which they put on floral decorations. Apuniba, as senior visiting principal, led the procession into and around the hamlet at a run amidst shouts of welcome and applause from his hosts. Then the carriers staked out the pigs at the edge of the dance plaza and piled most of the taro in the hamlet clubhouse. They displayed the rest on upright poles near the pigs. Distribution followed the programme for the total exchange as set out in Table 9: a pig, a pole of taro and betel-nut, and additional taro and betel-nut from the clubhouse, for each of the terminal principals except in the case of Exchange 3, which had taken place on the previous day, 19 May. (Ile'uba could not wait the extra twenty-four hours, so that he and his partner had merely given each other their pigs and taro without ceremony.)

About the same time, members of the visiting dance team gradually assembled in the bush outside Araka where they put on their regalia. They entered the hamlet at 1830 (two and a half hours earlier than was usual) and danced until sunrise. As already mentioned, they represented about a quarter of the Garia population and came from about six bush god domains: Yabapunaku-Eimanaku, Iwaiwanaku, Äliliwanaku, Pukusakunaku, Malainaku and Palakunaku. They performed the one dance Uluai under Yeyele'uma [Nali A] of Yabapunaku-Eimanaku. Even so, the gathering was depleted because of two factors. First, as Ile'uba had already transacted his exchange, some dancers from Kirili, Yaniba and Onea did not attend. Second, two

Table 11 (a) Those who carried Apuniba's pigs

Name	Settlement	Agnatic status	Domain	Relationship to Apuniba
Kasumala	Kumusiasi	Nali A	Yabapunaku-Eimanaku	close 'son' (linked agnate)
Walukuni	Iwaiwa	Nali B	Yabapunaku-Eimanaku	patriparallel cousin's son
Notoka	Olaiku	Keisibu	Äliliwanaku	close 'sister's son'
Apumala	Olaiku	Keisibu	Äliliwanaku	close 'sister's son'
Tupalia	Somau	Mosoli	Yabapunaku-Eimanaku	close 'brother'
Salapu	Somau	Ulawa	Yabapunaku-Eimanaku	close 'sister's son'
Iboinaku	Somau	Ulawa	Yabapunaku-Eimanaku	close 'sister's son'
Iwaiwanaku	E'ulu	Uliamuni	Iwaiwanaku	close 'son'

(b) Those who carried taro and betel-nut for Apuniba

Name	Settlement	Agnatic status	Domain	Relationship to Apuniba
Mauome	Iwaiwa	?	?	third wife
Uibulime	Iwaiwa	Nali B	Yabapunaku-Eimanaku	daughter
Wolosi	Iwaiwa	Wailagime	Munimuninaku	affine: patriparallel cousin's wife
Täli'alu	Iwaiwa	?	?	affine: patriparallel cousin's wife
Yausasi	Iwaiwa	Kuke	Munimuniaku	affine: patriparallel cousin's wife
Yeyebulime	Iwaiwa	Uliamuni	Iwaiwanaku	bush brother's daughter
Ulu'alime	Iwaiwa	?	?	close 'daughter'

deaths in Igurue prevented the people of Mubu and Iborau domains from bringing a team to dance Nisiri, for which they had a widespread reputation. Only a few of them could come: they sat at the edge of the dance plaza and sang the Abaiwala initiatory songs.[7]

After midnight the two hosts, Wowoli and his son Keisa, distributed cooked food, betel-nut and tobacco to the dancers. The formal proceedings, the exchange of the remaining pigs and taro, took place about 0700 on 21 May, about three-quarters of an hour after the dancing had stopped. Each principal gave his pig to his partner, while the relevant helpers stripped the food poles, and removed taro and betel-nut from the clubhouse. The visitors then carried home their booty and, after a short rest, slaughtered the pigs and cooked them together with the taro they had been given. Those who helped Apuniba were: his Nali B parallel cousins Muyäli and Imoguli, and their wives; his Mosoli 'brother' Labaia; his first wife's half-brother Pioba [Na'ina]; his wife Mauome, his daughter Uibulime, and a bush brother's daughter — most of whom had helped him before. Pieku had a similar band of helpers. When the work was completed, Apuniba and Pieku rewarded their female cooks with broth and portions of pork and taro, and then distributed the rest of the food. I set out Apuniba's distribution in Table 12. Those rewarded shared the pork and taro they received with others to whom they were in debt. Thus Salapu gave part of his portion to his true brother Iboinaku, Kasumala shared his with his Keisibu 'brothers' in Olaiku, and Apuniba distributed what he kept for himself (mainly the head, ribs and entrails) to junior Nali B agnates and other close kinsmen. Pieku's distribution was on the same lines.

Broadly, the Araka exchange was a success. It was marred but not seriously disrupted by three untoward events. First, because Keisa had to postpone the final ceremony by twenty-four hours, Ile'uba had to complete Exchange 3 on 19 May, so that some of the Kirili, Yaniba and Onea dancers did not go to

Table 12 Distribution of Apuniba's pig

One leg to Kasumala [Nali A] in return for previous services, for leading the Kaurai dance team in Iwaiwa, and for helping to catch and carry the pigs that went to Araka.

One leg to Poliloma [Miome] of Yaniba (Munimuninaku domain) in return for previous services: he had helped Apuniba with loans of garden land. He also provided coconuts (a rare delicacy in Garialand) for the Araka exchange.

One shoulder to Salapu [Ulawa], a close 'sister's son', to whom he was previously indebted, who had helped catch his pigs and carry them to Araka, and whose wife had helped with cooking.

One shoulder to Yeyele'uma [Nali A], who had led the Ulilai team both in Iwaiwa and Araka, had contributed taro and had lent Apuniba garden land near Somau.

The tongue to his Mosoli 'brothers' Tupalia and Labaia. Tupalia had helped catch and carry the pigs to Araka, while Labaia had led the Kanam team in Iwaiwa and had supervised the killing of the pig that came in return.

Portions of meat to his fellow agnates of Nali B, Mamauli, Muyäli, Imoguli and Lalagua, his Sogumu 'brothers' Walili, Ubilili and Watutu, his Yaukai 'brother' Obenaku, and his Kaka affine Mogulu, all of whom had helped him with contributions of food and in other ways.

Bundles of food (*mä'atu*) to all those who received gifts of pork and to other men and women who had helped in minor ways during the exchange.

Araka. Second, two sudden deaths kept many people in Igurue at home on the last night. These two factors diminished the number of dancers. Third, Apuniba was criticized for his treatment of his elderly parallel cousin Mamauli [Nali B], whom he had persuaded to lend him a pig for the exchange. He sent the beast he received in return to Onumaiba [Kaka] of Inam to settle a previous debt and then gave Mamauli a most ungenerous share of pork and taro as recompense. Mamauli claimed that he had been duped. Apuniba settled the score only after Mamauli's death, when he gave the latter's widow a pig previously owed him by people in Igurue.

Nevertheless, despite these deficiencies, the Araka festival bears out the main point I have already made. The pig exchange is a primary focal or multivalent institution in two distinct contexts: the *ad hoc* situation — the short-term relationships between a principal and his helpers on the one hand, and between the aggregations of persons supporting different principals on the other; and the long-term situation — relationships within the security circle, which ego has to reinforce, and those outside it, with distantly related and unrelated persons, which he has to create. In dealing with both these situations, I am concerned to show that the pig exchange, in all its manifestations, serves to create between ego and persons tied to him through it a sense of moral obligation (*nanunanu* and *eiyo*, Pidgin *tingting* and *sari*) that tends to prevent the occurrence of wrong actions between them.

The *ad hoc* situation

In ideal, and largely in actual, terms the pig exchange is conducted on the Melanesian principle of reciprocity. Wealth is traded for wealth on the basis of equivalence. Workers, cooks, carriers and dancers are rewarded with gifts of pork and food in proportion to their contribution to the ceremony, although any debts previously incurred have to be settled. Put another way, the exchange is an *ad hoc* focal or multivalent institution in that it cements relationships between ego and those members of his security circle who participate in it, and should therefore prevent all quarrels between him and them. They have a common interest: as the success of the exchange is to their benefit, they depend on each other for co-operation. I illustrate this argument by examining: the helpers' initial contributions of food and work to their principals, and the principals' final distribution of pork and taro to them; the several nights of dancing; and the final exchange.

In the festival described, once the principals had initiated proceedings and had called for contributions of food and work, as in any other major activity, they looked to their security circles as reservoirs from which they could draw to suit themselves as long as they met their obligations in return. All Apuniba's and Pieku's helpers were members of their security circles near Somau and Iwaiwa, irrespective of association with any particular bush god domain, although others living far away made no contribution, certainly at the outset. Agnates participated but did not dominate the scene. For Apuniba, Nali A and B agnates (Yeyele'uma, Mamauli, Lalagua, Muyäli and Imoguli) did a great deal in the early stages of the exchange. although Kasumala (then commuting between Komusiasi and Araka) and Tulamia (in Uria) showed no interest. Other kin were equally important: Apuniba's cross-cousin's son Poliloma [Miome] of Yaniba (Munimuninaku domain), his Sogumu and Mosoli 'brothers', his bush brother Pesesa [Sulu] of Munimuminaku, and his first wife's half-brother Pioba [Na'ina] of Yabapunaku-Eimanaku. Only one member of his security circle near at hand failed him: his true sister's son Kiwoliba [Uliamuni] of Iwaiwanaku, who was subsequently criticized. The same broad principles applied to Pieku, although, as he sent only one pig to Araka, he needed less help than Apuniba. His Kulosi agnates were important but at least two of them lived so far away that they were excused — Ausilapu in Nugu and Patuma in Kulubaitabulo — as were his sister's sons in Nugu and matrikin in Yaniba. By the same token, when Ubilili [Sogumu] of Iwaiwa was later a principal, two of his fellow agnates living in distant settlements — Äbalia in Yaniba and Wawaku in Uria — did nothing to help him. When Obenaku [Yaukai] of Iwaiwa sent a pig to Inam, none of his fellow agnates helped: he got his main support from his Uliamuni matrikin with whom he was living. In 1950, when Labaia [Mosoli] of Somau bought the rights to the Tiburu dance from Nugu, he received far more help from his two sisters' sons Salapu and Iboinaku [Ulawa], and a classificatory 'sister's son' Pinama [Waipa], than from his fellow agnates, all of whom lived relatively close to him.

Catching, carrying, slaughtering and cooking pigs are organized in the same way. They are jobs for any members of ego's security circle conveniently at hand. Thus Pioba, an affine, supervised the trussing of Apuniba's pigs to go to Araka and, with Labaia, a classificatory 'brother', the slaughtering and cooking of the beast he got in return. Again, in the distribution of pork, agnates are important only in so far as a principal is indebted to them for past services. Although Apuniba sent joints to Yeyele'uma and Kasumala [Nali A], who had led his dance teams, he presented two others to kinsmen outside Nali and, as reported, shared only the head, ribs and entrails with his junior agnates in Nali B. Pieku made the same sort of distribution. On these occasions, as in selecting formal exchange partnerships, principals balance important relationships that need buttressing against already existing debts. They wish to ensure a sense of moral obligation with as many members of their security circles as possible, especially with big men whose influence and support are of the greatest consequence to them. A skilful man avoids making the same distribution too often: although neglected relationships must be reinforced, it is pointless to reaffirm those that are already stable. As will be apparent in Chapter 6, balance and diversification are the essence of Garia politics.

Dance teams demand many more participants than technical work in an exchange. For Apuniba, thirty-four persons and, for Pieku, twenty-one persons provided food and betel-nut, caught pigs, carried to and from Araka, and cooked for the final distributions. Yet a dance team of fewer than twenty-five men and ten women is of no significance. The individual teams that performed in Iwaiwa from 16 until 19 May were considerably larger. The composite team that went to Araka on 20 May numbered about four hundred even without the dancers from Kirili, Yaniba and Onea who did not attend. Moreover, there should have been a Nisiri team of well over fifty from Igurue. Such teams can assemble initially because the principals are able to recruit from their dispersed security circles. Once again, agnation has its place but, in view of the numbers involved, it cannot dominate the organization of dance teams. As already noted, these teams come together on the same basis as those in gardens and hamlet populations: random common interest. The rights to stage a particular dance are vested in big men who have mastered the ritual secrets that guarantee its success, but the rights to participate in it are diffused throughout the community at large. To understand this, it is necessary to explain how particular dances are said to have come into Garialand.

The only extant dance said to have originated in Garialand is Abaiwala. Nisiri (Pidgin Kaima) was introduced from Asiasi near Kesawai in the Ramu Valley: as late as 1952-53 Garia were purchasing from that area new regalia claimed to be imbued with awesome power. Uluai is believed to have come from Igoi in Sopu country and, like Nisiri, to have been in Garialand for many generations. Finally, there are the coastal dances traded in from Madang and Bogati: Kanam, Subaku, Kaurai, Suluma-Mogoku, Silali, Tiburu and others. I witnessed the purchase of Tiburu in Somau-Iwaiwa from Nugu in 1950.

As suggested above, there are two kinds of rights to these dances, based on locality and sex: to assemble a team and perform ritual to ensure its success, which is the prerogative of male leaders: and to wear the regalia and perform the figures, in which also men are most conspicuous. Nisiri and Uluai are common to all Garia. Nisiri is almost exclusively a male preserve: only men are initiated into it and perform the leading roles, very few women taking part. In Uluai and the coastal dances, although men are still predominant, more women participate, dancing around the men who form the centres of the teams. By 1953 most of the imported coastal dances belonged to all Garia. They have been traded in from locality to locality on the following basis. A local big man announces his intention to buy the rights to a particular dance and, helped by members of his security circle, assembles the wealth generally accepted as proper for it: in 1950 four or five pigs, some twenty clay pots and wooden plates, £A10 in cash, taro and other foods, betel-nut and tobacco. He then invites the local leader who has agreed to sell him the rights to bring a team to his settlement, perform the dance during the night and collect the purchase price next morning. He learns the ritual at the same time. He is then free to teach the figures to all those who originally contributed to the transaction and also, in effect, to any member of his security circle who wishes to learn.

This flexibility obviously has important implications for the composition of dance teams. Rights to dances being regional rather than vested in specific corporate groups, a team assembled by any principal will consist of virtually anybody from his political region, incorporating even persons from outside his security circle, provided they have, or are related to others who have, the right to participate. A dance team is bound to be socially irregular, drawing, as I have said, on a far wider selection of persons than those who contribute food and labour, and normally more broadly based than a garden team, inclusion in which is limited by the individual's access to specific pieces of land on the site to be cleared. In any dance team, people from many settlements, even from those in no other way involved in the exchange, may exercise their rights to perform simply to keep in the public eye. They may even be actively recruited by a leader who wants to enhance his own prestige with a big following. This happens especially when a principal does not lead his own dance team, because he has too many other duties, and calls on an ambitious younger relative to take his place. Such a man would lose face by bringing up only a small team. In view of this, it is easy to understand why groups from Somau, Iwaiwa, Pukisak and Kopa'olo could perform separate dances for several nights and then join, together with people from Inam, to form a huge team for Uluai under Yeyele'uma at Araka at the close of the festival. Conversely, this can embarrass a principal, who can never tell in advance how many people will come to dance in his honour and have to be fed, particularly as previously unheralded teams may materialize at the last moment. Also, as occurred in the case of Apuniba and Pieku, he may have to cater for a totally unscheduled night's dancing. If his food supply is adequate, his reputation soars but, if not, he is disgraced. There are no ameliorating circumstances: ignorance of the number of guests is no excuse.

Virtually every dance assembly, therefore, has an undercurrent of anxiety.

It is not organized around corporate groups under the control of specific leaders but is a motley throng, at first sight basically anarchic but in reality an aggregation of individuals between whom there are networks of interpersonal relationships. Yet, because these networks cannot link all the persons taking part in it, quarrels may occur if arrangements go wrong. The maintenance of order depends on the ability of the principals to fulfil obligations between themselves, and between themselves and their respective followers: the exchange of pigs and taro on the one hand, and the distribution of pork and cooked food on the other. These relationships are focal to the extent that they serve this function although, as emphasized, there are invariably loopholes. I illustrate this by analysing the chains of interpersonal ties within the Araka exchange: those between the principals themselves; those between the principals and their helpers; those between the different bands of helpers; and the position of individuals with no close ties to any party.

The terminal principals in the Araka exchange were all unrelated and able to eat each other's pigs. Hence, before its culmination (the establishment of *sawaiya/nalaya* ties) on the morning of 21 May, they could not act in concert to guarantee a peaceful outcome. Yet this gap was bridged in a way typical of, and most important in, Garia society: Wowoli and Keisa of Ubesuanaku domain, the central figures and middlemen through whom all the pigs (except those sent to and received by Ile'uba of Múnimuninaku) were channelled, were sufficiently closely related to all the other principals for their considerable prestige to hold the exchange together. They were linked to Pieku through his enatic tie to Muli, while Oninagu was their classificatory 'son'/'brother', who had provided Keisa temporary cultivation rights in Mubu domain. They had the same kinds of intermediary relationships with Apuniba and Ätobai, Apuniba and Anuai'apu, and Munia and Kinigara. Had anything gone seriously wrong, they could have exerted influence on the other principals to maintain or restore social harmony.

Even so, this on its own might not have been enough and it is essential to consider the other contexts mentioned. Thus, between each principal and his helpers there were bonds of common interest in the pigs to be exchanged: all would share in the renown and the pork, and therefore desired a smooth transaction. The same consideration applied to relations between the separate bands helping the different principals. This factor reinforces the potential exchange partnerships between the various principals and is especially important in the last context to be considered. As noted, many people who have no close ties with any principal may participate in dance teams or are even persuaded to do so to augment individual retinues and prestige. Their material reward is limited: a meal each night they dance and the personal satisfaction in having been seen in regalia. Should they be affronted, it depends on the degree of reticulation of the other relationships discussed whether or not they can be restrained from making trouble.

Hence, if everything goes more or less according to plan, a pig exchange is an *ad hoc* focal or multivalent institution which engenders and sustains amicable relations over a wide area. Garia say: 'When we exchange pigs, the mountains become one. Everybody — men and women — comes to dance'. As I have stressed, the Araka exchange endorsed this argument. About a quarter of the Garia population congregated in a hamlet inhabited, at that time, by twenty-three people and conducted the ceremony with remarkably little friction: the untoward incidents I have already reported did little to mar the final outcome. This situation is repeated about a dozen times a year in different settlements throughout Garialand. From May until late July 1949 I observed a number of exchanges which brought the central Garia (among whom I did my field work) into direct contact with virtually all other members of the language group. In more theoretical terms, during the dry season, exchanges activate intersecting security circles throughout all Garialand and even across the linguistic borders into neighbouring groups.

Not every exchange is conducted so smoothly. In 1949 I recorded three ugly incidents. The first was due to a principal's failure to fulfil his obligations, the second to a purely fortuitous accident, and the third to the principals' inability to control their irregularly composed dance teams. In the first case, at an exchange in Kopa'olo in mid-June, one principal could not catch his oversized pig with the result that his partner immediately took his dance team home to Uria, cancelled the exchange, and threatened sorcery. The rift lasted for well over a year. In the second, a Somau-Iwaiwa team visited Kolu (Unoba domain), where its members had few kinship and affinal ties. Consequently they were afraid of sorcery. A Kolu leader seemed to endorse their fear when he addressed the dancers at midnight: 'True, we of Kolu do use sorcery against you, but tonight we are exchanging pigs and you need not fear'. Next morning, when the visitors were going home, one lad slipped and fell on the track, made greasy by overnight rain. When he got home, he became very ill: as he had had an argument with the Kolu people about a girl he wanted to marry, he and everybody else suspected sorcery — especially his 'brother' Labaia [Mosoli], who 'cured' him by 'removing' an arrowhead from his stomach.[8] Nobody openly laid the blame on any particular person in Kolu: anyone in the press of people in the village could have been responsible. In the third case, a Kolu team visited Aiyauku on the Garia-Girawa border in July. The principals could not stop their dancers, few of whom were interrelated, from brawling. One man was so badly injured that he had to be carried to hospital in Madang.

Nevertheless, such incidents are not sufficiently numerous to negate the very positive role of the pig exchange in the field of *ad hoc* social control. It consolidates ego's relationships with the members of his security circle who live in his immediate vicinity: they help him with food and labour, and dance in his honour. Also it temporarily expands his security circle by attracting unrelated persons to his dance team and permanently augments it by creating enduring exchange partnerships, which I discuss in the following section. Because virtually every participant has an interest in its successful and peaceful conclusion, it generally does act to prevent serious ill-feeling and conflict within the amorphous crowd that assembles to celebrate it. The general euphoria carries on for some time after it is over. Even so, its effectiveness goes well beyond the immediate situation. In the long term, it helps to reinforce essential relationships within ego's security circle in ways which we can understand only by studying them diachronically and in the context of the rules of land tenure presented in Chapter 3.

The long-term situation

The long-term significance of the giving and exchanging of domestic pigs was summarized for me in 1950, even if incompletely, in a spontaneous statement by a reliable informant, Pioba [Na'ina] of Yabapunaku-Eimanaku domain:

> This is our system: I should give the first pig I raise to my true mother's brothers, although they should send it on elsewhere and kill and eat the one they get in return for it. My true mother's brothers' children should receive the next. My close 'mother's brothers' children' should get the one after that. Later I should give my distant kinsmen pigs which they may kill and eat. When I am an old man, all my kinsmen will have eaten pork at my hands and be as one with me *(apunō kilenini)*. If I am involved in a dispute, they will come to my aid and say: 'Ah they are angry with the man who sent us pigs, our *sawaya* . . .'

at which he made a significant gesture as if with a bow and arrow.

In structural terms, as I have indicated, the pig exchange enables ego periodically to buttress and even extend his security circle. This is important in two ways: it minimizes the likelihood of the parties to specific relationships behaving improperly towards each other; and, by the same token, it affords them greater mutual protection in conflict situations. In a word, they are forced to 'think on' one another. To explain this, I analyse the process of giving and exchanging pigs within the social framework I have described in earlier chapters: the genealogical structure of ego's security circle, the titles to land associated with specific relationships within it, and the creation of exchange partners outside it.

Ego's genealogical security circle consists of his close patrikin and matrikin — in theory, up to the level of the fourth ascending generation — details for whom I presented on pp. 56-7. To recapitulate briefly, close patrikin are members of ego's own patrilineage, members of others enatically linked to it and of those to which he is enatically linked through his father, and persons who share with him common enatic links to patrilineages on his father's side. Close matrikin are members of those patrilineages to which he is enatically linked, and persons sharing with him common enatic links, on his mother's side. In addition, there are his affines: all those linked to him by marriage, again theoretically up to the fourth ascending generation. Within this structure *over time,* the only permanent element is ego's patrilineage, membership of which he inherits and transmits *in perpetuo.* The relationships with other members of his genealogical security circle that he transmits to his patrilineal descendants are transient in the sense that they change generation by generation. They begin as immediate but then successively become *close, quite close, quite distant* (when they leave the security circle) and finally *distant* (after which they are completely forgotten). Yet the cycle is replenished by new marriages: ego's affines become his son's matrikin and part of his sons's son's patrikin. Beyond the genealogical and affinal structure of his security circle are his exchange partners (see Figure 7). The pig exchange is a vital means of reinforcing and expanding this structure. Briefly, to anticipate the argument, ego may send out a pig for any one of several reasons: as an instalment of bride price, to purchase land rights, to cement relationships with *quite close* kin still important to him, or to create new (and possibly reinvigorate old) exchange partnerships (*sawaya/nalaya* bonds).

It is most convenient to regard the total process as beginning with ego's marriage, when he sends his affines the first of a number of payments initially to establish rights over his wife but also, in many cases, to acquire additional permanent usufructuary rights for his sons on her brother's patrilineage land. Should he die before completing these payments contracted for either purpose, his sons must shoulder the debt. This explains the Garia rule which Pioba enunciated and to which I referred in Chapter 3: that a boy's first pig should go to his mother's brother — to complete his father's affinal obligations and his own land purchase or, if these liabilities have been met, to express respect and acknowledge clientship.

These payments affect affinal and kinship ties within the security circle over several generations. I have already described how they create affinal bonds, changing distant kinship ties fraught with suspicion and potential hostility into safe, if formal, relationships. This in itself is so well known that it needs no further elaboration. Yet it must be noted that correct observance of the rule of exogamy is of great consequence for social control. It has a multivalent function in that, provided ego marries a girl who is at most only *quite distantly* related to him, he will enlarge his own security circle, and properly establish that of his children, by creating affinal bonds with people with whom he was not positively connected in the past. If he ignores this regulation and marries a girl too nearly related to him, he and his children will forfeit this advantage: their respective security circles will be attenuated because persons already close relatives will become his affines and their matrikin. This is a positive sanction for marrying correctly. The additional payments ego and his sons make for land rights have a comparable function in social control: they provide socioeconomic content to otherwise purely nominal consanguineal relationships and thus ensure a strong sense of moral commitment. As this is not immediately obvious, I devote some space to its analysis. Once again, I deal separately with northern and southern Garialand.

In *northern Garialand,* as described in Chapter 3, a maternal uncle, in return for these additional payments, usually transfers permanent usufructuary rights on a number of his own patrilineage strips to his sister's son(s), whose patrilineal heirs may inherit them *in perpetuo.* Yet he and his fellow agnates retain residual rights over the land. For some five additional generations his nephew(s) and his/their patrilineal descendants must refer to the land by the name of his own patrilineage, and defer to its members (the agnates) in all cases of further alienation and disputes arising over it. Only after this period may the nephew's/nephews' descendants absorb the land into their own patrilineage estate, changing its name and themselves exercising guardian rights over it. This process has two effects. First, it creates for ego additional bush brotherhood ties, which are based not on kinship but on common economic interests. He claims such relationships wherever he has considerable holdings. I have discussed this in Chapter 3. Second, it knits members of different patrilineages — clients and guardians — in a system of interlocking rights to land that make it unlikely that they should forget their bonds of kinship.

The crux of this interlocking system is the duality of rights which I described in Chapter 3, and which bind together the agnates and enates of a cognatic stock in relationships of interdependence. In the first place, the agnates express their unity as a corporate patrilineage through their guardian rights over the land strips that bear their name. In the second, both agnates and enates, as free-ranging individuals, may exercise permanent usufructuary rights on these strips, agnates as the result of continuous automatic inheritance and enates as the result of purchase followed by automatic inheritance. In short, individual agnatic and enatic landholders must recognize the corporate authority of the patrilineage within the stock. Once again, this process cannot be understood synchronically but must be examined through time. As I have suggested, the pattern of inheritance and acquisition of land rights is consistent with that described for ego's kindred. Ideally, it can be tabulated as follows:

1. *Patrikin of the close grade*

   (a) *Ego's own patrilineage*

Apart from exercising individual usufructuary rights over some strips bearing the name of his patrilineage, ego and his fellow agnates have common guardian rights over all such strips irrespective of the status (as agnates or enates) of the individual landholders. He and his fellow agnates are responsible for the interests of enatic landholders, who in turn must defer to them.

   (b) *Members of patrilineages enatically linked to ego's own*

These persons are: ego's Z sons and agnatic descendants of his FZ, FFZ, FFFZ and FFFFZ. Where they enjoy permanent usufructuary rights on strips bearing his patrilineage name, they are in a dependent relationship with him and his fellow agnates as under 1 (a).

   (c) *Patrilineages to which ego is enatically linked through his father*

These are those of ego's FM, FFM, FFFM, FMM, FFMM, FMFM and FMMM. Where he enjoys permanent usufructuary rights on strips bearing the names of these patrilineages, he is in a dependent relationship with their members. This is normal, however, in the cases of only FM, FFM and FFFM patrilineages (see 2(a) below).

   (d) *Persons who acknowledge, with ego, common enatic links through their fathers to patrilineages listed under 1(c).*

Although such persons belong to patrilineages other than his own, they share with ego dependent relationships to the patrilineages listed under 1(c) whenever they have permanent usufructuary rights on land bearing their names.

2. *Matrikin of the close grade*

   (a) *Patrilineages to which ego is enatically linked through his mother*

These are those of ego's M, MM, MFM, MMM, MFFM, MFMM, MMFM and MMMM. Where ego acquires permanent usufructuary rights on land bearing the names of these patrilineages, he is in a dependent relationship with their members. As noted, normally he does not acquire such rights except from his M, and occasionally MM, patrilineage. The others are not important in this context.

   (b) *Persons who acknowledge, with ego, common enatic links through their mothers to patrilineages listed under 2(a)*

Wherever such persons — for example, MZ sons — have acquired,

like ego, permanent usufructuary rights on land bearing the names of these patrilineages, they share with him a dependent relationship.
Outside ego's security circle, the system can be tabulated ideally thus:

3. *Patrikin of the distant grade*
    (a) *Patrilineages still acknowledging vague enatic links with ego's own beyond the fourth ascending generation*
    For example, descendants of ego's FFFFFZ. Such persons would normally have given up or be giving up their dependent relationship with his patrilineage.
    (b) *Patrilineages to which ego still acknowledges vague enatic links through his father beyond the fourth ascending generation*
    For example, FFFFM patrilineage. Again, ego would normally have given up or be giving up his dependent relationships with such patrilineages.[9]
    (c) *Persons who still acknowledge, with ego, common vague enatic links through their fathers to patrilineages beyond the fourth ascending generation*
    Ego would not normally be tied to such persons by common dependent relationships.

4. *Matrikin of the distant grade*
    (a) *Patrilineages to which ego still acknowledges vague enatic links through his mother beyond the fourth ascending generation*
    I recorded no case of a man buying permanent usufructuary rights from such patrilineages. Dependent relationships do not exist at this social range.
    (b) *Persons who still acknowledge, with ego, common vague enatic links through their mothers to patrilineages beyond the fourth ascending generation*
    Ego would not normally be tied to such persons by common dependent relationships.

This system of interlocking land rights is of crucial importance from the points of view of both the diachronic structural process introduced in Chapter 2 and recapitulated on p. 150, and self-regulation or social control. First, *ideally* land rights should follow the same pattern within ego's security circle through time as do his consanguineal ties to its members. Just as after each generation kinship ties are realigned — ego's *quite close* patrikin becoming *quite distant* to his son, and the gap being filled by his own matrikin becoming patrikin, and his affines matrikin, to his son — in the same way, personal land rights originally acquired from his FFFM patrilineage should be changed to full guardian rights by his son or son's son, within whose security circle there will now be fewer buttressed relationships. But the gap can be filled, and the system restored, if his son inherits rights which he himself acquired from his mother's brother and in his own turn acquires such rights from his own maternal uncle. I illustrate this in Figures 8 and 9.

Second, like the pig exchange itself, interlocking land rights have an im-

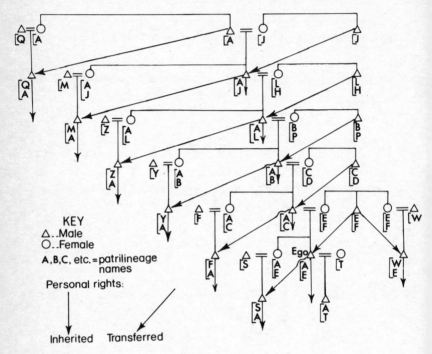

Figure 8 Acquisition and inheritance of usufructuary rights

Categories of kin (as in text, pp. 152-3):

1. *Patrikin of close grade*
   (a) A.
   (b) Descendants of S, F, Y, Z and M.
   (c) C, B, L, D and P. Others omitted.
   (d) Common enatic links to C, B, L, D and P. Not shown.

2. *Matrikin of close grade*
   (a) E and F. Others omitted.
   (b) Descendants of W. Others omitted.

3. *Patrikin of distant grade*
   (a) Descendants of Q.
   (b) J.   (c) Common enatic links to J. Not shown.

4. *Matrikin of distant grade*
   (a) and (b) omitted here.

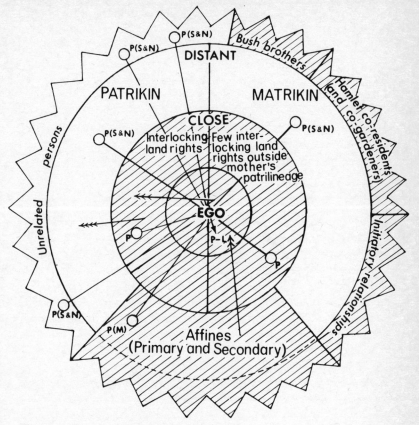

Figure 9 Pigs, land rights and security circle

Shaded areas represent ego's human security circle.

➞ P-L:	Pigs sent to mother's brother for land rights.
⊶ P:	Pigs sent out of goodwill to patrikin and matrikin of the close grade to cement relationships and, in the case of patrikin, strengthen usufructuary rights to land.
⊶ P (M):	Pigs sent as marriage payments to primary and secondary affines.
⊶ P (S&N):	Pigs sent to create exchange parternships both within and outside the already existing security circle.
⟶➤	Affines become ego's son's matrikin and bring him usufructuary rights on their land.
⟶➤➤	Immediate matrikin become ego's son's close patrikin in the next generation: acquired rights are inherited by ego's sons and their agnatic heirs.
⟶➤➤➤	Close patrikin become distant patrikin and leave the security circle: personal usufructuary rights are absorbed by the beneficiary patrilineage, which assumes guardianship. Gap left in structure is filled by ego's son's acquisition of rights from his own matrikin.

portant focal or multivalent role. Reciprocal guardianship and clientship engender a strong sense of moral obligation between the two parties that may not entirely eliminate quarrels but generally helps to resolve them quickly when they do occur. Enatic clients are wise to defer to agnatic guardians in matters other than land concerns. Guardians, if offended, can always remind them, often without subtlety, that their titles are only recent. Hence, as suggested in Chapter 3, prudent clients make a point of sending occasional pigs to guardians even one or two generations after the completion of the original transaction to avoid this kind of embarrassment. Nevertheless, the system is not as inclusive as this might suggest for two reasons already discussed. On the one hand, ego normally purchases rights from his M patrilineage but rarely from those of his MM and beyond: his son will thus not inherit buttressed relationships with members of these patrilineages. On the other, not everybody in every generation acquires rights from his maternal uncle. Those who do so not only are short of land but also aspire to leadership or some degree of local prominence, for which they need economically buttressed relationships, while the unambitious are generally content to rent or borrow additional garden sites and rely on powerful kinsmen for protection. For economic reasons, rising men turn to relatives with large estates but few sons and, for political reasons, try to forge links with the most influential. They leave relationships with unimportant kin dormant.

I illustrate the foregoing argument by reconsidering Genealogy 2 and Table 2. By 1949, through acquisition and subsequent inheritance of permanent usufructuary rights, Sogumu agnates were variously clients of Tulua, Asina (Kailala), Oyesinō, Kaka, Wailagime, Usa and Mosoli patrilineages and, by August 1980, after a good deal of soul-searching had acquired permanent joint rights on Limau land. The most ambitious and prominent Sogumu agnate was Watutu, who personally had acquired strips from Wailagime and Usa, and from Kailala for his son Munimala. He had a strong ally in his true maternal uncle, Polilipa [Wailagime-Usa] of Munimuninaku domain. By comparison, Walili and Ubilili had achieved status before the war — as plantation foreman and medical *Tultul* respectively — whereas Äbalia and Wawaku were satisfied to remain unimportant men. Yet Sogumu, despite their lack of patrilineage strips, had their own enatic clients: agnates of Nali B and Na'ina, whose forebears had acquired permanent usufructuary rights from their own.

In *southern Garialand,* as is obvious from my previous analysis, the situation is bound to be more irregular than in the north. For reasons already given, I have no knowledge of Kamai'asa. In three of the other five domains — Iborau, Mubu and Koli — there can be no true system of interlocking permanent land rights, for the process of individual acquisition from outside the patrilineage is so infrequent as to be of negligible importance. Neverthe-less, the inhabitants of these domains compensate for this lack of reinforced but dispersed cognatic ties: they derive their own sense of security from the greater local concentration of affinal and kinship links. As we saw, this does not promote exclusive and active political groups but it does give the individ-ual a cushion of support and the self-confidence this entails.

In Malainaku and Pukusakunaku, which have both kinds of landholdings — small strips to the north and huge tracts to the south — the situation is idiosyncratic. Those with rights in both areas take advantage of both systems. For instance, although Imoguli was meant to renounce his natal agnatic sta-tus, Nali B, in favour of the one he had purchased, Au, circumstances enabled him to retain both and exploit a wide range of security circle relationships buttressed by dispersed land rights. As Nali B agnates, he and his sons had Nali and Sogumu strips in Yagapunaku-Eimanaku and Iwaiwanaku do-mains and, as Au agnates, they had personal strips in northern Malainaku as well as joint rights to the huge estates in southern Malainaku and Kamai'asa they held in common with Yoiyasi and Limau agnates. In addition, his sons claimed a residual interest in their original Salasi land at Kolese in Koli domain, while Papoku [Nali B], whose father had acquired Muli land in Ubesuanaku and Kutia domains, asserted that they too had a part share in it because Imoguli had contributed to the purchase. As my earlier account implies, even though some ties were growing weaker, by the 1970s Nali B agnates could exercise geographically extensive economic and political influ-ence (see Genealogy 3 and Map 9). Likewise, when Labi and Naguni even-tually acquired permanent joint rights on Limau land, they followed the lead of Nali B and kept agnatic status in Sogumu.

The full structural connotation of Pioba's statement to me in 1950 (see p. 149) should now be clear. In a pig exchange, ego may be consolidating or extending his security circle by completing a bride price, by purchasing land rights, by reinforcing close and strategically vital relationships (assuring guardian patrilineages that he acknowledges his enatic client status or merely currying favour with the politically important), or by creating exchange part-nerships with his distant kin or unrelated persons who can advance his inter-ests. So far I have concentrated on the role of the pig exchange in marriage and land payments. I now discuss the formal exchange partnerships (*sawaya/ nalaya* bonds), which leaders in particular, and ordinary men on a more modest scale, establish between themselves.

The last sentences of Pioba's statement refer to the general Garia view that the expansion of ego's security circle through the creation of exchange part-nerships represents the culmination of his career while he is alive. Ideally, he should turn his attention to them only after he has met his obligations to his affines, matrikin and any other relatives who have legitimate claims on him, unless he believes that he can evade some of these responsibilities with impunity. In this he needs considerable political acumen: the ability to balance recognized moral standards against immediate considerations of his own advantage. His aim is to strike partnerships with big men who can protect and be of service to him but with whom he has no already existing close consanguineal or associational ties. He should be able to present himself also as an established or impending big man who in his turn has benefits to confer, if he is to get any response. To be of value to both parties, these relationships have to be contracts between actual or potential equals. Once they have been struck, as I have already pointed out, they impose stringent discipline on both partners, who are now the equivalent of close kin to each other. They should always support one another in any emergency: they can no longer harbour mutual suspicion or temptation to aggression. They should not marry each other's *immediate* female relatives, especially sisters and cross-cousins. They may, if they wish, exchange pigs again in the future, although informants regarded this as unnecessary unless an already existing partnership needed to be rejuvenated for a specific purpose, as in the case of Apuniba, whose aim was also to acquire rights to Muli land from Wowoli of Ubesuanaku domain. Otherwise, I was told, it is more important to create new relationships.

Although, in the *ad hoc* situation, it contributes to cordial relations between their respective bands of helpers, an exchange partnership is established essentially between individual principals. It may have no long-term effects: it does not automatically renew itself unless their sons make deliberate provision for it by a further exchange of pigs. Partners always encourage their sons to do this when they can see continuing advantage — as, once again, in the case of Apuniba, who saw that his son Papoku continued the tie with Wowoli's son Keisa to clinch his rights to the acquired Muli land by acknowledging client status. Yet, if the sons do not choose to follow this course, the partnership lapses: such moral obligation as they feel for each other is no more than inherited but unbuttressed sentiment. The signal for the termination of the relationship is often intermarriage, which automatically creates close kinship bonds. Nevertheless, as a final comment, even death itself does not excuse ego from any commitments to send out pigs that he made when he was alive. His immediate heirs are expected to honour those obligations he could not meet, so that his funeral may be the grand finale of, rather than a mere postscript to, his career in the exchange cycle. Although they too benefit from this by consolidating or even extending their own security circles, they must divest themselves of several of the pigs they inherit from him. They should send beasts to any of his affines or close kin who have not previously received them but have legitimate grounds for assuming that they would have done so had he lived or, if he met these obligations before he died, to other people with whom he agreed to establish exchange partnerships. This completion of his exchange commitments after his death and two other features of his funeral emphasize a theme that I stressed at the beginning of Chapter 2 but had to reserve for a later context: the close interdependence between the human and superhuman realms of the cosmos. By way of return, those who receive pigs at or after ego's funeral should perform services for him which I discuss more fully in Chapter 8: they should ensure that his spirit arrives safely in the land of the dead and, should foul play be suspected, divine the identity of the sorcerer responsible so that he may be avenged.

This effectively concludes my analysis of Garia human society *per se,* which I summarized in Chapter 2 in largely abstract terms as basically a mesh of ego-centred security circles. I have now filled out this model by giving it cultural content, by describing the dynamics of the main categories of relationships within it: ego's ties with kinsmen, affines, bush brothers and exchange partners (see again Figure 9). Yet there are still implications to be considered in two fields: social structure and sociopolitical control.

In the field of social structure, the immediate implications are for the genealogical security circle. In Chapter 2 I pointed out that the Garia kindred was biologically but not socially truly bilateral because, despite the recognition of ties through both father and mother, there was still an ultimate bias towards patriliny and patrilaterality. I now review this initial statement, made in the context of abstract social relationships, against the background of social action. Clearly, the most important factor here is land tenure, because of which ego's patrikin are socially accentuated at the expense of his matrikin. His patrilineage is the kernel of his security circle: it determines his primary social identity and, in its guardian role over the land and ritual formulae bearing its name, is the only genuine collective to which he belongs. Beyond this, in northern Garialand, he may inherit originally acquired rights to land strips bearing the names of his FM, FFM, FFFM and FFFFM patrilineages, whose members are included in his patrikin. On the distaff side, he acquires rights normally from his M, and occasionally from his MM, patrilineage, leaving other, even close, matrikin relationships (which become patrikin relationships for his sons) unbuttressed, although he may strengthen some of them, in his own generation only, by sending out pigs. In southern Garialand the role of the patrilineage in land tenure is even more sharply defined for the reasons I have elaborated. *In toto,* social structure is theoretically cognatic but has a strong *de facto* agnatic and patrilateral emphasis.

In the context of social control, the structure I have analysed is also a moral system or framework of moral obligation. As I have shown, Garia describe social conformity as a by-product of moral obligation *(nanunanu* and *eiyo),* which is expressed through proper behaviour towards others, instilled into the individual by means of education and socialization, upheld by the sanctions of shame and popular criticism, and ultimately derived from the principle of reciprocal self-interest. As I mentioned previously (p. 133) and have argued in an earlier publication (Lawrence 1971b; cf. Lawrence 1969 and 1971a), moral obligation is not even theoretically universal in Garia society. Ego does not owe it to everyone he knows — not even to everybody in his political region. He restricts it to members of his security circle. In addition, however, even within this limited social range he may not be strictly impartial. Although, ideally, he is brought up to observe moral obligation towards all persons with whom he has close ties — for example, all kinsmen up to the fourth ascending generation — in fact, he may discriminate in favour of those persons with whom he has reinforced as against purely nominal relationships. In major undertakings and disputes he is perhaps more likely to support affines, close patrikin and immediate matrikin to whom he is bound by interlocking land rights, bush brothers and exchange partners than other kinsmen, however close. In this context the focal institution is the pig exchange, which consolidates all these relationships: it forces ego to behave in such a way as to induce others to 'think on' and show proper concern for himself. This reciprocal attitude operates to contain, and control the conduct of, most disputes in Garialand. This is the subject of the following chapter.

6

Sociopolitical Control: Disputes in Human Society

My discussion of the social range of moral obligation at the end of Chapter 5 can be restated in complementary terms. Self-regulation affords ego considerable protection within his political region. In the main, it predisposes members of his security circle not only to refrain from harming him but also actively to support him in situations of conflict as far as they are able. Yet this does not guarantee him total immunity for two obvious reasons. In the first place, self-regulation cannot eliminate all quarrels between members of a security circle: even close kin occasionally have serious altercations. Some persons are impervious to moral obligation, especially if only nominal, socially unbuttressed relationships are involved, and will break the rules if they think that they have little or nothing to lose. In the second, as I have stated in several earlier passages, by no means every inhabitant of ego's political region belongs to his security circle and thereby owes him moral obligation. There are invariably some people with whom he has no close ties and may expect to have his most serious disputes as result of wrongs of commission (positive wrong actions), for which he or his opponents are responsible. This leads to retaliatory action on the part of the individual whose rights have been infringed, or who believes that they have been infringed.

Retaliatory Action in Human Society

However tempting, it is wrong to compare retaliatory action in Garia society with jurisdiction in western courts on three grounds: the social interpretation of the offences involved; the nature of the action taken; and the means of controlling disputes. In each of these contexts, western legal concepts are irrelevant.

First, as I foreshadowed in Chapter 5, the basic classification of offences in western law has no meaning in Garia society. In Anglo-Australian and American codes, most offences are placed in either one of two broad categories: *crimes* (treason, murder, theft and so forth), held to affect all members of the body politic, and hence punished by and in the name of the state; and *torts*, involving only the individual citizen-isolate and necessitating only personal restitution. As there is clearly no such entity as a Garia state and, in any society based virtually entirely on kinship, marriage and descent, there can be no such person as a genuine citizen-isolate, the foregoing western terms are inapplicable. Radcliffe-Brown (1952: 212-19) recognized this as true for all stateless societies and, writing in 1933 but, in fact, paraphrasing Durkheim (1964: 70-110), tried to overcome the difficulty by positing two kinds of offence specific to 'primitive society': public and private delicts. A public delict normally leads to the 'organized and regular' reaction of 'the whole community', whose representatives fix responsibility and inflict punishment on the guilty person. In a later publication (1940: xv), he argued that 'in collective actions . . . in which the community judges and the community inflicts punishment, we may see the embryonic form of criminal law'. By the same token (1952: 212-19), a private delict affects only the individual and, as in western law, is settled by restitution or compensation.

Certainly for Garia society Radcliffe-Brown's classification also is largely irrelevant.[1] On the one hand, the concept of a purely public delict implies the existence of a fully public demesne coterminous with linguistic or other diacritical boundaries. There cannot be such a phenomenon among the Garia for obvious reasons. In the secular realm of the cosmos, as we have seen, because of the mesh of intersecting security circles, which are the crux of social structure, there are no corporate political groups to take the kind of action Radcliffe-Brown assumed. Indeed, there are not even precise sociopolitical boundaries between the different language groups. Hence, although the Garia have a common set of values defining certain types of conduct as good or bad, they have no processes of collective or communal reaction. Later, I describe a youth's alleged attempt to seduce the wife of a close 'mother's brother'. One informant told me before the moot[2] that, although, like everybody else, he regarded the lad's behaviour as utterly reprehensible and inhuman ('the conduct of a pig or a dog'), he himself was not outraged and would not attend the moot because he was not related to either party. As will be seen, retaliatory action is taken initially on an individual basis and its strength depends on the network of purely interpersonal relationships between those involved in the case at issue. There is only one possible exception to this generalization — an act of sacrilege rather than a secular offence. As already mentioned, it is said that in the past any woman who witnessed Male Cult secrets was immediately put to death, without protection of her kinsmen, and her body thrown away to rot, without ceremony or mourning, in the bush. Should other women inquire about her fate, they were told that the spirits of the dead had devoured her. Nevertheless, even this example is controversial. None of my oldest informants had ever witnessed an incident of this kind. Moreover, their accounts, which included legend and even fantasy, made it clear that such 'executions', although generally endorsed, were not decided at public moots but were the spontaneous reactions of males involved in particular initiatory ceremonies. No corporate bodies played any part.

On the other hand, the concept of a private delict implies that the individual is a citizen-isolate in the western sense: a self-sufficient person, who has equal rights with all other citizen-isolates before the law, and who is thereby personally responsible to the state (society as a whole) for his actions in this context. Such a person cannot exist in Garia society, once again because of the ramification and convergence of ego-centred security circles. Ego's interests intermesh with those of a variety of persons, so that any offence, even if initially it involves only one person, may drag in others. In a few instances delicts may be purely private: petty altercations between husband and wife, and cases of minor theft and the obviously accidental killing of domestic pigs, which I discuss below. When the parties have previously been at peace with each other they may settle quickly. Yet often they and their supporters weave such incidents into wider patterns of already existing hostility, interpret them as the immediate consequences of previous conflict, and manipulate them as just causes for squaring old accounts. Unless neutral kinsmen can negotiate a settlement, the two litigants may suddenly find themselves surrounded by bands of supporters eager to escalate to their own advantage what may have started as a petty irritation. In short, Durkheim's and Radcliffe-Brown's categories are useless in this context: serious disputes are neither strictly public nor strictly private but tend to attract, largely on an individual basis, those members of the litigants' security circles who believe that their interests are at stake, even though they may realize that the parties they support are technically guilty.

Second, the principles underlying action taken in western law courts and Garia retaliatory action are different. In western society a plaintiff who brings his case to court normally does so through a solicitor. Thereafter his self-help is minimized: lawyers conduct his case and a state official (judge or magistrate) determines the settlement, which, having surrendered his right to 'take the law into his own hands' in return for the state's protection, he is bound to accept, subject to his right of appeal.[3] But, in Garia society, without state and a structure of centralized and delegated authority, there can be no comparable process. Hence, self-help has to be maximized: the plaintiff himself must initiate and carry through retaliatory action on his own behalf with whatever support he can get from his security circle.

My description of the main types of retaliatory action in Garia society follows but also amends my earlier account (Lawrence 1971b: 87-8). Of the positive wrong actions previously listed, I have already mentioned two that are likely, sometimes but not always, to concern only individuals: theft and the killing of domestic pigs. As I have already suggested, where they involve persons otherwise on good terms, they are settled with minimum discord. If his garden or other property has been robbed and he does not know the thief's identity, ego may either display a cordyline leaf to shame the thief should he return or, if the loss is considerable, resort to 'preventive magic' (oi'oi osa) to cause illness or death. If he knows the thief's identity, he will call him out and demand compensation, which is usually paid at once unless, as hinted, he and the defendant are already on bad terms and the offence fuels already existing conflict. Again, rules concerning domestic pigs are explicit. Ego is free to shoot any such beast that has invaded his garden: the owner takes its carcass and disposes of it as he wishes. Yet should he, even inadvertently, shoot it in a settlement or the bush, he is at fault: he takes and may dispose of the carcass as he wishes but must present a live pig of the same size to the owner. Unless, as in the case of theft, acts of pig-killing are fed into pre-existing disputes, most people abide by these rules without grumbling, although occasionally an owner whose pig has been shot in a garden may try to bluff it out by blaming the dilapidation of the fence. I have never known such tactics succeed.

The other offences previously listed — proscribed marriage, abduction of widows, default in pig exchanges, adultery, bodily violence, and homicide (by physical means[4] and sorcery) — are much more common and socially disruptive in that they are likely to involve more people than only the two original litigants. The plaintiff may initiate proceedings by calling a moot, an acephalous gathering of members of the security circles of the parties concerned who reach a decision by means of consensus. His most effective weapon is sarcasm, which he uses to channel local criticism, hitherto only diffuse gossip, against the defendant. The moot may recommend the following:

1. For proscribed marriage: that the husband return his wife to her kin.

2. For the abduction of a widow: that the woman be returned, or that bride price be paid, to her first husband's next of kin.

3. For default in a pig exchange: that the obligation be honoured in full.

4. For adultery: limited physical violence, such as ritual wounding; compensation in pigs, valuables and, nowadays, money; or nowadays a game of football.

Should the defendant refuse to appear at a moot or reject its ruling, the plaintiff may take direct action in any of the following ways:

1. For proscribed marriage: ritual wounding of the husband or wife or mild sorcery (to cause illness but not death).

2. For abduction of a widow: an attempt to retrieve the woman, which may lead to a fight or a sorcery feud.

3. For default in a pig exchange: a fight or a sorcery feud.

4. For adultery: physical violence or homicide (by physical means or sorcery); a retaliatory act of adultery; and nowadays a game of football.

Of these types of retaliatory action I need comment on only two: sorcery and football. I discuss sorcery in detail in Chapter 7. Here it is sufficient to mention that it has three forms. *Ämale* (Pidgin *saguma*) is regarded as the most dangerous and, as mentioned in Chapter 1, is said to be 'shot' from a bow *(puriä)* with the aid of a god. *Se'u* (Pidgin *poisin*) is the common form of contagious magic whereby the practitioner steals something intimately associated with his victim and destroys it in, or heats it over, a fire to cause death or illness. *Oi'oi osa* (literally 'bad ritual'), for which I have no specific details, can cause illness, death, or the destruction of property. All types of sorcery can be cured by a healer. Football is based on Association Rules or soccer, which was introduced by Europeans into the labour compounds before 1942 but which in Garia villages now follows the traditional pattern of organized conflict.[5] The two litigants choose from their security circles teams nominally of eleven men each and appoint a referee (Pidgin *wisilman*). The game may last for two hours and its aims may vary. If both parties want to settle, they 'play with moderation' *(pe'upe'unu kikwobu,* Pidgin *kik isi):* the players follow basic soccer rules but allow the scores to end up equal, the plaintiff being satisfied if his side wins prestige by kicking the first goal. But, if either party wants to perpetuate the dispute and disgrace his opponent, he will 'play rough' *(soksok/oma kikwobu,* Pidgin *kik kiros),* trying to score the first goal and running off with the ball as soon as his team is well in the lead.

Third, the means of controlling the conduct of disputes in western courts and Garia society are radically different. In western courts the principle of control is centralized authority. Judicial decisions and punishments are the prerogative of the state and, because all citizens are equal before the law, should be impartial. The judicial focus is on the nature of the offence: the status of, and personal realationships between, the litigants and other socio-political factors are ideally irrelevant. In any class of offence, courts should punish the guilty in exactly the same way: it should not matter whether the litigants are close kin or complete strangers.

For obvious reasons this situation cannot obtain among the Garia. My general comments on Papua New Guinea in this context (Lawrence 1969 and 1971a) are fully relevant here. The conduct of disputes in Garialand is governed by factors that are repudiated by western law and that have only limited importance in the total structure of modern western society: the social range of relationships between the interested parties — the litigants and their supporters. Social range is based initially on the genealogical closeness or distance of kinship and affinal ties, the degree of intensity of bush brother-hood, and so forth, although it can be affected by other considerations: ego's everyday association with members of his security circle; its members' willingness and ability to support him; the number of big men among them; and residence, which makes it easy or difficult for them to come together with him. Barnes (1961) describes this kind of 'law' as unashamedly 'politically active'. It leads to the following general formula: in the majority of disputes in Garia society, the closer the effective relationship between the litigants, the less socially disruptive they will be, fewer people being involved, retaliatory action being less severe and settlement therefore easier. Conversely, a dispute at greater social range, with a more tenuous relationship between the liti-gants, involves more people, leads to tougher retaliatory action, and therefore tends to be more difficult to solve.

In disputes at close range, ideally two factors should operate. First, the litigants should remember that their relationship ultimately represents mu-tual advantage and hence mutual moral obligation. They belong to one se-curity circle, and to cause each other irreparable harm would weaken their positions against outsiders. Second, others interested in such a dispute also belong to this joint security circle and cannot split easily into two groups, each supporting one side exclusively. Should either litigant or his close supporters lose restraint, they blanket the dispute and ensure settlement as soon as they

Sä orumu: garden leader with a bowl of *musa,* 1952

Sä orumu: garden leader planting sugar cane, 1952

Wulu ceremony: garden leader breathing spell into *komai*, 1952

Garden leader breathing spell into *wulu* spray, 1952

can. Hence, in these disputes, retaliatory action tends to be mild so that, once the litigants have let off steam, agreement is easily reached. A moot should lead to compromise and compensation. Should it fail and the plaintiff resort to direct self-help, he is allowed only limited physical violence (at most, wounding in the upper arm or thigh with a multipronged arrow) and expected to use only weak sorcery (enough to cause illness but not death).[6] Homicide at this range is unthinkable and morally condemned but, should it occur (as may occasionally happen), it is normally settled by compensation. By the same token, football matches should be free of turmoil.

Epstein, A. L. (1974: 12) agrees that 'the social range of offences' and 'the social relationships and interests of the parties involved' are the main forces governing disputes in traditional Papua New Guinean societies. Yet he comments that my statement that a closer social range makes a dispute easier to settle (Lawrence 1969: 32) may be an oversimplification: ' . . . the closer the relationship between the parties the greater the likelihood of any dispute reviving old resentments and thus making the containment of the case more difficult'. A settlement may be only 'a temporary truce'. The caution is salutary but, in the Garia context, it modifies rather than refutes my original formulation. Certainly, in at least two cases I recorded, Epstein is right. As already mentioned, Nali A agnates were permanently dispersed after Yerema's aggression against Yolekauma. In another example, which I describe in detail later on, a main participant went beyond the accepted limit of physical violence and caused the disruption of ties between two sets of linked agnates for at least two generations despite the periodic efforts of the joint security circle to patch them up. Yet in most cases at this social range that I recorded, this situation did not arise: quarrels flared up but were soon extinguished because the litigants and other people concerned kept retaliatory action well in hand, within the threshold of accepted self-help. On these occasions the operative forces were those I have outlined above and in previous publications (Lawrence 1969, 1971a and 1971b).

With the extension of social range, more serious disputes occur. They are less easy to control because the gaps in the networks of interpersonal relationships between the participants are larger. As litigants are now at best only tenuously related or associated, they have no strong sense of reciprocal moral obligation: they have nothing to lose by an open breach and feel free to kill each other. More people are now involved and, at least initially, form two opposing bands, one supporting the plaintiff and the other the defendant.

These opposed bands are not corporate groups represented by the inhabitants of bush god domains or even sets of agnates (patrilineages). As I have stressed, the inhabitants of a domain may not be linked by security circle ties or, if they are, their loyalties may be diversified by relationships outside it.

This may be true also of a set of agnates: centrifugal enatic bonds can break down unilineal solidarity. Once again, loyalties are based on interpersonal relationships within the security circle. The absence of automatic group allegiances imposes on the individual an increased burden of personal choice. He must make his own decision about his role in every dispute within his political region. He must feed his own ties with both litigants and their supporters into what I have called his kinship computer. Although, as I shall show later, he may subsequently modify his position, at the beginning of the dispute he must judge tentatively whether it is not his concern so that he may stay aloof, whether he can unequivocally support either side, or whether he should adopt an indeterminate position. The type of retaliatory action used in each case derives very largely from the aggregate of such individual choices.

Even in disputes between unrelated persons, the most common forms of self-help have always been moots, demands for compensation, sorcery and, in the past, wounding and limited homicide. Unrestricted warfare or killing was unlikely because of a factor to which I have already alluded: the invariable presence of neutral kin. All ego's serious quarrels occur within his political region, which from his point of view is an area of fairly intense genealogical interrelatedness and interpersonal association. Some people are bound to be connected to both sides, as, for instance, 'brothers' of the plaintiff and at the same time 'cross-cousins' of the defendant. In such circumstances, ultimate compromise is more likely than obdurate confrontation. The interest of neutral kin is clearly to limit or end a serious dispute: they do not want either litigant, who belongs to their security circles, to be killed or badly injured, or their ties with other members to be endangered. Traditionally, such persons urged the two parties to hold a moot and settle by means of compensation. Should they have to take part in any fighting, they avoided or protected kinsmen and affines on the other side. If possible, they refused to join in and, as soon as an opportunity arose, prompted the two bands to make peace. Nowadays, they play the same role in football matches. Their effectiveness has always depended on their numbers, personal prestige, and determination to bring the conflict to an end.

Hence, because of these convergent or bridging relationships, most disputes in Garialand are either settled or kept within reasonable bounds until they eventually disappear. The main exception is the sorcery feud, which is conducted largely on the basis of mutual suspicion and accusation and, as I shall show, may continue for a long time if an epidemic provides a suitable sequence of deaths. Moreover, although informants asserted that, without neutral kin, disputes could lead to unrestricted warfare (the killing of all human beings and livestock, and the destruction of property), they could remember no actual example and my own observation (Case 5 below) strongly suggests that this kind of situation can have occurred only very rarely. Garia never fought for land and, as people had little contact with those outside their political regions, it is unlikely that they were often in conflict with them. This is reflected in linguistic usage. Unlike other Papua New Guinean peoples (Williams 1930, Read 1955 and Berndt 1964), Garia make no terminological distinction between limited and unlimited homicide (feud and war). Their only word is *oma,* which they translate into Pidgin variously as *kiros* (anger) and *stilpait* (ambush, literally 'steal-fight'): the aggressor and one or two supporters normally waylaid the victim along a bush track, shot him down from behind a tree, and then made good their escape.

I now illustrate these general principles with five cases which I recorded or reconstructed in the field. Each one illustrates a dispute at the different social ranges I have suggested and the forces that control its conduct: the quick settlement of a dispute within a close kinship network; a case involving persons with a joint security circle but not so closely related as to make settlement easy; a case bearing out Epstein's point that when close kinsmen overstep the accepted limits of retaliatory action the ensuing rift can persist for generations; a protracted sorcery feud; and a case in which the litigants not only were unrelated but also lived so far apart that there were no neutral kin and no traditional procedures by which the plaintiffs could redress the wrong done them.

Case 1: The Wawaku-Pioba Affair (see Genealogy 6)

This case lasted from 20 until 21 October 1949. It was a quarrel between close kin and, despite its initial bitterness, was quickly settled and forgotten. Wawaku [Sogumu], properly of Iwaiwanaku domain but living in Ulilainaku (in Uria village), was visiting his brother Ubilili in Iwaiwa and helping him prepare a strip in Garden 12 (see Map 4) on the border between Iwaiwanaku and Yabapunaku-Eimanaku domains. Ubilili had borrowed the strip from his 'brother' Pioba [Na'ina], a Sogumu enate living at Onaiyau just south of Iwaiwa. The track to the garden went through this hamlet.

Wawaku had gone from the garden to Iwaiwa to get an axe and bushknife that he and Ubilili needed. On his return, he was followed by two of Ubilili's dogs, one full grown and the other a puppy. A dog belonging to Mutiti [Uliamuni] of Iwaiwa had preceded him and attacked Pioba's newly weaned piglet near Onaiyau. Ubilili's dog joined it in the kill. Wawaku chased the two dogs away but Pioba, angered by the death of his piglet, seized his bow and arrow and shot the puppy, which had taken no part in the affair. Wounded, it ran to Wawaku's feet. Pioba, intending to finish it off, fitted another arrow to his bow, but accounts of what happened next differed.

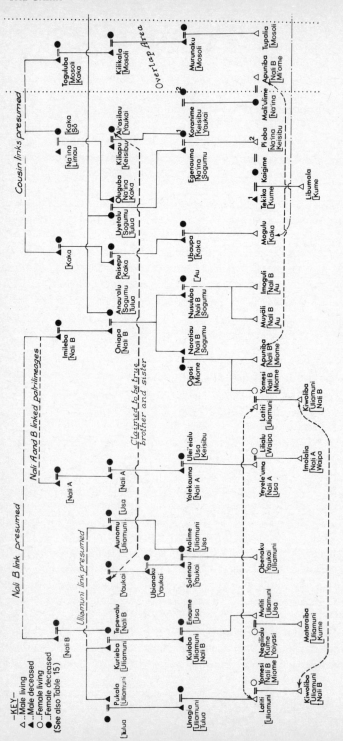

Genealogy 6 The Wawaku-Pioba Affair

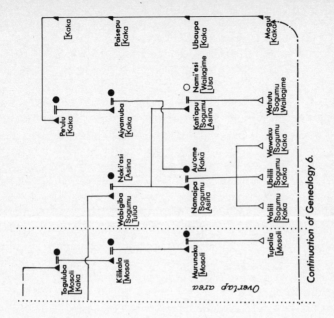

Continuation of Genealogy 6.

Wawaku's version was that he upbraided Pioba thus: 'Why have you shot this puppy? It did not kill your piglet'. Pioba replied: 'Why did you bring all these dogs and kill my piglet?' Pioba then drew his bow and aimed at Wawaku's chest. Pioba's explanation was that when he aimed his second arrow at the puppy he saw that it was at the feet of his younger 'brother' Wawaku and therefore laid his weapon aside.

Wawaku called a moot on 21 October. During informal discussions before it began, it became clear that it was impossible to establish what had really happened. Those initially favouring Wawaku (Watutu [Sogumu] and Imoguli [Nali B] argued that it was a case of attempted murder and should be reported to the District Office in Madang, while those sympathetic to Pioba (such as his 'brother' and affine Apuniba [Nali B]) claimed that he had aimed his arrow only at Wawaku's thigh and that the two parties should settle the affair by means of a small monetary exchange. Others gave no immediate opinion: for instance, Ubilili had not witnessed the incident and was acutely embarrassed because his true brother Wawaku was accusing his close 'brother' Pioba, whose garden land he had borrowed for the forthcoming year and who, as an enate, had client rights on Sogumu land. My private view was that Pioba was telling the truth but that there were genuine grounds for misunderstanding: when the incident occurred, Pioba was higher up the hillside than Wawaku so that, in aiming his second arrow, he might have cursorily swept it across Wawaku's chest.

I set out those who attended the moot in the Aubanuku (Iwaiwa) club-house in Table 13. Their interrelationships can be computed from Genealogy 6. The moot's outcome was a foregone conclusion. Nearly all the participants belonged to each other's security circles, while those who, like Mutiti, did not were so closely linked to the litigants through secondary channels that they could still bring influence to bear. Although Wawaku was prepared to bring a most serious charge against Pioba, a close Sogumu enate and client on Sogumu land, everybody else made it clear that he wanted a quick decision, that would save both litigants' faces and settle the matter for good. Neither Watutu nor Imoguli repeated at the moot their earlier intemperate remarks, and Imoguli played a leading role in the final compromise settlement.

Wawaku began by explaining how the dogs had killed the piglet and then asserted that Pioba, after wounding the puppy, had levelled the second arrow at his chest. Pioba maintained a dignified silence. Thereafter there was a brief conciliatory discussion which led to the general view that, as nobody other than the two litigants had seen what had happened, it was impossible to apportion blame. Everyone wanted an end to a distressing quarrel between close kin. Ubilili, whose position I have clarified, and Imoguli, adroit in the politics of compromise, urged monetary compansation. It was eventually agreed that Mutiti should compensate Pioba for the piglet killed by his dog and that Pioba should give a sum to Wawaku to obliterate any suggestion of intent to kill him. The participants then formed two parties to contribute cash as follows: a sum of 11s for Wawaku from Pioba (4s) helped by Yeyel-e'uma (1s), Obenaku (1s), Apunuba (2s), Imoguli (1s) and Libumala (2s); and a sum of 10s for Pioba from Mutiti (5s) helped by Muyäli (2s), Imoguli (1s) and Obenaku (2s). As the two litigants hesitated to accept the money, Ubilili summarized the consensus of the moot: 'I want to finish this business quickly. Both of you take the money, and let there be an end to it!' And so it has turned out: Sogumu, Na'ina and Nali have never quarrelled since.

It is worth noting the behaviour of three persons. First, Walili, Ubilili's and Wawaku's true elder brother and the senior Sogumu agnate, did not attend the moot. He was not personally involved and believed that Ubilili and Imoguli would find a solution. Second, Imoguli, despite his initial po-lemics, finally identified with both Wawaku and Pioba, contributing one shilling to each: his part in the compromise solution enhanced his reputation. Third, Obenaku also expressed complete neutrality by contributing cash to each party, although, as he was not a big man, he took little part in the debate.

Table 13 The participants in the Wawaku-Pioba moot

Name	Agnatic status	Bush god domain	Remarks
Pioba	Na'ina	Yabapunaku-Eimanaku	close 'brother' of Sogumu and Nali B; also affine of Apuniba (q.v.)
Wawaku	Sogumu	Iwaiwanaku	close 'brother' of Pioba and Nali B
Ubilili	Sogumu	Iwaiwanaku	true brother of Wawaku; close 'brother' of Pioba
Watutu	Sogumu	Iwaiwanaku	true parallel cousin of Wawaku; close 'brother' of Pioba; and close 'brother' of Mutiti through Usa
Yeyele'uma	Nali A	Yabapunaku-Eimanaku	close link to Pioba but not Wawaku. Had close ties (through Usa) with Watutu and (through Nali) with Apuniba, Muyäli and Imoguli; he was also a true affine (through Nali A) of Walili [Sogumu]; thus he could influence both Sogumu and Nali B, who were related to Pioba
Imolalia	Nali A	Yabapunaku-Eimanaku	true son of Yeyele'uma
Apuniba	Nali B	Yabapunaku-Eimanaku	close 'brother' of Pioba, Ubilili, Wawaku and Watutu (through Sogumu); also husband of Pioba's half-sister;* close 'brother' of Mutiti (through Nali) and true mother's brother of Kiwoliba, Mutiti's close 'son'
Muyäli ⎱ Imoguli ⎰	Nali B	Yabapunaku-Eimanaku	close 'brothers' of Pioba, Ubilili, Wawaku and Watutu (through Sogumu); close 'brothers' of Mutiti (through Nali) and close 'mother's brothers' of Kiwoliba
Mutiti	Uliamuni	Iwaiwanaku	no close tie with Pioba or Wawaku, but close ties with Apuniba, Muyäli and Imoguli (through Nali); close 'father' of Kiwoliba
Mataraiba	Uliamuni	Iwaiwanaku	true son of Mutiti
Kiwoliba	Uliamuni	Iwaiwanaku	close 'son' of Mutiti and close 'brother' of Mataraiba; true sister's son of Apuniba, and close 'sister's son' of Muyäli and Imoguli

(continued)

Table 13 — *continued*

Name	Agnatic status	Bush god domain	Remarks
Obenaku	Yaukai	Yabapunaku-Eimanaku	close 'cross-cousin' of Pioba (through Yaukai) and of Mutiti (through Uliamuni); claimed, with Wawaku, a common enatic link to Kaka, whose land he sometimes borrowed
Mogulu	Kaka	Iwaiwanaku	close 'brother' of Pioba, and close 'cross-cousin' of Ubilili and Wawaku; very close association with Pioba
Tupalia	Mosoli	Yabapunaku-Eimanaku	close 'brother' of Pioba and 'cross-cousin' of Ubilili and Wawaku (through Kaka)
Libumala	Kume	Totogulunaku	son of Pioba's wife Kaigime by her first husband

*The couple were technically too closely related to marry, but they were adamant and eventually were allowed to proceed.

Case 2: The Yelibubu Affair (see Genealogy 7)

This case was first advertised about 3 October, and finally settled on 23 October 1949. As forecast, the two litigants belonged to each other's security circles, although the concentration of neutral relationships was not as great as in the previous example and could not ensure an immediate settlement. The final decision needed patience and deviousness.

Yelibubu [Yoisili] of Pukusakunaku domain, unmarried and about sixteen, had left his father's settlement Kopa'olo because his patrilineage was virtually extinct. Apart from himself, only his classificatory 'father' Aiyapa and 'sister' Kililasi were alive. He went to Iwaiwa, where he was brought up by Konoiba and Ilomala [Yoiyasi], who treated him as a close 'sister's son' because his mother Wauwasi had been an agnate of Kume (Totogulunaku domain), to which they claimed an enatic link through their father Koloiba. The arrangement was mutually satisfactory. Childless, they welcomed him as a junior dependant. Without close kin, he appreciated the status and protection they afforded him. Continuous association compensated for the lack of a close consanguineal tie: he observed proper respect behaviour towards them, especially avoiding the use of their personal names. Yet, when he was about fourteen or fifteen, he flouted the initiatory taboos by having

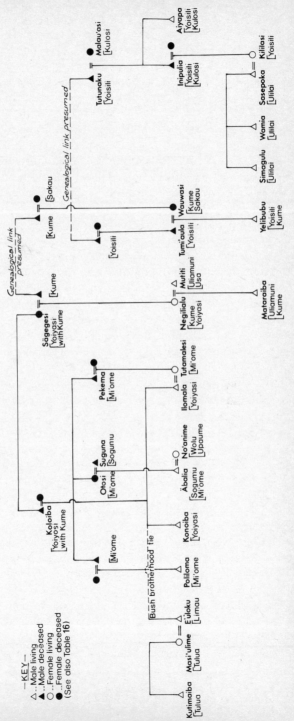

Genealogy 7 The Yelibubu Affair

sexual relations with a woman in the bush. Konoiba and Ilomala helped him out of this peccadillo by compensating the aggrieved husband with money. He became the subject of dire predictions. Because of his act of sacrilege, gods and spirits of the dead would punish him: he would never be proficient in any ritual activity — for agriculture, initiation, dancing and sorcery. If he reached manhood — and there were those who doubted even this — he would be just a nobody.[7]

In late September 1949 it was alleged that Yelibubu had tried to seduce Tutamalesi, Ilomala's wife, in her own house. In Iwaiwa he had formed an association with Kapapua [Keisibu], who, as an *émigré* from Äliliwanaku domain, also was glad to have an additional junior dependant. On the day before handing over the first instalment of the bride price for his son's marriage, Kapapua asked Yelibubu to go from Yagili'ese'u (where they both lived) to Aubanuku (another ward of Iwaiwa) to tell people that there would be a dance that night in honour of the event. It was alleged that on his return he stole into Tutamalesi's house with some cooked pork, which he had acquired from the provisions for the feast next day and on which he had put a love spell.[8] She screamed and people ran to the house. Everyone assumed that he had violated her. He fled to Kopa'olo, to the protection of his Ulilai affine Sasepoka, who had married his 'sister' Kililasi. The affair culminated in a moot outside the Aubanuku clubhouse in Iwaiwa on 23 October. More than two hundred people attended. I set out the main participants in Table 14.

Ilomala initiated proceedings against Yelibubu with support from his brother Konoiba and his closest 'affines', Poliloma and Äbalia, who were respectively Tutamalesi's true parallel cousin and true cross-cousin, although they had no close tie with Yelibubu. Yelibubu's associates in Kopa'olo — Aiyapa [Yoisili], his 'brother-in-law' Sasepoka, and the latter's brothers Simagulu and Wamia — acknowledged his potential guilt and urged him to appear, although they gave him what backing they could. Aiyapa attended the moot but was too old to take part. Hence Sasepoka and his two brothers were initially Yelibubu's main allies, bringing him to Aubanuku and protecting him in a situation in which tempers were running hot. Later, others such as Mataraiba joined them in this role. Unwilling to disgrace their 'sister's son' in public, Ilomala and Konoiba left their case with Poliloma and Äbalia. Hence, although the moot was attended by members of the security circles of both litigants, many of whom were interrelated, proceedings were left in the hands of their respective affines: Sasepoka and his brothers for Yelibubu; and Poliloma and Äbalia for Ilomala. Tutamalesi was the only woman present. She and Yelibubu were made to stand in front of, and facing, the gathering, about three metres apart.

Poliloma began by challenging Tutamalesi: 'Did you have sex with Yeli-

Table 14 Main participants in the Yelibubu moot

Name	Agnatic status	Bush god domain	Remarks
Ilomala	Yoiyasi	Malainaku	husband of Tutamalesi, true brother of Konoiba, and close 'mother's brother' of Yelibubu
Konoiba	Yoiyasi	Malainaku	true brother of Ilomala and close 'mother's brother' of Yelibubu
Yelibubu	Yoisili	Pukusakunaku	close 'sister's son' of Ilomala and Konoiba, and 'brother' of Mataraiba; but not related to Poliloma and Äbalia
Tutamalesi	Miome	Munimuninaku	wife of Ilomala, patriparallel cousin of Poliloma, and cross-cousin of Äbalia
Poliloma	Miome	Munimuninaku	true patriparallel cousin of Tutamalesi and hence a very close 'affine' of Ilomala; no close tie with Yelibubu
Äbalia	Sogumu	Iwaiwanaku	true cross-cousin of both Poliloma and Tutamalesi (through Miome), and hence very close 'affine' of Ilomala; no tie with Yelibubu
Sasepoka	Ulilai	Pukusakunaku	close 'affine' of Yelibubu
Simagulu ⎱ Wamia ⎰	Ulilai	Pukusakunaku	true brothers of Sasepoka
Mutiti	Uliamuni	Iwaiwanaku	a 'part-affine' (*asai*, see Figure 3) of Yelibubu, having married his mother's 'sister', and a close 'affine' of Ilomala and Konoiba, having married their true cross-cousin Negilialu
Mataraiba	Uliamuni	Iwaiwanaku	true son of Mutiti; close 'brother' of Yelibubu; and close 'sister's son' of Ilomala and Konoiba
E'uloku	Limau	Malainaku, Iwaiwanaku, Yabapunaku-Eimanaku, Siliwanaku, Pukusakunaku, and Kamai'asa	bush brother of Ilomala and Konoiba, and therefore a close 'mother's brother' of Yelibubu
Kutimaiba	Tulua	Iwaiwanaku	E'uloku's wife's true brother; Yelibubu's 'mother's brother' by association

bubu? Everyone says you did'. Tutamalesi replied: 'Yelibubu gave me pork but we had no sex. People lie! I am not a dog!' Poliloma now lost all sense of discipline: 'Don't answer me back!', he yelled as he struck her and Äbalia punched Yelibubu. Then Sasepoka, Wamia, E'uloku and Mataraiba broke up the scuffle and prevented further disturbance. Wamia said to Äbalia: 'Settle the case and then hit him with the flat of your hand'.

Poliloma then challenged Yelibubu: did he have sex with Tutamalesi? Yelibubu replied that he had gone to her house to give her some pork, which she ate. Then she held his penis and said: 'Let us have sex!' He had an erection but was ashamed to do anything because she was his 'mother'. When he refused her, she screamed and everyone came running. Tutamalesi interjected that he was lying: she had thought that the pork was just a gift to her as his 'mother' and so she ate it. But he had tried to seduce her.

This represented a clear impasse in which nobody could prove guilt, although feeling ran against Yelibubu. Mutiti, who was tied by marriage to both Ilomala and Yelibubu, and whose son had already helped protect Yelibubu from physical violence, intervened: 'I gave the lad (Yelibubu) the pork. I watched him. He did not eat it all. He took part of it away and gave it to Tutamalesi. I ask you: why does a man give pork to another's wife?' The moot accepted this as 'proof' of Yelibubu's wicked intention and upbraided Tutamalesi for her lack of principle in accepting the meat. She then tried to run away but was caught and brought back to the moot.

Thereafter, with Yelibubu's guilt 'established', several people — such as Kutimaiba [Tulua] and Ubilili [Sogumu] of Iwaiwanaku domain, his classificatory 'mother's brothers' — mildly upbraided him. But then E'uloku [Limau], who as Ilomala's bush brother rated as a close 'maternal uncle' to the boy and had already defended him in the scuffle with Äbalia, intervened sternly: 'Yelibubu, in the past you had sex with a woman. Who paid the compensation?' Yelibubu replied: 'My "mother's brothers" '. E'uloku became dramatic: 'Name them', he challenged — an attempt to shame the boy by forcing him to repeat personal names forbidden to him. Yelibubu did not reply, so that E'uloku, having made his point, went on: 'All right, Ilomala — how much?' Yelibubu answered: '5 shillings'. E'uloku again: 'And Konoiba — how much?' Yelibubu mumbled: '10 shillings'.

The discussion then turned to Tutamalesi, Ilomala suggesting to Poliloma that Yelibubu be forced to marry her. Poliloma rejected this: 'The boy is too young to marry my "sister". You keep her. She must work for you!' Ilomala accepted this. But the question remained: what was to be done about Yelibubu? During this time Äbalia had been strutting up and down periodically slapping the lad's face and abusing him. Eventually Konoiba, who had so far held his peace, addressed Yelibubu: 'Where is your true father? Dead. Who raised you? My brother and I. We became your true "mother's brothers". Before this you had sex with a woman. Who paid the compensation? My brother and I! Her husband wanted to send you to gaol but we had the case settled here. Now you try to seduce your "mother's brother's" wife. What sort of conduct is that? You have treated us with contempt. All right, Ilomala and I helped you with money. Now you can repay it to us: 10 shillings to me and 5 shillings to him'.

The moot approved this suggestion. Yelibubu could provide 12 shillings. He gave 10 shillings to Konoiba and 2 shillings to Ilomala, whom he still owed 3 shillings, which was a considerable sum in Garialand in 1949. Hence it was agreed that he should go to work near Madang to earn some money and pay off his debt. Tempers now cooled and the moot became quieter, but Äbalia wanted to strike Yelibubu again. Although Wamia was prepared to allow this with the flat of the hand, his brother Sasepoka, Yelibubu's 'affine', persuaded the moot that the boy had suffered enough indignity as it was and that he should be allowed to depart. As Yelibubu started back to Kopa'olo, Wamia spat a final remark: 'Go home, you lecherous little rascal!'

Case 3: The Ukapu-Keisibu Affair (see Genealogy 8)

This case began probably during the 1920s, when Australian administration was not yet fully effective in the Bagasin Area, but within the living memories of my informants, several of whom participated in its opening stages as young men. It petered out in the 1960s. It was one of the last examples of traditional homicide in Garialand and is interesting because, as I have forecast, it illustrates Epstein's point: that when close kin (in this case, the two linked sets of Keisibu agnates or patrilineages) ignore conventions about retaliatory action towards each other, bitterness and conflict may last for several generations.

The first stage of the affair occurred when Motili [Ukapu] of Kutia domain quarrelled with Patiti [Keisibu] of Äliliwanaku over an adultery. Patiti died and his close kin accused Motili, who was in no way related to him, of sorcery. Three of them ambushed and shot him: Ibagia [Mosoli] of Yabapunaku-Eimanaku, who subsequently became *Luluai* of Somau, was a close 'cross-cousin' of Patiti, and at the same time commuted between Somau and Olaiku; Yerema [Nali A], properly of Yabapunaku-Eimanaku domain but living at Araka in Ubesuanaku, Patiti's close 'brother-in-law' through Keisibu;[9] and Kotokoto [Keisibu], Patiti's true brother. After the funeral there was a moot, which was inconclusive and was followed by a token fight with bows and arrows. The combatants were ranged as follows: For Patiti — the Keisibu agnatic descendants of Kopenau and Muguliba (Kotokoto, Kapapua and

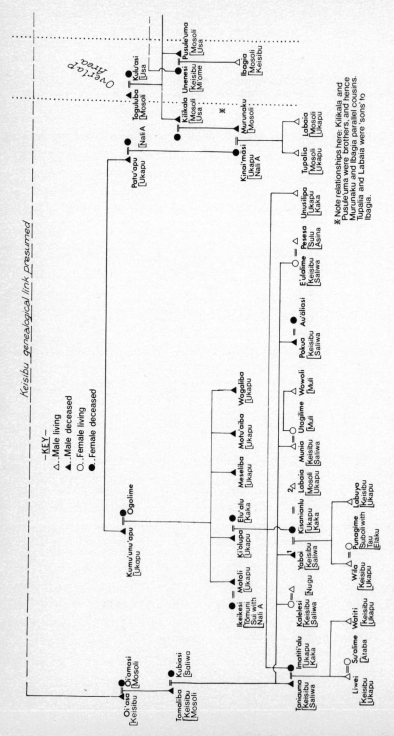

Genealogy 8 The Ukapu-Keisibu Affair

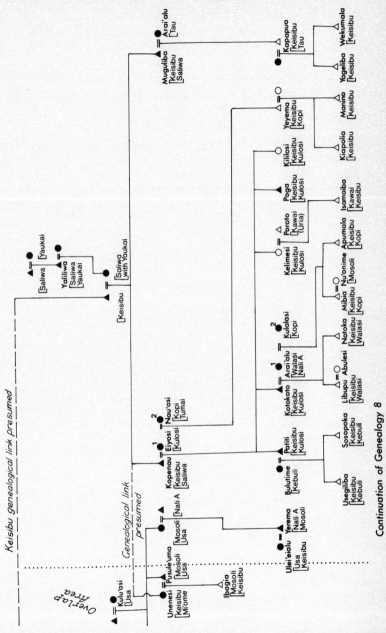

Continuation of Genealogy 8

Yeyema), supported by their 'cross-cousin' Ibagia [Mosoli], and 'brothers-in-law' Yerema [Nali A] and Poroto [Kawai], the last of Ulilainaku domain; and for Motili — Ukapu agnates (Kiolupa, Meseliba, Moto'aiba and Wagiliba), Keisibu agnatic descendants of Oi'asa (Taniauma and Yaboi, who were affines of Ukapu, and Munia and Pokua, who stood by their true brothers), Wowoli [Muli] of Ubesuanaku, whose sister had married Munia, and Tupalia and Labaia [Mosoli], who were sister's sons of Ukapu.[10]

Although at the beginning of the dispute the principals were not related to each other, subsequently, as can be seen from the foregoing lists and Genealogy 8, many close kin were distributed between the two bands of supporters. Because of this the moot should have reached a reasonable settlement and even the ensuing fight should not have caused a permanent rift between them. Yet there was an incident of the kind that no sociopolitical system can entirely eliminate. Although most of the combatants, out of concern for relatives on the other side, aimed their arrows high, Yaboi [Oi'asa section of Keisibu], over-zealous for his Ukapu in-laws, deliberately wounded his 'parallel cousin' Kotokoto [Kopenau-Muguliba section of Keisibu] in the head. Kotokoto recovered but the two sections of Keisibu were for a long time totally estranged. Muguliba and Kapapua had already emigrated to Yagili'ese'u in Iwaiwanaku domain, where they had purchased rights to Tau land, and from this time on kept very much to themselves. But now the agnatic descendants of Oi'asa, although still claiming rights to their Keisibu holdings in Äliliwanaku, left the domain for Kutia and Yabapunaku-Eimanaku, and the protection of their Ukapu affines, eventually settling in Somau village.

Feelings between the two agnatic sections of Keisibu became progressively more bitter. After a few years of uneasy peace, Yeyema [Kopenau-Muguliba section of Keisibu] seduced Auäliasi, wife of Pokua [Oi'asa section of Keisibu]. Then Yaboi and Kotokoto died. Although no member of either section was prepared openly to accuse any member of the other of using lethal sorcery within the linked patrilineage, thereby proclaiming the total loss of all moral obligation and concern, suspicion and gossip were nevertheless rife. Members of the two sections kept out of one another's way.

Mutual enmity continued throughout the war and into the next generation. It flared up again early in 1949 when Patiti's son Usegiliba [Kopenau-Muguliba section of Keisibu] seduced Punagime, wife of Wila [Oi'asa section of Keisibu]. At the subsequent moot he invoked a new 'law' attributed to Yali of the Rai Coast, the figurehead of the Cargo Movement in the southern Madang Province: that people should not bother the Administration with petty disputes but settle them in their own way (cf. Lawrence 1964: 172-3). He offered 10 shillings as compensation, which Wila refused with disdain. There was no settlement and the dispute smouldered. Towards the end of 1949 Wila retaliated by seducing Abulesi, wife of Libupu [Kopenau-Muguliba section of Keisibu], Usegiliba's true parallel cousin. There was another moot. Usegiliba, as defendant in the previous case, Libupu's elder 'brother' and a rising big man, brought the case against Wila. In the debate he flouted the wishes of Imoguli [Nali B], who was an established and prominent leader and who urged settlement by means of a pig exchange. He won agreement that instead there should be a game of football between teams fielded by Wila and himself in Uria village, which at that time had the best playing field in the locality.

Although intended to be 'friendly', the game promoted a good deal of wrangling which led to the introduction of players from outside the immediate Somau-Iwaiwa area. Initially it was hoped that both teams would consist of closely related persons who would preserve order and not come to blows on the field. But now the danger was that the participation of outsiders might weaken the concentration of security circle relationships and create the possibility of a brawl. The issue arose when Usegiliba wanted to set the date of the match as the first Saturday after the moot on the grounds that a 'friendly' contest could and should be organized quickly. In this he had a clear advantage. Virtually all Kopenau's agnatic descendants supported him, lived in Olaiku and, with his coaching, had become the best footballers in northern Garialand. Also, their self-confidence was strengthened by their certainty of divine favour: Usegiliba had mastered the ritual that was believed to win him the patronage of his bush god Äliliwanaku in these encounters. But Wila's position was very weak. Although he could rely on Labaia, who had married his widowed mother Kisanialu, to invoke Yabapunaku to the same end, he could count few expert footballers among his local kinsmen, bush brothers and affines. To cap it all, his true parallel cousin Liwei, irresolute at the best of times, used his quite close marriage tie to an Ätaba man in Usegiliba's team as an excuse to keep in the background. Wila was faced with the likelihood of disgrace either because he could not field a team at all or because his team might not score even a single goal. He prevaricated: he managed to postpone the match until the following Monday on the grounds of his sudden illness.

Usegiliba now blundered and lost his commanding position. He came to Wauwau in Somau, where his opponents had their headquarters, and publicly insulted Wila's wife. He announced that, as she had no man to uphold her good name and had had sexual relations with himself, she should go to him as his wife. As he put it crudely, they had seen each other's sexual organs. The Garia, certainly in public, are prudish, so that local opinion was outraged by these remarks. Nevertheless, Wila now had the chance he needed. He felt justified in seeking support beyond his geographically close kin by turning to his affines, his wife's Suboli, Eläku, and Tau relatives in Yaulilinaku, Iwai-wanaku, Palakunaku, Unoba and E'uruanaku domains (Onea, Iwaiwa, Inam, Kolu and E'unime). He had won an important tactical point, for his in-laws could provide him with enough seasoned players at least to make the game even.[11] I set out the members of the two teams in Table 15.

Even after Wila had equalized the contest by bringing in his affines from outlying domains, there was still a good deal of lobbying. Because of the general fear that these people might make it harder to control the game, a band of neutrals put pressure on both sides to keep order: for example, Ibagia [Mosoli] of Yabapunaku-Eimanaku, and Kapapua and Yageliba [Keisibu], who were living in Iwaiwanaku. (I discuss the importance of their roles in a later context.) They continually visited both Usegiliba and Wila in an attempt to promote compromise. In the event, Usegiliba was ready to settle the dispute — admittedly for the time being and on his own terms, for the prowess of his football team still afforded him significant advantage. Thus, in the actual game, he made sure that his men scored the coveted first goal and then made as if to terminate play by running off with the ball. The spectators insisted that the match be resumed and several prominent people co-operated to preserve order. Thus when a fight seemed imminent, Yalokai, Wila's 'affine' and a big man from Unoba, called out, *'Jeba Keisinō!'*, 'I am of Keisibu!', stressing a remote enatic link to both Usegiliba and Wila. Gradually Usegiliba surrendered his lead and allowed the scores to end up equal before the final whistle, when he and Libupu shook hands with Wila. Both sides then retired to eat food provided and cooked by their supporters. Those

Table 15 Teams in the Uria football match

For Usegiliba and Libupu

Name	Agnatic status	Bush god domain	Relationship to Usegiliba
Usegiliba	Keisibu	Äliliwanaku	captain
Libupu	Keisibu	Äliliwanaku	true patriparallel cousin
Mibia	Keisibu	Äliliwanaku	true patriparallel cousin
Sosopoka	Keisibu	Äliliwanaku	true brother
Notoka	Keisibu	Äliliwanaku	true patriparallel cousin
Kiapolia	Keisibu	Äliliwanaku	true patriparallel cousin
Isamaiba	Kawai	Ulilainaku	true cross-cousin
Pilaku	Ätaba	Ulilainaku	bush brother
Yuri	Ätaba	Ulilainaku	bush brother
Kasumala	Nali A	Yabapunaku-Eimanaku	close 'cross-cousin'
Karoli	an adopted immigrant from the Rai Coast		

(continued)

Table 15 — *continued*

For Wila

Name	Agnatic status	Bush god domain	Relationship to Wila
Parawa	Sua	Yaulilinaku	captain, 'affine' (through Suboli link)
Obenaku	Yaukai	Yabapunaku-Eimanaku	close 'brother'
Mataraiba	Uliamuni	Iwaiwanaku	close 'affine'
Kukupia	Limau	Malainaku, Iwaiwanaku, Yabapunaku-Eimanaku, Siliwanaku, Pukusakunaku, Kamai'asa	close 'affine'
Watutu	Sogumu	Iwaiwanaku	close 'cross-cousin' and exchange partner
Siopai	Mosoli	Yabapunaku-Eimanaku	close 'brother'
Ulabunaku	Silei	Mamunaku	close 'affine'
Isimala	Suboli enate	E'uruanaku-Unoba	close 'affine'
Ilokai	Suboli enate	E'uruanaku-Unoba	close 'affine'
Yosep	Suboli enate	E'uruanaku-Unoba	close 'affine'
Yalokai	Suboli enate	E'uruanaku-Unoba	close 'affine'

who cooked for Wila were a heterogeneous aggregation of cognates and affines. Those who cooked for Usegiliba were older members of the Kopenau-Muguliba section of Keisibu living in Olaiku, augmented by kinsmen and bush brothers from neighbouring settlements.

The football match was the last serious episode of this protracted dispute, although Usegiliba made his presence felt until the early 1960s. About October 1952, and then about ten years later, he seduced Liwei's wife Sualime [Ätaba] of Ulilainaku domain, technically his 'sister' through a bush brotherhood relationship. In 1952 there was an inconclusive moot and, in 1962, an Administration court case at Usino Patrol Post because the incident occurred during the building of the airstrip. Pilaku and Yuri [Ätaba], Liwei's 'affines' and Usegiliba's bush brothers, blanketed these two disputes. As far as I am aware, the two agnatic sections of Keisibu have remained at peace ever since.

Case 4: The Ulawa-Olei-Wailagime-Suboli Sorcery Feud (see Genealogy 9)

This dispute, which was expressed through a number of accusations of lethal sorcery, was a response to a sequence of deaths in northern Garialand probably caused by the influenza epidemic between 1945 and 1949 that I mentioned in Chapter 1. An early settlement was vitiated by subsequent unexpected deaths. The quarrel continued unimpeded because both 'victims' and 'culprits' were unrelated. It petered out when the participants were made to realize that they had reached a *reductio ad absurdum:* that they could continue their vendetta only if they were prepared to assume that a man would use powerful sorcery against his close kin.

During the Japanese occupation, Nulua [Waipa] of Siliwanaku domain, at that time living in Somau village, was betrothed to Maunime [Sogumu] of Iwaiwanaku. But later, when he was recruited to carry supplies for the Allied Forces, she had affairs with several men, one of them Liwai [Ulawa] of Yabapunaku-Eimanaku, who lived in Iwaiwa and announced that he intended to make her his second wife. When Nulua came home and learnt what she had done, he broke the contract. Her brother Watutu, also home from war service, arranged for her to marry Sinene'uma [Olei] of Onea (Yaulilinaku domain). About three years later Sinene'uma died: his close kin openly suspected that Liwai had used sorcery *(ämale)* but brought no formal charge. The affair came to a head when Liwai himself died. On the day Liwai fell ill Sinene'uma's Olei 'brother', Noloba of Onea, was seen with a bow and arrow near Iwaiwa. As sorcery *(ämale)* is believed to be 'shot' with the aid of these weapons, he was immediately charged with Liwai's 'murder'.

At a moot in Somau village, Poliwa [Ulawa], Liwai's true parallel cousin, Sasauba [Kamai], a close enate of Ulawa (in which he claimed *de facto* agnatic status) and hence 'father' of Liwai, and Ibagia [Mosoli], a very close 'affine' of Sasauba and hence of Ulawa — all of Yabapunaku-Eimanaku — made the formal accusation. Noloba defended himself with skill, consistently denying the charge and countering it by claiming that it was equally plausible that Liwai had 'killed' Sinene'uma out of jealousy. The case was agreed to be 'not proven' either way and was settled by an exchange of pigs — a solution strongly backed by two Ulawa agnates, Salapu and Iboinaku, whose father's mother had been Olei and who therefore had to act as neutrals, arguing against any hasty assumption of Noloba's guilt. Despite this, Noloba left Onea for Kolu, where he became *tultul* and used his mother's brother's Eläku land in E'uruanaku domain.

Certainly after Noloba's departure the dispute would have evaporated had not Kokopula's son Yobibia [Wailagime] of Yabapunaku-Eimanaku domain suddenly died in Somau village. He was Maunime's true cross-cousin and hence Sinene'uma's close 'affine'. Kopopula was too old and infirm to take action, but his younger brother Polilipa and the latter's son Pesese'uma, who lived in Yaniba (Munimuninaku domain), accused Ulawa agnates of having used sorcery against him on the groundless suspicion that he had helped Noloba murder Liwai by the same means.

After Yobibia's death Olei were eliminated from the dispute, which now became in effect a slanging match between Wailagime agnates in Yaniba and Ulawa agnates in Somau. Ibagia [Mosoli], who had supported Ulawa against Noloba, now effaced himself because Wailagime were enates of Mosoli, as did Salapu and Iboinaku for the same reason. In Yaniba, Polilipa and Pese-se'uma openly voiced their suspicions, so that when Liwai's true father's brother Walusi died, Ulawa publicly denounced Wailagime but denied any part in Yobibia's 'murder'. Pesese'uma died just after my own arrival in Garialand in April 1949. At the funeral Polilipa, utterly heartbroken, accused Poliwa [Ulawa] of killing him by sorcery, at the same time disowning responsibility for Walusi's death.

Later Salapu [Ulawa], his wife To'abulime [Ätaba], and his half-brother Kuaki [Ulawa], all living in Somau (Yabapunaku-Eimanaku domain), fell ill but were 'cured' by Salapu's true mother's brother Labaia [Mosoli], who was famous for his skill in this field. People were soon murmuring that Polilipa had again taken revenge on Ulawa. This caused some scandal be-cause, although he was not related to Kuaki, he was a close 'mother's father' to Salapu through a common Mosoli enatic link. The charitable allowed that because of this he had 'shot' Salapu only once — enough to make him sick but not to kill him. Despite obvious temptation, he had not entirely forgotten his kinship obligations.

Yet this turn of events helped kill the dispute which, without another death, could logically go no further. Polilipa, by nature kind, was embar-rassed: he did not wish to be thought guilty of unwarranted aggression against a close relative. With tactful suggestions from neutral kinsmen such as his true sister's son Watutu [Sogumu], with whom he was very close, he turned the quarrel away from Ulawa in Somau to unspecified persons in Onea. He let it be known that Pesese'uma's ghost had told him in a dream that the true 'murderer' lived in Onea and that the cause he had been seeking was previous trouble over a pig which had belonged to Sigogoma [Suboli] of Yaulilinaku domain and which he (Pesese'uma) had shot when it ravaged his garden. Sigogoma then had resorted to a form of sorcery (*oi'oi osa*)[12] that caused Pesese'uma's wife Saniasi to go insane and hang herself. Later Sigogoma died. People in Onea had falsely assumed that Pesese'uma had 'killed' him in revenge and they had now 'shot' him (Pesese'uma) in return.

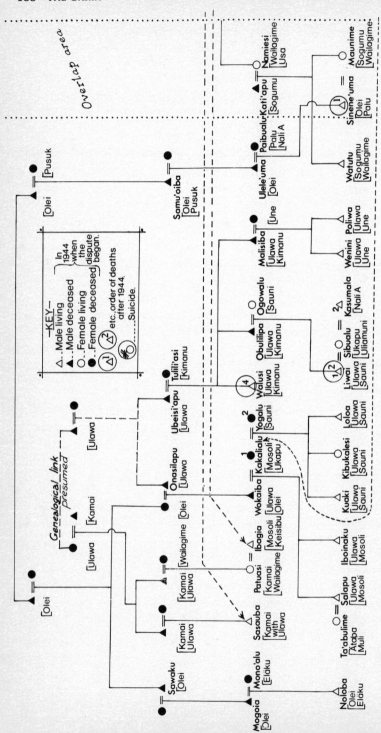

Genealogy 9 The Ulawa-Olei-Wailagime-Suboli Sorcery Feud

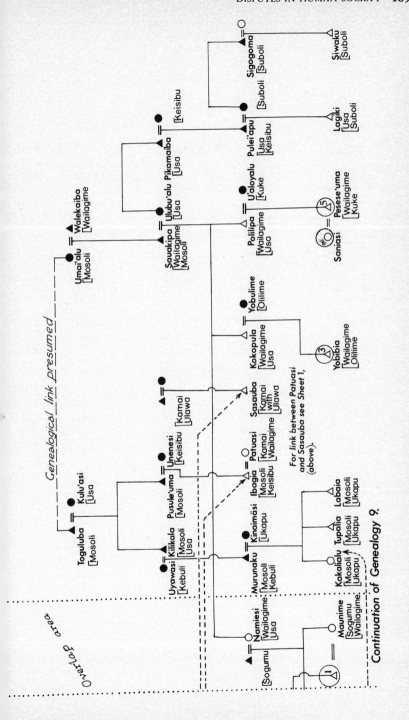

Continuation of Genealogy 9.

The dispute had exhausted itself. Polilipa could lay no charge against a specific person in Onea. Sigogoma had been an elderly recluse with few living kinsmen apart from his pre-adolescent son Siwaku and his true sister's son Lagiki [Usa], neither of whom could be held responsible for Pesese'uma's death. Siwaku was too young and Lagiki, who lived in Iwaiwa as a committed supporter of the Lutheran Mission, was close 'brother' to Pesese'uma, who had been an Usa enate. Polilipa died early in 1952 before I returned to the field. There was some talk that Sō agnates in Onea had 'shot' him in revenge for one of their women he was said to have 'murdered' as wanton compensation for his son. But those concerned killed the gossip by exchanging pigs and, as far as I am aware, never took the matter further.

Case 5: The Sogumu-Negri Affair (see Genealogy 2)

In this dispute the litigants were not only completely unrelated but also geographically so distant from each other that there could be no neutral kin to regulate it. It took place at a time when Australian administration had been unquestionably re-established after the Pacific War so that its circumstances were inevitably artificial. Nevertheless, it is of genuine academic interest in that it illustrates the problems that arise, and the ways in which people respond to them, when conflicts occur at this social range.

I had heard whispers about the affair before leaving the field in July 1950 but learnt the full details only when I returned more than two years later. In June 1950 Yaikolu [Kuauba], a young indentured labourer, returned to Yaniba in Munimuninaku domain. Handsome, conceited and sexually experienced — he had already been in prison for a homosexual offence[13] — he began to make his presence felt. He shot a pig belonging to E'uloku [Limau] of Iwaiwa and then became involved with No'anime [Wolu], wife of Äbalia [Sogumu], properly of Iwaiwanaku but living in Yaniba (Munimuninaku). Although he was not related to Äbalia and No'anime, he was a secondary affine of Walili (Äbalia's parallel cousin), who had married his widowed mother. Yet he did not allow this consideration to restrain him. Äbalia discovered the liaison either late in 1950 or early in 1951 and called a moot in Iwaiwa. During the debate and in full public view he killed Yaikolu with a cassowary-bone dagger which he had secreted in his clothing. Another parallel cousin Watutu, now *Tultul* of Iwaiwa, took him to the Supreme Court in Madang, where he was sentenced to five years in prison and No'anime was ordered not to remarry until he was released.[14]

The Sogumu agnates quickly came to terms with Kuauba. They feared reprisal for Yaikolu's death and, as soon as the Madang court case was over, sent a pig, food, valuables and £A6 as compensation with the proviso that, should Äbalia die in prison, Kuauba should send them an identical payment. As a secondary affine, Walili effaced himself and left the negotiations in the hands of Watutu, who claimed a special tie with Kuauba through Wailagime, of which he was an immediate enate: Kuauba stock was said to be originally descended from a Wailagime woman. The Kuauba men respected Watutu's delicate position and accepted the compensation on the terms offered.

The problem now lay with Äbalia's wife No'anime. Watutu, as spokesman for Sogumu, initially wanted her to live in Ula'ulu in Orinaku, her own bush god domain, where she had relatives to care for her. But she had other ideas. Her widowed mother Nenegiasi [Upaume], also from Orinaku, had remarried at Negri in Girawaland, along one of the main routes to Madang. On their return from the court hearing she got Watutu's agreement that she should stay in Negri with Nenegiasi. It was not long before she was having an affair with Asiauma, *Tultul* of Mauru, a nearby settlement. He grandly said that he would marry her.

The Sogumu agnates, speaking on behalf of Äbalia's security circle, took a reasonable view. They realized that Äbalia would not come home for several years and welcomed the chance to be rid of his faithless wife. They said that they would not oppose the new marriage but would ask Asiauma to return them what they had already paid out, as bride wealth and death compensation, on No'anime's account: £A35 or seven pigs.[15] They were irritated only because he would not come to Iwaiwa to seal the bargain and they could not put pressure on him to do so. Their problem was that, because of the *Pax Australiana,* Nenegiasi had been able to remarry in Girawaland, at a social and geographical range far wider than would have been possible for women of Orinaku and Iwaiwanaku domains in the past. Hence there were no neutral kinsmen directly linking them with Negri and Mauru. They had nobody who could put moral pressure on Asiauma to attend their moot and hear their proposals. Their only course was to bide their time for another year until an Administration patrol visited Garialand in November 1952. They took their case to the officer-in-charge on the grounds that he was the only force that could compel Asiauma to come to them. The patrol officer sent out a policeman, who brought him in to attend a hearing at the Administration Rest House at Ubiolo in Somau.

The hearing, which took place on 4 and 5 November 1952, was a blend of traditional processes of social control and Australian court procedures. The patrol officer presided. He was attended by: Ibagia [Mosoli], the retiring *Luluai;* Watutu, *Tultul* of Iwaiwa and soon to be *Luluai;* Aleinaku, Medical *Tultul* of Negri; and Asiauma, *Tultul* of Mauru. No'anime was also present. Walili, as the senior Sogumu agnate, was at the hearing but kept silent out of respect for his Kuauba secondary affines. The other Sogumu agnates kept in the background, leaving Watutu to argue their case. Watutu was supported by two of Äbalia's and one of his own 'affines': Pulutona [Upaume] of Orinaku, No'anime's true cross-cousin; Ulabunaku [Silei] of Mamunaku, her close 'mother's brother'; and Onumala [Kailala] of Yabapunaku-Eimanaku, with whom he had a dual relationship as a fictive 'brother' through Asina and as a close 'brother-in-law' through Kailala. Onumala was also potentially useful to him because he had a few kinsmen with whom he planted gardens in Amasua in Girawaland, although not as far afield as Negri and Mauru. All these people sat well to the front of the gathering. When Onumala voluntarily and competently interpreted for No'anime, who had little Pidgin, the patrol officer did not object.

The patrol officer explained that, as he had no magisterial powers, he could give no decision in the dispute but, at best, he could help the parties concerned find a solution for themselves. If they could not do this, he would have to send them to the Court for Native Affairs in Madang.[16] Watutu then explained Sogumu's position as I have already outlined it. He, his fellow agnates, and the rest of Äbalia's security circle did not want to make trouble. As Äbalia would be away for several years it would be wiser for his wife to remarry. All they wanted was to recoup what they had expended on her, especially as they had not benefited by children of the marriage: £A35 or seven pigs. Asiauma replied that he could not contemplate marriage on such terms: he could not raise such wealth and would therefore relinquish No'anime. Yet she remained adamant: she would not leave Asiauma, who had promised to marry her, and would not wait for Äbalia to return. As this was an obvious impasse, the patrol officer ruled that the parties should go to Madang and closed the hearing.

During the rest of 4 November there was much discussion behind the scenes. It emerged that Asiauma planned to resign his headmanship and join the police, and that No'anime was unwilling either to go to Madang or to return to Iwaiwa. She was clearly confused: if she went to Madang, the magistrate would imprison her; and, if she lived in or near Iwaiwa, Äbalia, who had already killed Yaikolu, might return to kill her also. When she was told that he could as easily kill her in Negri or Mauru, she replied that she would not live in or near Iwaiwa because Yaikolu's ghost (kaua) would undoubtedly seek revenge and automatically regard her as equally guilty as Äbalia for the original murder.[17] Finally, when she realized that she would have to obey the patrol officer and go to Madang, she changed her mind: her duty was to stay in Iwaiwa and look after the gardens and other property of her 'brother-in-law' Watutu. She would not go back to Negri.

The patrol officer reconvened the hearing next day. When he learnt about No'anime's change of heart he rescinded his order for her and Asiauma to go to court in Madang, but his problem was where she should live. He rejected Watutu's advice that she should go to Ula'ulu, as it would make it too easy for her to run away, and instructed her to stay in Iwaiwa, in the household of Watutu's first wife Onasilime. No'anime honoured her undertaking until about February 1953, paying only occasional visits to Negri to see her mother and care for her sow which was about to farrow. But she then resumed her liaison with Asiauma, who did not, after all, join the police. The *Luluai* of Negri, not wanting trouble with the Administration, sent word to Äbalia in prison, who took legal action to prevent their marriage before his return to Garialand. But No'anime was determined about the man of her choice: as soon as Äbalia was free, she opted for Asiauma. Äbalia died soon after and Sogumu recovered none of the original bride price or compensation for Yai-kolu's death.

The Forces controlling Disputes in Human Society

I now analyse the cases I have described to illustrate two issues that I have continually stressed. First, whereas leadership is crucial in the process of self-regulation, it has only limited importance in the settlement of disputes. Second, the Garia system of sociopolitical control is a function of the ego-centred security circle, expressed in the politics of individual choice and neutrality, which accentuate the balance between personal self-interest and social self-regulation, and which are the essential factor in the conduct and settlement or, at least, control of most disputes.

Leadership

As I have argued in Chapter 5, big men are essential for integrating the social order. They are catalysts in focal and multivalent activities and institutions that are the cornerstone of self-regulation in human society. They are the pivots of garden teams and settlement populations. They initiate the pig exchanges that cement affinal ties and subsequent consanguineal links within the close grade of ego's kindred based on interlocking land rights, and that extend his security circle by creating *sawaya/nalaya* bonds. In Chapters 7 and 8 I demonstrate that they play a comparable role in man's relations with the superhuman realm of the cosmos: they perform the rituals that create and perpetuate relationships between ego, his deities and the spirits of his departed ancestors. They are essentially cosmic persons: they operate in both the human and the superhuman realms of the cosmos, promoting interaction and collaboration between all its inhabitants — gods, ghosts and men.

Yet, as I stressed in the same context, the leaders' formal role in the secular realm is restricted in two ways. First, they have only limited policy-making functions: they mainly set in motion and co-ordinate socially accepted activities, which are routine in that they are culturally predetermined. Second, they perform no strictly judicial duties. In the five disputes I have outlined, no leader represented society at large or any specific group within it, handing out decisions binding all its members. Certainly, big men used their influence to advance the interests of those persons in their security circles whom they were supporting, but they did so only as individuals. They were *primi inter pares:* their power and influence were open to challenge both by their rivals helping other persons and even by their juniors. This was especially clear in Case 3: Usegiliba [Keisibu], a young but aspiring big man, was able to put down a well established leader, Imoguli [Nali B]. As a footballer, he had a monopoly of a new but highly prized skill and, therefore, won his point. Finally, as for any other person, a leader can make his presence felt in any dispute only to the extent that his security circle alignments allow.

The politics of individual choice and neutrality

Just as leaders represent neither Garia society *in toto* nor specific parts of it, in the same way there can be no system of segmentary group politics, with units of the same order balanced in opposition. In none of the examples I have presented — indeed, in none of the cases I recorded in the field — was there any suggestion of automatic or compulsory group solidarity in the bush god domain or patrilineage. This needs no further elaboration. In any dispute ego's position is determined by his kinship computer: by his personal ties to the adversaries and their supporters on the basis of his place in a mesh of intersecting security circles articulated mainly by multiple descent names. He should always help any member of his security circle — agnate, enate, bush brother, affine or exchange partner — especially if the relationship is reinforced by land interests and as long as no tie with his opponent gets in the way. This, in theory, does not entirely eliminate the possibility of bush god domain and patrilineage solidarity, although it makes both unlikely and unnecessary. What is more to the point, it accentuates the politics of neutrality.

As is implicit in the foregoing argument, because participants' roles in any dispute are based on individual choices and convergence of interests, the role of neutral kin — those related to both disputants and their supporters — is of crucial importance. Such persons in large measure determine its conduct and prevent it from getting out of hand. Even though it implies no judicial role, to exert such influence is the mark of a genuinely big man. Men such as Yerema [Nali A], in the past, and Usegiliba [Keisibu], in more recent times, won renown for their aggressiveness: they were discussed with a sense of awe that camouflaged underlying disapproval and distrust.[18] Hence, especially at times of social turmoil, those who were known for their skill in negotiating and manipulating solutions to disputes, either in moots or before disputants confronted each other — men such as Imoguli [Nali B] and Ubilili [Sogumu] — enjoyed a greater and more permanent reputation.

Neutrality *(obolo pulobu,* Pidgin *stap namel —* literally, 'to be in the middle') demands great political skill. As his aim is to achieve compromise between the adversaries, a go-between must be completely pragmatic and flexible, suiting his commitment to the situation as it develops. I realized this in November 1949, as the result of a personal experience. With considerable reluctance I accepted an invitation from the people of Nugu to adjudicate in a local dispute on the condition that I might organize the moot in my own way. At the moots I had previously attended, supporters of both parties and neutrals sat down together indiscriminately: there was no pattern from which I could gauge the numerical strength of those committed to any one particular position. I insisted, therefore, that the participants formed three groups: those for the plaintiff; those for the defendant; and neutrals. Grudgingly the people acquiesced, and I counted 22, 16, and 15 respectively. Yet later I realized that it was a meaningless exercise that had caused the participants acute embarrassment. During the discussion of the case several people changed their positions radically: those who were initially supporters of the plaintiff or defendant suddenly spoke as neutrals, while those initially neutral espoused one or other of the disputants, as unforeseen issues forced them to respect relationships they had previously overlooked. In fact, the overt disorganization of a moot is essential for neutrals. Unlike the hard-core supporters of either side, they prefer to melt into the background until they have surveyed the whole field of action and found a suitable opportunity to offer an acceptable solution. As I have already foreshadowed, they cannot finally programme their kinship computers until they have heard at least some of the debate in a moot or have observed the protagonists' behaviour in other forms of retaliatory action such as football and can judge the wisest course of action they can take. By the same token, they make excessive use of allusive language *(kuna ila'ila,* Pidgin *tok bokis)* so that their statements are not restricted to fixed interpretations until they can openly declare themselves.

Neutrality sheds light on a further aspect of social control which Gluckman (1954) was the first to point out, albeit for the rudimentary Lozi state in Zambia. Paraphrasing him in a previous publication (Lawrence 1971a: 23-4), I commented on the contrasting aims in dispute settlement in western law courts on the one hand, and traditional Papua New Guinean societies on the other. Whereas in western law the aim is to guarantee the individual and equal rights of the citizen-isolate, with emphasis on the nature of the offence committed and abstract, impartial justice, in Papua New Guinea there is no concept of *fiat justitia, ruat coelum* but a clear recognition that the sky must be kept up. In settling a dispute, the aim is to restore the social order by patching up relationships that have been damaged or broken. The nature of the offence is of secondary importance. What matters is that, for the good of all concerned, the adversaries should be induced to resolve their differences. Far from there being abstract, impartial justice, the forces of self-regulation, which western courts dismiss as irrelevant, cannot be divorced from retaliatory action, which varies therefore with every situation. They are its controlling principle, determining its nature and severity according to the social range and circumstances of the dispute, and often preventing it from overstraining the social order.

This is particularly true of the flexible Garia cognatic structure that makes it inevitable that in virtually every conflict there are persons with divided loyalties. They bring the pressures of self-regulation to bear on the litigants and their immediate supporters. Even if they cannot always specify the type of self-help to be adopted, they can generally keep it within bounds and thereby steer the litigants to a reasonable solution. In a normal dispute, unless either litigant flouts the conventions I have discussed, the more intense the degree of neutrality deriving from cross-cutting relationships, the more it is likely that this situation will obtain, as the five cases described illustrate.

Case 1, involving only close kin, was crystal clear. Pioba [Na'ina] and Wawaku [Sogumu] represented both Yabapunaku-Eimanaku and Iwaiwanaku domains. Yet neither was living in his own domain at the time. The money exchanged to settle the dispute was provided, on both sides, largely by representatives of Yabapunaku-Eimanaku, only Mutiti [Uliamuni] representing Iwaiwanaku. In the moot nobody could produce evidence of Pioba's guilt and, because of the clearly divided loyalties of virtually all the participants, the result was a foregone conclusion. Under pressure from Ubilili and Imoguli, the moot quickly adopted a settlement by means of compensation and forced it on the two adversaries when they showed signs of not accepting it. This was typical of many quarrels at close range that did not develop into protracted vendettas.

In Case 2 there was considerable irregularity. Those ranged against each other came from a number of bush god domains and patrilineages. The neutrals were less concentrated. Yelibubu was not a very close relative of

Ilomala and Konoiba, whose direct backers Poliloma and Äbalia were not connected to his own defenders. The two sets of immediate supporters left to themselves might well have started a brawl. Yet there were enough neutrals at the moot to control it. Mutiti, Ubilili, E'uloku and Mataraiba showed their disapproval of Yelibubu, and allowed him to suffer some disgrace and physical violence, but protected him from serious harm. His Ulilainō defenders took their cue from this. They acknowledged his 'guilt' but acceded to the neutrals' policy of permitting but limiting retribution.

In Case 3, although the Kopenau-Muguliba and Oi'asa sections of Keisibu patrilineage were early protagonists, Patiti was avenged by a heterogeneous trio from his security circle. Yet, despite the estrangement of the two sections because of the skirmish that got out of hand, by 1949 there were influential neutral kin who could contain the dispute. Ibagia [Mosoli], who had stood for the Kopenau-Muguliba section at the outset, now did his best to protect Wila's interests. He did so partly because he was *Luluai* of Somau, partly because he was linked to Wila through Labaia, and partly because Usegiliba was now clearly the prime aggressor. He urged moderation on both sides but, without openly opposing him, made sure that Usegiliba did not manipulate the football game exclusively to his own advantage by supporting Wila's introduction of his E'unime-Kolu 'affines' to equalize the contest. In the end he identified with Wila by helping to cook for his team. He was given moral support by Kapapua and Yageliba (patrilineal descendants of Muguliba), who had become neutrals in the dispute because of their enatic tie through Tau with Wila's wife. By the same token, Liwei's allegiance to Wila was undermined by his own affinal link with a member of Usegiliba's football team. Another interesting person in this context was Yalokai of Kolu. During the match he supported his 'affine' Wila but used his influence as a distant Keisibu enate to maintain order. Somewhat later he identified with the Kopenau-Muguliba section by supporting Usegiliba in a sorcery divination at a funeral.

In Case 4 there were no clearly defined groups confronting each other. Ulawa agnates never fully united against Olei or Wailagime agnates because two of them, Salapu and Iboinaku, were enates of the former and linked through Mosoli to the latter. The case against Noloba was brought in the name of Ulawa by only one of its agnates, supported by an enate with *de facto* agnatic status and the latter's very close 'brother-in-law'. Subsequently, this case almost perfectly illustrated the rules given me by informants. Those who died and those accused of 'murdering' them were quite unrelated until the very end. Yet this introduces an additional point: as this case suggests, sorcery disputes are often conducted only on the basis of mutual suspicion, so that neutral kin play a less important role in them than in moots or at times of physical conflict. There is no open or concrete situation in which they can take part. Thus, when Noloba was charged with Liwai's 'murder' at a moot, neutrals such as Salapu and Iboinaku could make their positions clear and presence felt. Yet, after the next few deaths, there were no moots: aggrieved kinsmen merely aired their speculations, and left gossip and rumour to do the rest. Neutrals could not exercise influence. It was only when Polilipa's close 'daughter's son' Salapu fell ill that they had a chance to bring the dispute to an end.

Case 5 was, as far as I could judge, completely outside tradition. The dispute occurred at a social range so great that, before the *Pax Australiana* made distant journeys safe, it would have been impossible for a widow from central Garialand to remarry so far away and so help create such a situation. Yet, from a purely traditional view, two things are of interest. First, even at this range, neither all residents of Iwaiwanaku domain nor all Sogumu agnates overtly expressed their solidarity against Asiauma of Mauru. Walili, the senior Sogumu agnate, did not dare offend his Kuauba secondary affines. Indeed, Watutu, who led the case before the patrol officer, got his main support from outside his bush god domain and patrilineage: from two of Abalia's and one of his own 'affines'. In view of this, I doubt whether whole bush god domains or patrilineages have often combined for this kind of political action. Second, as he explained to me, Watutu in asking the patrol officer to intervene was seeking *not* abstract, impartial justice but a substitute for neutral go-betweens who could prevail on Asiauma to come to Iwaiwa and negotiate with him. He was trying to assimilate the Australian politico-legal system to his own traditional process of social control.

In conclusion I return to a point I made earlier in this chapter. As virtually all disputes in traditional society appear to occur at sufficiently close range for at least some of the participants to be interrelated, most of them are finally solved or eventually fade into oblivion. Even when, as Epstein, A. L. (1974: 12) points out, closely related adversaries are bitterly estranged because one of them has gone beyond the accepted limits of retaliatory action, there are still enough restraints to prevent widespread social collapse. We are dealing with another version of Evans-Pritchard's (1940: 296) 'ordered anarchy' in what, as noted earlier, Fortes (1970: 102) has aptly designated 'a kinship polity'.[19] But, in contrast to the African Model, the participants in this system are invariably individuals whose irregular and mercurial alliances are determined by the networks of interpersonal relationships I have called security circles. They are induced to compose their differences by skilful intermediaries who, as I have just argued, are ineffective only when deaths attributed to sorcery have not been debated in open moots. As this involves the belief in non-secular forces, it is now convenient to introduce the next stage of the inquiry: the putative or superhuman realm of the cosmos, in which leaders or big men enjoy a special, even privileged, position.

7

Religion: the Putative Realm of the Cosmos – Superhuman Beings

I do not offer a precise definition of Garia religion because, like other Melanesians (cf. Lane and Lawrence in Lawrence and Meggitt 1965: 251 and 198), the people themselves have no collective term for it in their own language. Implicitly, they regard it as just one aspect of their generalized and integrated cosmic structure rather than a separate, specialized institution. It impinges on most facets of their workaday lives. So far, I have presented it only as an exordial explanatory mode: the people's account of the origins of their physical environment and sociocultural system. I now approach it in the manner suggested at the beginning of Chapter 2, treating it as a second system of relationships within the total cosmic order: a network of conjectural ties between human and superhuman beings, all of whom co-exist in the same natural environment. As such, religion is not merely an oblique reflection of human society, but also essentially a putative addition to it. In other words, I take up the last three questions posed in the Introduction about the nature of this superhuman realm. In this chapter I attempt to answer the first: this realm's conceived structure. I begin by classifying the types of superhuman beings the Garia acknowledge. I then describe a youth's introduction to them through initiation. Next, I show how initiation buttresses and extends his secular security circle by creating the special relationships with other human beings I mentioned in Chapter 2. Finally, I delineate his fictive superhuman security circle: the gods, ghosts and possibly personal double, whom he regards as the complement of his human security circle in his political region. In Chapter 8 I explore the second and third of the questions posed: the maintenance and restoration of order in this wider cosmos, which men believe to depend on their own performance of ritual or interaction with superhuman beings.

Superhuman Beings: Gods, Ghosts and Demons

We now recognize that the view of early European colonists that indigenous Melanesian religions were based entirely on fear was gross misrepresentation. The Garia, who are probably typical of the region in this respect, are pragmatic about their religion. They regard many, if not all, superhuman beings as potentially beneficent if they are ritually honoured but as potentially dangerous only if they are annoyed. Ego sees this in the same terms as in the case of his human security circle: he has to establish positive relationships with specific deities and spirits.

In more general terms, Garia regard their natural environment as both benign and minatory. It is benign in that there is always food, even if it is sometimes inadequate, and human and animal populations are usually maintained. It is minatory in that there are always economic and social risks: destruction of crops by wild pig, landslides and drought, crippling illness and premature death. The people have to explain and keep these dangers at bay. Thus they conceive within the cosmos forces more powerful than human, some always potentially friendly but others always inimical. They personify them as various types of superhuman beings who may work for their advantage if correctly approached and manipulated, or for their ruin if ignored or displeased.

Garia acknowledge four broad categories of superhuman beings: creator deities (*oite'u*, Pidgin *masalai*), ghosts or spirits of the dead (*kopa* and *kaua*, Pidgin *tambaran*), demons and personal doubles. In two cases they classify demons as gods (*oite'u*) but, in all others, they call both demons and personal doubles *norugoiba* and *sigiasi* (Pidgin *wailman/wailmeri bilong bus*, 'wild men/women of the bush') according to sex. As I have emphasized both in the Introduction and at the beginning of Chapter 2, they do not conceive any of these beings as inhabiting a supernatural or transcendental realm: as living apart from and on a higher plane than the earth. They see them as essentially terrestrial: as beings living, and often associating freely, with men and women in the natural environment.

Gods and goddesses are described as corporeal: normally as either quasi-human beings, animals, reptiles, birds or fish with conventional physical attributes (skin, flesh, bones, blood and hair), although they may change their form at will. If attributed human form, they are said to wear clothes and ornaments, and carry tools and weapons appropriate to their sex. Yet, however mundane, they have very great power. They can do things impossible for human beings, even sorcerers: they can travel vast distances in the twinkling of an eye and perform prodigies of physical strength. As I have already explained, they created artefacts, food plants, animals and institutions instantaneously, and then revealed them to men in dreams or through personal association. Again, as I have mentioned and shall argue later in greater detail, they enter into reciprocal relationships with men in response to ritual, guaranteeing the success of otherwise purely secular activities. They inhabit sanctuaries (oite'u weise, Pidgin peles masalai), generally stands of large trees (such as ficus), cliff faces, boulders and river pools.

Ontologically, deities are said to be quite different from spirits of the dead. They are conceived as independent creator spirits who have always existed in their own right, and never as metamorphosed ghosts who were once living men and women. During life the human body has its own soul (enumu, Pidgin dewel), sometimes confused with its own shadow (enumuguku). At death the soul becomes a spirit of the dead: either kopa (the spirit of a person who has died from natural causes or sorcery) or kaua (the spirit of a person who has died as a result of physical violence). Both kopa and kaua are very powerful: like deities, they can travel at great speed and do things well beyond ordinary human capacity. Yet they are never creators. Again, like deities, they are said to be corporeal, although they are cold to touch and visible mainly to big men. They can assume a variety of forms other than human: as animals, reptiles, birds or insects. When they do take human form, they have clothes, tools, and weapons proper to their sex.

Traditionally, a corpse was exposed on a tree platform. When it had decayed, the sons of the deceased — especially in the case of a prominent man — collected and preserved its bones for the purpose of honouring the ghost, although after several generations, for reasons I give below, their descendants discarded them for those of the more recent dead. Under pressure from the Australian Administration, however, after the 1920s the Garia adopted the practice of burying people either in village cemeteries or in the bush near the land they were working before they died. Both kopa and kaua go initially to one of three lands of the dead, supervised by Obomwe, the snake goddess who gave birth to mankind: Nesua by the River Mobo for spirits from western and south-western Garialand: Waliwau[1] near Totoba for those from the northern and central areas; and Sie near Nugu for those from the east and south-east. Yet, just as the living change their settlements, ghosts also may move freely from one land of the dead to another if they wish to be with other kinsmen. In addition, they may roam the bush at will or visit living relatives, especially in dreams. *Kaua,* always vengeful, are greatly feared: they continually haunt the land in search of those who killed them and whom they wish to strike down in their turn. I discuss this in detail in Chapter 8.

The life of the dead in Nesua, Waliwau and Sie replicates, and thus validates, that of the living. Ghosts inhabit orderly settlements, residing with the kinsmen of their choice and enjoying the same statuses as when alive, as big men or ordinary folk. They raise wild pig and, as their household fowls, *ile'u* birds (black of plumage and long of tail), whose cry is said to presage imminent death. Yet the Garia have no concept of ghostly immortality. As the pig myth (p. 135) indicates, ghosts may be killed. In any case, they survive the deaths of their human bodies only for a period. There are no remote ancestors.[2] Both *kopa* and *kaua* spend only two or three generations in the lands of the dead. They then turn into flying foxes or bush pigeons, which even their true descendants may kill and eat with impunity. This final metamorphosis takes place when a ghost is no longer significant for secular society: when its successors have forgotten its name and nickname, and consequently throw away its bones. Later in this chapter I analyse the structural implications of this belief.

Although men believe that they can incorporate creator deities and ghosts in their security circles, they claim at best only ambivalent relationships with the two other categories of superhuman beings they recognize: demons and personal doubles. Demons are invariably hostile. The snake god Sikikiba tries to make garden sites infertile. The monster Kesene tries to waylay ghosts on their first journeys to the lands of the dead. Non-specific 'wild men and women of the bush' *(norugoiba* and *sigiasi)* are invariably malicious to human beings. Finally, each human being is said to have his or her personal double (also, as noted, *norugoiba* or *sigiasi* according to sex), who inhabits the bush and is distinguishable only by having inordinately long fingernails. Some informants asserted that ego's personal double was potentially friendly, while others adopted an entirely contradictory position. Once again, I set this issue aside until Chapter 8, in which I discuss the ways in which men try to come to terms with superhuman beings by means of ritual.

Childhood and Initiation

Ego's life cycle falls into four stages. A male child is called *nono* and a girl child *momugo* (Pidgin *pikaniniman/meri*). With initiation, when he is about ten years old or more, a boy becomes a youth *(tenemai*, Pidgin *manki)* and, after menstruation, a girl, becomes a maiden *(maguna,* Pidgin *liklik meri).* A married man is called *apu* (Pidgin *man)* and a married woman *ui* (Pidgin *meri).* When they have several children, husband and wife are 'true' man and woman *(apu/ui meru,* Pidgin *draipela man/meri* or *man/meri tiru).* An old man is *sakau'apu* (Pidgin *lapun man)* and an old woman *sakau'ui* (Pidgin *lapun meri).* A leader or big man is *kokai'apu* (Pidgin *bikpela man)* or, especially when he is old, *kanaba* (Pidgin *masta).*[3] I am concerned here mainly with youths: their development through childhood and progressive isolation from women, followed by initiation and training in religious secrets.

Every child is placed under the protection of superhuman beings even before it is born. While his wife is pregnant, ego must taboo certain foods, especially game meat, as ordained by the gods. After she has been delivered, he performs ritual to promote the baby's health. But he may not see his wife, who is attended by any female relatives or affines available, for about three days, after which they both take the child to a stream to cleanse it and themselves of the pollution of parturition. Thereafter, not only the father but also the maternal uncle (as is logical in a cognatic society) each give it a separate name — often in the case of a boy, but never in that of a girl, the name of a deity to whom either of them has rights, such as a bush god or one of those presiding over artefacts or food plants. Gods so selected should act as a boy's personal tutelaries, although at this stage he may learn no more about them than their open names. Their esoteric names, like all religious secrets, cannot be entrusted to him until his formal education during and after initiation. Young children are told about gods, ghosts and demons — to respect the first two and avoid the third — but that is all.

Otherwise, a boy's and girl's first ten years of life are largely secular. As soon as it is sentient, a child is given toilet training and taught kinship terminology and behaviour. Yet parents and older relatives are never autocratic: they frequently indulge and rarely discipline. While girls tend to stay with their mothers, who continually instruct them in feminine roles, boys form their own play groups but still learn through imitation. They join mock dance and hunting teams, but very often accompany their parents to the gardens or other work sites, where, with a minimum of direction from their elders, they take part in everyday tasks and gradually accept adult responsibilities. By early adolescence they have mastered most of the secular skills essential for survival.

Yet, as I have argued generally for the southern Madang Province in previous publications (Lawrence 1959; 1964; and 1965), the people rate these secular skills as only routine knowledge that anybody, given time, may acquire and that, in itself, does not confer distinction. 'True' knowledge is the gradual mastery of mythology and ritual that harnesses the power of deities and ghosts to vital secular undertakings. It is the exclusive possession of adult males who have been through several stages of initiation (genuine education). Women may know about mythology and dances in honour of the dead but may never learn the arcane details of religion. In the present context I concentrate on the process by which youths are believed to acquire 'true' knowledge. I reserve the discussion of its nature or content and cosmic significance for Chapter 8.

In the past, adolescence brought great changes to both girls and boys, all of whom now ceased to go naked. After menstruation girls put on fibre-skirts and remained exclusively with their mothers and elder female relatives, who prepared them for marriage in their later teens. Youths had to go through a series of ceremonies, which began when they first adopted clothing (the bark-girdle), and might last for a decade and end in their early twenties, when they also were getting ready to marry. Since 1949 these rules have been modified. Most children of either sex older than four or five now wear European clothes, blouses and skirts for girls, and shirts and shorts for boys.

Yet what has always been most important for youths from this time on is their segregation from all nubile women, to which I drew attention at the beginning of Chapter 4 and which I now examine in detail. This rule, despite some relaxation during the last three decades, has left an indelible stamp on male–female relationships, which are at best ambivalent. On the one hand — particularly in a cognatic society — men must recognize the sociopolitical importance of women at least as kinship links: as persons who have made possible vital relationships within their human security circles. On the other, boys are now taught that, in contrast to their structural role, women are subordinate and dangerous to them. I have already described how husbands do not cohabit with their wives. They visit them at night for what are, in effect, fleeting sexual encounters, the evil effects of which they must wash off next morning. They do not fraternize with them at work, and leave them to perform many of the heavy household tasks, such as carrying food and firewood. Their continual fear is 'menstrual disease' (*ui yaui po suba*, Pidgin *sik bilong meri mun ikilimem*), which they can catch from all nubile women, and which will cause them to waste away and die. Hence, apart from those they enjoy among themselves, men should have socially close relationships only with post-menopausal women: sons with widowed mothers and elderly husbands with elderly wives. But this promotes a paradox. First, despite male sexist hubris and taboo, women are prized objects. As is clear in Chapter 6, adultery is a common offence that enhances the male ego. Men boast about their triumphs. Second, in both betrothal and adultery, men are particularly pleased when women make the necessary initial advances to them. This is a bulwark against their own inner sense of insecurity: a vindication of their own physical attraction and witness to the potency of the elaborate sex rituals lavished on them to promote it during the initiatory ceremonies, which I now describe.

Traditionally, there were three separate initiatory ceremonies: Abaiwala, Oitu (Nisiri)[4] and Nalisägege. As foreshadowed in Chapter 1, by 1949-50 only the first two had survived Lutheran Mission influence. I was able to observe a good deal of Abaiwala and Oitu (Nisiri), but not of Nalisägege, which the people had abandoned virtually entirely in the 1930s. During their revival of traditional religion in 1948 (Lawrence 1964: 201-3), they made no attempt to reintroduce it, claiming that the other two ceremonies were quite adequate for their purposes. Although a few men can still remember the melodies of its songs, no informant was ever able to give me a clear account of the ceremony itself. As I have already made plain, initiation serves two functions: it reinforces and increases a boy's secular security circle by creating for him special relationships with those who go through the ceremonies with him or who supervise him; and it introduces him to his super-human security circle — specific deities and spirits of the dead. In the people's eyes, the second function is the more important. Above all, initiation brings a youth under the protection of his ghostly forebears, and fits him to learn the myths and ritual which will give him beneficial ties with the deities to whom he has rights through his father and maternal uncle. In the past he was trained also in sorcery, especially *ämale* (Pidgin *saguma*), its most lethal form. He ate medicines and learnt spells by which he could turn invisible and then 'shoot' or 'project' (*wolobu*, Pidgin *siutim*) arrow-heads or other missiles painlessly into his victim's body to cause illness or death. He learnt curing (*auwobu*, Pidgin *windim sikin*) and the other forms of sorcery — *se'u* (Pidgin *poisin*) and *oi'oi osa*, which are based on sympathetic magic — during the years after he entered the initiatory cycle (Lawrence 1952).

A boy's initiation begins when he is about ten. His father tells him that soon he must wear clothes, avoid physical contact with nubile women (even his true sisters), take food (cooked or raw) only from other men or post-menopausal women, and preferably cook for himself. He tells him also that he should leave his mother's house for the men's club — although, as we have seen, the boy may now begin to move from settlement to settlement. These rules become more rigid with the onset of formal initiatory ceremonies, which have several stages. First, together with other novices, the boy is introduced to Abaiwala. He joins in the men's singing in the cult-house, and is allowed to watch the operation of penile incision *(omunigi walinigebu,* Pidgin *siutim kok)* performed on the older initiands, so that he will not be afraid when his own turn comes, and to attend but not join in the public part of the ceremony. Second, several years later, he goes through the full Oitu (Nisiri) festival. Third, after a further three or four years, he experiences the complete Abaiwala ceremony. By 1949-50 this concluded a boy's initiation but, before then, there was a fourth stage, the now forgotten Nalisägege, which was specifically designed to invite the spirits of the dead to the settlements and thank them for their protection of the new harvest by playing music and dancing in their honour.

I observed the Abaiwala in central Garialand in February 1950, the month in which it is normally celebrated because the new harvest makes feasting possible. People from Iwaiwanaku, Palakunaku, Yabapunaku-Eimanaku, Munimuninaku, Äliliwanaku, Ulilainaku and Mubunaku domains took part. The overt occasion for the ceremony is the manufacture of a new slit-gong for any settlement in need of it. This takes place in the bush during the wet season. Either the craftsman or the man who commissions the new artefact must organize a team to haul it to the settlement for which it is destined. As it is very heavy and bush tracks are very rugged — in the ceremony I watched, the slit-gong was made near Nugu and had to travel to Yaniba via Uria — he needs a large labour line, which he must reward with gifts of cooked pork and other food. His call for helpers signals the beginning of the ceremony, which has two parts: the esoteric and the public.

The esoteric part of the ceremony starts when the adult males of the settlements involved summon novices and initiands to attend their clubhouses. Once again the response reflects Garia cognatic structure. Some youths go to their fathers' clubs, while others remain in those in which they are currently sleeping and are sponsored by any senior kinsmen showing interest in them. Yet others prefer to return to the clubs most closely associated with their patrilineages, even though their agnatic forebears may have emigrated and settled elsewhere.

As soon as they have assembled in a clubhouse, novices and initiands come under the direction of the older men, one of whom is accepted as most skilled in organizing the rituals to be performed and therefore as leader. They have to observe the taboos I have outlined. For the first day the boys must fast, and for the rest of the ceremony may not drink water or eat food cooked in water. They are allowed only roasted food and sugarcane. They are not permitted to wash. During the first night they must squat around the fire and sweat profusely. Like the food taboos, this is an essential preliminary to the forthcoming ritual which is designed to ensure their physical maturity and success in sorcery and other religious skills. In the past they were then given their first sorcery medicine, *naguli* (the bark of a tree from the Ramu Valley), which was bespelled with the secret name of Yeyaguliba, the god who invented the black art. Also, under the supervision of the men, squatting on their haunches and beating short lengths of bamboo on the floor, they sing the songs sacred to Maulemu, the god of Abaiwala.

Next morning novices and initiands go to a river near their clubhouse to observe or undergo the operation of penile incision.[5] Each initiand, naked, sits with his legs apart, while a ritual expert *(esiapei)* — any skilled male who is not an immediate relative — takes a miniature bow *(itete)* and arrow, bespelled with the secret names of Maulemu and Yabapunaku (the deity who is said to have brought the artefact to Garialand from Bogati), and shoots the lad's glans penis several times so as to draw blood. The arrow-head is a thorn so padded that it cannot penetrate deeply. Thereafter the men take novices and initiands back to their clubhouses, where they eat a little roasted food and chew sugarcane. Any contact with water would neutralize the ritual performed on their behalf: the spells to Maulemu and Yabapunaku for the efficacy of penile incision, which should guarantee that they become sexually attractive men and, in the past, those to Yeyaguliba, which should enable them to become sorcerers. These dietary regulations are maintained for the rest of the ceremony.

For three more days and nights novices and initiands remain in the clubhouses, singing the sacred songs and eating sparingly. On the third night, in the past, they ate another bespelled sorcery medicine, *a'au,* a mixture of bush herbs. On the afternoon of the fourth day the initiands and those novices whose sponsors wish it are prepared for the public ceremony, the hauling of the slit-gong. Like the men, they have their new bark girdles, and shell and bone ornaments, brought to their clubhouses, where the leaders bespell each item with Maulemu's secret name and then pile it with the others as the *Abaiwala Enumu,* the 'soul of Abaiwala'. No woman may see the *Enumu:* the ritual power concentrated in it to promote male potency would make her very ill. All night, men, initiands and novices sing near the *Enumu,* and initiands and novices eat betel-nut, lime and the flowers of two shrubs, *ulu-lasa* and *poko'egitani,* sacred to Maulemu and once again bespelled with his secret name. The aim is to induce the god to 'think on' *(nanunanu,* Pidgin *tingting)* the *Enumu* and those who will wear the girdles and ornaments next day — especially the initiands — and imbue them with his power.

On the fifth morning, men, initiands and novices end their singing, dismantle the *Abaiwala Enumu,* and take their girdles and ornaments to the stream where they are to decorate themselves. The ritual experts *(esiapei)* supervise the initiands, painting their faces, placing ornaments on their heads and around their necks, piercing their nasal septa with small bones, putting their bark-girdles on them, and setting yellow cockatoo feathers in their hair. (Novices are dressed less elaborately and do not have their nasal septa pierced.) These preparations completed, men and initiands from all participating settlements line the track along which the slit-gong is to be hauled, some carrying miniature bows *(itete)* and arrows, and others cassowary bone daggers impaled with red fruit *(mauō)*. The leaders organize and inspect their teams, walking up and down, breathing yet more spells, spraying potions from their mouths, and here and there adjusting someone's attire. The teams come together in the bush clearing where the slit-gong has been made and take position along both sides of a rattan rope attached to it. Those who cannot find places form up in the rear but in front of the novices, who may only watch the ceremony.

Meanwhile, women from the settlements taking part, who have spent their morning painting their faces, and decking themselves in ornaments and new fibre-skirts in the bush away from their menfolk, suddenly come on the scene. They carry netbags filled with red fruit *(mauō)* and, when the men and the initiands go to the slit-gong, they follow some fifty to ninety metres behind. When everyone is in position, the men on the rope start hauling and singing the Abaiwala songs. They pull a little and then rest a little, dancing sideways from the rope and then back again. Then they haul once more. Laboriously, ceremonially, with the aid of rollers, they bring the slit-gong to the main track. At the same time, the women form two lines on each side of the men and pelt them with *mauō* fruit. The men describe this loosely as 'play' *(nela,* Pidgin *pelei)* but also recognize that it has a further significance: the effect on the women of the sex ritual heaped on the men, and especially the initiands, and the women's consequent pleasure in their appearance. The pelting is normally random but occasionally an unmarried girl singles out an older youth — or even a married woman a married man — for special attention, indicating her physical attraction and paving the way to marriage or adultery. Eventually, after many hours of labour, the dancers haul the slit-gong in triumph into the settlement for which it has been made. They break formation and accept gifts of pork and food, which their hosts have cooked for them and which they carry home. After a final night's singing in their clubhouses, they eat this food and relax the taboos imposed during the ceremony, which is now concluded.

Initiation into Oitu (Nisiri) may take place at any time in the dry season after the end of Abaiwala. The ceremony is as elaborate as Abaiwala and directed to the same general end: to place initiands under the protection of the spirits of the dead and Wese Oite'u (the Fish God), the deity who invented it. Once again, the ritual is intended to induce the god to promote their physical maturity and sexual potency, and to further their training in general religious practices, including sorcery in the past. Yet, in contrast to Abaiwala, Nisiri — the public part of the ceremony held immediately after Oitu itself—is always incorporated in an ordinary pig exchange simply as one of its dances.

Every year after the beginning of the pig exchange season, leaders bring together lads who have witnessed but not fully participated in Abaiwala, and prepare them for Oitu (Nisiri). The total ceremony lasts about six days. For five nights and days men and initiands sit around clubhouse fires in the settlements participating. Once again, initiands taboo all contact with water, including boiled food: they take only roasted food and sugarcane. They have to sit near the fire and sweat so that the ritual performed for them and their sorcery training will be effective. In the past, on the third night, they were given the sorcery medicines *naguli* and *a'au,* and a first portion of *oitu musa,* a concoction of herbs sacred to Wese Oite'u and bespelled with his secret name. They ate the second portion of *oitu musa* on the fifth night. In 1949-50, however, I was assured that initiands were allowed only *oitu musa.* During the whole period, instructed by the men but unaccompanied by any musical instruments, the initiands sing Unuma and Kali, songs originated by Wese Oite'u himself.

On the sixth morning the men take the initiands to a stream and dress them in the ornaments for the Nisiri dance except only the *sara* or high wicker 'masts',[6] which the performers strap on their backs. They also make the *oitu,* a representation of Wese Oite'u, out of cooked taro and yam, bespelling it with his secret name and blowing short bamboo flutes in his honour. They then break up the *oitu* and give the initiands pieces of it to eat. Finally, initiands remove their ornaments and take them back to their clubs, where that evening they put them on again and also fasten wicker 'masts' on their backs. They join the Nisiri dance team and help to celebrate a normal pig exchange.

Initiation: the Extension of the Human Security Circle

I discuss the religious significance of the two initiatory ceremonies I have described in the next section. In this section I am concerned only with their purely social or secular importance. From this point of view, the two ceremonies serve the same general functions as pig exchanges: they mobilize heterogeneous aggregations of people and hold them together by means of networks of interpersonal relationships, some of which they in fact create. I illustrate this by analysing the Abaiwala ceremony which was held in central Garialand in February 1950 and on which I have based my general account. As noted, people from seven different bush god domains took part: on the final day they assembled to haul the new slit-gong over a distance of about six kilometres through rugged mountain country.

The purely human or social relationships that emerge in or are created by initiatory ceremonies are as irregular in terms of bush god domain representation and genealogical ties as in the case of garden and pig exchange teams, and settlement populations. As I have said, there is no rule prescribing the clubhouse in which a youth should prepare himself for either initiatory ceremony. In the Abaiwala celebrated in and around Somau-Iwaiwa in 1950 initiands exercised a wide range of choice. In neither village did the people use all the clubs available: they preferred strong assemblages to emphasizing local ties. In Somau all participants congregated at the Wauwau clubhouse: agnates of Mosoli, Ukapu, Waipa, Osi, Ulawa, Mamu and Keisibu (Oi'asa section) cognatic stocks. Of these only Mosoli and Ulawa represented Yabapunaku-Eimanaku domain, in which the clubhouse was situated. In Iwaiwa all participants gathered at the Mamainesiau clubhouse: agnates of Sogumu, Nali A and B, Yaukai, Uliamuni and Limau cognatic stocks. Of these only Nali A and B and Yaukai were primary representatives of Yabapunaku-Eimanaku, in which once again the clubhouse was built. The Olaiku clubhouse in Äliliwanaku domain had a slightly more regular pattern. It was used by the agnatic descendants of Kopenau and Muguliba in Keisibu cognatic stock, including Yageliba and Wekumala (see Genealogy 8), who lived in Yagili'ese'u (Iwaiwa), had remained neutral in Usegiliba's football match at the end of 1949, but preferred to attend the Abaiwala ceremony with their closest patrilineal kin. Present also were Siga and Sui agnates, the latter not representatives of Äliliwanaku domain. The E'ulu club was unique on this occasion: it was used exclusively by Kulosi agnates (except for those permanently resident in Nugu), all of whom were representatives of Yabapunaku-Eimanaku domain.

The distribution of bush god domain representatives throughout the clubhouses during the Abaiwala ceremony in the Somau-Iwaiwa area in February 1950 correlated with that of the special relationships it established: those termed *mali'omei, sagomei* and *esiapei*. I discuss each of these relationships in turn and then consider a fourth: the *nawe'omei* bond created by the Oitu (Nisiri) ceremony. *Mali'omei* are those who put on the bark-girdle for the first time together. Hence all the initiands in each of the clubs mentioned enjoyed this relationship with each other: for example, in Mamainesiau, agnates of Sogumu, Nali A and B, Yaukai, Uliamuni and Limau. *Sagomei* are those who have their penes incised and are trained in sorcery together by the same experts. *Esiapei* is the reciprocal term used between initiands and those who train them in sorcery, incise their penes, and dress them in bark-girdles for the first time. As by 1950 training in sorcery was no longer offered publicly, these two relationships were said to refer only to penile incision and being dressed in bark-girdles. Moreover, as at that time few were skilled in the operation of penile incision, all the youths in the Somau-Iwaiwa area (from the Mamainesiau, Wauwau, Olaiku and E'ulu clubs) went to the same ritual expert, Usegiliba [Keisibu] of Äliliwanaku. They all shared *sagomei* relationships with one another and a communal *esiapei* relationship with him. Even so, beyond this, they all had *esiapei* relationships with those senior kinsmen in their clubhouses who had formally dressed them in bark girdles for the first time. The same pattern emerged in the Oitu (Nisiri) ceremonies held in central Garialand in 1949-50. The *nawe'omei* relationship between those who ate *oitu* together was established between the irregularly related initiands attending the same clubhouses. Finally, of course, in a large number of cases, these initiatory relationships merely reinforce already existing kinship bonds but, where they do not, they represent entirely new ties and hence expand the human security circles of the individuals concerned.

Initiation: Ego's Introduction to his Superhuman Security Circle

In Garia eyes, however, the overriding importance of initiation is religious rather than social: the introduction of youths to the realm of superhuman beings so that they have the opportunity to acquire 'true' knowledge, not the mere secular skills they have previously gleaned but the lore of ghosts and deities. Youths are placed under the protection of their immediate forebears, and are progressively taught the myths and ritual that will grant them beneficial relationships with particular deities within their political regions. The gods and ghosts with whom they legitimately claim such bonds represent their superhuman security circles, the other system of relationships within the cosmic order in which they see themselves as involved and to which I have previously referred.

At first, a boy's instruction is only general and, should he show no aptitude or ambition, it will never be more. Yet should he aspire to leadership, it becomes more intensive, especially after he has participated fully in the Abai-wala ceremony. Whereas unmotivated youths now drop out, he will undergo, outside formal initiation, special periods of serious religious tuition during which he must observe all the taboos described earlier. Normally, provided he has the requisite knowledge, a father will be his sons' first teacher: he will instruct them in the myths for the creation of the physical environment and human beings, but more particularly in myths and ritual for the two initiation ceremonies, their bush god(s), and deities for food plants, livestock, artefacts and dances. But a youth may not be restricted to only one teacher or set of ritual formulae. He may turn to older agnates, who may have greater learning than his father. Furthermore, as in the case of permanent usufructuary rights to land, he may turn for additional rights to ritual, especially in the economic field, to his maternal uncle. I discuss this later but point out in this context that, although leadership is democratic and the sons of the obscure often become prominent, those whose fathers and other senior relatives are established big men do, in fact, have an advantage.

The Garia pantheon generally reflects the elastic structure of Garia society. There are, of course, the pan-Garia gods I have already introduced: Sinatu the lizard and Mubu the python (shapers of the physical environment), Obomwe the snake (initiatrix of human life and death), Maulemu (Abaiwala), Wese Oite'u (Oitu and Nisiri) and Yeyaguliba (sorcery). Again, most of the deities presiding over the dances discussed in Chapter 5 also belong to this category in that rights to them have been traded throughout the whole area. All these gods have common myths and — with the exception of Sinatu and Mubu, who no longer influence human affairs — are honoured with uniform ritual. Rights to bush gods obviously have a more restricted geographical range, although they can be acquired through a number of enatic links as well as through the patriline. A bush god is common to all persons with permanent usufructuary rights to land in his domain, whether they be agnates or enates of the relevant cognatic stocks. Especially in northern Garialand, where holdings are fragmented and scattered, ego's rights to bush gods are likely to be equally widespread. This can be true even of those he inherits patrilineally. Two obvious examples are Limau agnates, who ideally claim seven bush gods — Iwaiwanaku, Malainaku, Kamai'asa, Pukusakunaku, Yabapunaku, Eimanaku[7] and Siliwanaku, although they concentrate only on the first two — and Au agnates who ideally claim three — Malainaku, Pukusakunaku and Kamai'asa, although they concentrate only on the first. Yet some Au agnates (recruited from Nali B) can claim three additional bush gods — Iwaiwanaku, Yabapunaku and Eimanaku — in whose domains they have Sogumu and Nali holdings.

The pattern is even more intricate in the case of economic deities, especially those for food plants. In the whole of Garialand there are eight taro deities, of whom some people may claim rights to more than three. Rights to these deities are said to follow the same pattern as those to land. In northern Garialand, on which I base the following analysis, within each cognatic stock the agnates (the patrilineage) claim their own exclusive set of secret names for these deities.[8] They regulate the use of these names just as they regulate rights to land bearing their descent name: both permanent individual usufructuary rights and residual joint guardian rights. They inherit rights to use secret names of deities from their fathers but allow them to go outside the patriline normally only to true sisters' sons who have paid handsomely for land rights and have demonstrated their devotion in other ways. Once again, a sister's son who has been taught these secret names may transmit them to his own sons but must obtain the corporate permission of his maternal uncle's patrilineage to reveal them to his non-agnatic kin. The donor patrilineage's period of guardianship over alienated secret names is said to be the same as that for alienated landholdings, about five generations, after which the original beneficiary's agnatic descendants assume full collective control. Thus, in theory, the ritual formulae for taro that a youth learns from his father or mother's brother may be based on either secret names for different deities or different secret names for the same deity derived from a number of patrilineages in the past.

My description of the inheritance and acquisition of rights to taro ritual is based largely on what informants told me. If their statements, which were always consistent, were correct, clearly the process is labyrinthine. The examples of ritual formulae I did obtain bore them out: sets of secret names for the taro deity Ibinime given me by a few closely related men with whom I was on intimate terms showed exactly the kinds of variations I have already suggested. Yet I could not substantiate their claim by making a wide survey and tabulating the necessary information from a large number of people, as I was able to do in the case of landholdings. Garia regard ritual secrets as a priceless possession and believe that they can impoverish themselves by revealing them to outsiders, who may use them to lure the relevant deities away from themselves. Indeed, in view of this belief, it would have been not only unwise but also contrary to the generally accepted ethics of field work to try to broaden the scope of my inquiries. Nevertheless, I attempt to indicate how potentially complex the process of inheritance and acquisition of rights to bush gods and taro deities can be by presenting one example: the agnates within Sogumu cognatic stock in 1949-50. I set out the details in Table 16 (see also Genealogy 2). It can be seen that Sogumu agnates at that time, had they taken the trouble to realize them in every generation, had a wide range of ritual rights: an aggregate of eleven bush gods and an aggregate of seven taro deities. In addition, they claimed rights to other economic deities—for example, the god of pottery.

Since 1945 at least, my informants asserted, the foregoing has represented the whole of virtually every youth's education. Yet, in the past, there was the further branch of learning, which, as I have hinted, is nowadays imparted

Table 16 Sogumu agnates: potential rights to bush gods and taro deities, 1949-50

Name	Descent names	Bush gods	Taro deities
Äbalia	patrikin: Sogumu	Iwaiwanaku	Ibinime, Liyu, Unaile
	Tulua	Iwaiwanaku	Ibinime, Liyu, Unaile
	Asina	Yabapunaku, Eimanaku	Ibinime, Liyu, Unaile
	Oyesi	Yabapunaku, Eiminaku	Ibinime, Liyu, Unaile
	matrikin: Miome	Munimuninaku	Ibinime
	affines: Wolu	Orinaku	Ibinime, Liyu, Unaile
	Upaume	Orinaku	Ibinime, Liyu, Unaile
Walili	patrikin: Sogumu	Iwaiwanaku	Ibinime, Liyu, Unaile
	Tulua	Iwaiwanaku	Ibinime, Liyu, Unaile
	Asina	Yabapunaku, Eimanaku	Ibinime, Liyu, Unaile
	Oyesi	Yabapunaku, Eimanaku	Ibinime, Liyu, Unaile
	matrikin: Kaka	Iwaiwanaku	Ibinime, Liyu, Unaile
	affines: Nali	Yabapunaku, Eimanaku	Ibinime, Liyu, Unaile Ibinime, Liyu, Unaile
	Usa	Munimuninaku	Ibinime
	Wailagime	Munimuninaku	Ibinime
	Keisibu	Äliliwanaku	Ibinime, Liyu, Unaile
Ubilili	patrikin: Sogumu	Iwaiwanaku	Ibinime, Liyu, Unaile
	Tulua	Iwaiwanaku	Ibinime, Liyu, Unaile
	Asina	Yabapunaku, Eimanaku	Ibinime, Liyu, Unaile
	Oyesi	Yabapunaku, Eimanaku	Ibinime, Liyu, Unaile
	matrikin: Kaka	Iwaiwanaku	Ibinime, Liyu, Unaile
	affines: Limau	Malainaku, etc.*	Ibinime, Liyu, Unaile, Teteine, Iniburi
	Usa	Munimuniaku	Ibinime
Labi ⎫	patrikin: Sogumu	Iwaiwanaku	Ibinime, Liyu, Unaile
	Tulua	Iwaiwanaku	Ibinime, Liyu, Unaile
Naguni ⎭	Asina	Yabapunaku, Eimanaku	Ibinime, Liyu, Unaile
	Oyesi	Yabapunaku, Eimanaku	Ibinime, Liyu, Unaile
	Kaka	Iwaiwanaku	Ibinime, Liyu, Unaile

(continued)

Table 16 — *continued*

Name	Descent names	Bush gods	Taro deities
	matrikin: Limau	Malainaku, etc.*	Ibinime, Liyu, Unaile, Teteine, Iniburi
	Usa	Munimuninaku	Ibinime
Wawaku	patrikin: Sogumu	Iwaiwanaku	Ibinime, Liyu, Unaile
	Tulua	Iwaiwanaku	Ibinime, Liyu, Unaile
	Asina	Yabapunaku, Eimanaku	Ibinime, Liyu, Unaile
	Oyesi	Yabapunaku, Eimanaku	Ibinime, Liyu, Unaile
	matrikin: Kaka	Iwaiwanaku	Ibinime, Liyu, Unaile
	affines: Kopa'asamana	Ulilainaku	Ibinime, Liyu, Unaile, Siliguku, Apai
Älitolo	patrikin: Sogumu	Iwaiwanaku	Ibinime, Liyu, Unaile
	Tulua	Iwaiwanaku	Ibinime, Liyu, Unaile
	Asina	Yabapunaku, Eimanaku	Ibinime, Liyu, Unaile
	Oyesi	Yabapunaku, Eimanaku	Ibinime, Liyu, Unaile
	Kaka	Iwaiwanaku	Ibinime, Liyu, Unaile
	matrikin: Kopa'asamana	Ulilainaku	Ibinime, Liyu, Unaile, Siliguku, Apai
Watutu	patrikin: Sogumu	Iwaiwanaku	Ibinime, Liyu, Unaile
	Tulua	Iwaiwanaku	Ibinime, Liyu, Unaile
	Asina	Yabapunaku, Eimanaku	Ibinime, Liyu, Unaile
	Oyesi	Yabapunaku, Eimanaku	Ibinime, Liyu, Unaile
	matrikin: Wailagime	Munimuninaku	Ibinime
	Usa	Munimuninaku	Ibinime
	Mosoli	Yabapunaku, Eimanaku	Ibinime, Liyu, Unaile
	affines: Kulosi	Yabapunaku, Eimanaku	Ibinime, Liyu, Unaile
	Keisibu	Äliliwanaku	Ibinime, Liyu, Unaile
	Kailala	Yabapunaku, Eimanaku	Ibinime, Liyu, Unaile
	Sō	Munimuninaku	Ibinime

(continued)

Table 16 — *continued*

Name	Descent names	Bush gods	Taro deities
Nanaula	patrikin: Sogumu	Iwaiwanaku	Ibinime, Liyu, Unaile
	Tulua	Iwaiwanaku	Ibinime, Liyu, Unaile
	Asina	Yabapunaku, Eimanaku	Ibinime, Liyu, Unaile
	Oyesi	Yabapunaku, Eimanaku	Ibinime, Liyu, Unaile
	Wailagime	Munimuninaku	Ibinime
	Usa	Munimuninaku	Ibinime
	Mosoli	Yabapunaku, Eimanaku	Ibinime, Liyu, Unaile
	matrikin: Kulosi	Yabapunaku, Eimanaku	Ibinime, Liyu, Unaile
	Keisibu	Äliliwanaku	Ibinime, Liyu, Unaile
Munimala	patrikin: Sogumu	Iwaiwanaku	Ibinime, Liyu, Unaile
	Tulua	Iwaiwanaku	Ibinime, Liyu, Unaile
	Asina	Yabapunaku, Eimanaku	Ibinime, Liyu, Unaile
	Oyesi	Yabapunaku, Eimanaku	Ibinime, Liyu, Unaile
	Wailagime	Munimuninaku	Ibinime
	Usa	Munimuninaku	Ibinime
	Mosoli	Yabapunaku, Eimanaku	Ibinime, Liyu, Unaile
	matrikin: Kailala	Yabapunaku, Eimanaku	Ibinime, Liyu, Unaile
	Sō	Munimuninaku	Ibinime

*The other bush gods are: Iwaiwanaku, Yabapunaku, Eimanaku, Siliwanaku, Pukusaku-naku and Kamai'asa. This table is based on the position in 1949-50. By 1980 Labi and Naguni had accepted agnatic status in Limau and thereby gained full rights to additional bush gods: Malainaku and Kamai'asa, in whose domains they now had permanent joint land titles.

only clandestinely: sorcery. Traditionally, as described, novices and initiands ate sorcery medicines during the Abaiwala and Oitu (Nisiri) ceremonies. Thereafter, as for other ritual skills, they had to decide whether to persist with or drop out from further training. Those who opted to become sorcerers apprencticed themselves to an instructor *(esiapei),* who was normally a close but not immediate kinsman. He took them to a secluded shelter in the bush, made them observe the normal initiatory taboos, and gave them intensive doses of the two medicines, *naguli* and *a'au.* He then taught them the secret names of the god Yeyaguliba and how to use them as spells that would make them temporarily invisible. Finally, he made them demonstrate their mastery of the ritual and the potency of the medicines they had eaten by having them purloin objects from other people without being seen. Those who passed this test were deemed proficient in *ämale,* the most powerful form of sorcery: by turning invisible they could 'shoot' arrow-heads from their bows or 'project' other missiles from their hands, painlessly into their victims' bodies to cause either illness or death. A single 'shot' or 'projection' would only make a person ill, while several more would be bound to kill him. Even so the apprentices had to master three further skills: 'curing' *(auwobu,* Pidgin *windim sikin)* those who had suffered *ämale* attacks, and *se'u* (Pidgin *poisin)* and *oi'oi osa,* the second and third but less important forms of sorcery. For 'curing', they were shown how to make a funnel of *kemia* leaves, place it over that part of a patient's body where the pain was evident, breathe Yeyaguliba's secret names, and so 'remove' the arrow-head or other offending missile, which they had then to show to other persons who had watched the operation. *Se'u,* as mentioned, is based on ordinary contagious magic, but I never obtained information about the techniques for *oi'oi osa,* which, in fact, is said to be the least used. Those who passed these tests became accredited sorcerers with the title of *au'apu* (Pidgin *man bilong saguma).* Those who failed, like those who opted out at the beginning of a course, were labelled *mä'apu* and were said to be 'just like women' (Lawrence 1952).

Initiation not only introduces young men to the pantheon: the pan-Garia deities, their bush gods, and those presiding over the economy and other sociocultural institutions in their political regions. It also, as stressed, makes them fully aware of the spirits of the dead: ghosts of the forebears of the cognatic stocks of which they are either agnates or enates, and of their bush brothers. From his earliest years a boy is taught to respect and honour his ancestors. All dances are performed to this end and, with the exceptions of Abaiwala and Nisiri, he may always join in them. In ordinary dance teams mothers carry infants in netbags on their backs, and parents may deck out older children, especially boys, in shell and bone ornaments, so that they too can participate. Fathers may allow favourite sons to carry their prized lime-gourds in lieu of hand-drums. Such children dance close to their parents, imitating their movements as best they can. Once a boy has been through the Oitu (Nisiri) ceremony and is preparing for his second Abaiwala, he begins to learn about and participate fully in rituals honouring the spirits of the dead. Above all, he is taught that the life of the dead is not remote and that ghosts — in much the same way as big men (see Chapter 8) — enjoy a dual cosmic role. On the one hand, ego places the spirits of all his close kinsmen, on both his father's and mother's side, together with the deities to whom he has ritual rights, firmly in his superhuman security circle. On the other, in a very real sense, because of his strong genealogical ties with them, he also regards them as virtually an extension of his secular security circle into the superhuman realm.

I discuss the benefits the dead are believed to confer on the living in return for ritual honour in Chapter 8. Nevertheless, it is essential to introduce in this context one service in the field of land tenure and agricultural ritual that ghosts are said to perform for the living because of its bearing on the structure of both the human and superhuman security circles. Although the living members of a patrilineage exercise guardian rights over the land strips, blocks or tract bearing its descent name and their hereditary esoteric formulae, their authority is guaranteed by the power attributed to their deceased agnatic forebears, who are the ultimate custodians. These ghosts watch over the patrilineage's landed estate and ritual, and take action against outsiders who encroach on them.

Once again I base my analysis on the situation as it is conceived in northern Garialand. For reasons I have already given, the period during which the dead can be concerned with the affairs of the living is limited to two or three generations. This is most relevant to the pattern of ghostly custodianship of land and ritual rights, which is closely linked to that of a patrilineage's human guardianship. When these rights have been alienated, after about two generations from the initial act of transfer, the true identities of the original maternal uncle and his sister, who made it possible, are generally lost: their personal names are forgotten or, at best, superseded by equally transient nicknames. After another generation, their ghosts no longer exist, having become flying foxes or bush pigeons. The relationship between the two relevant patrilineages — the agnatic descendants of the original donor and beneficiary respectively — is now only quite close and will be distant after two or three more generations. During this period the agnatic successors of the original beneficiary do not change the name of the land and ritual in question partly out of respect for the original donor patrilineage but also for fear of those of its ghostly forebears who have not yet disappeared, may still jealously preserve their residual custodian role, and are therefore likely to retaliate against those who challenge it. It is only after that, at about the level of the fifth descending generation, when all the spirits likely to be interested in the inaugural relationship have vanished for ever, that they can regard the original ghostly custodianship as irrelevant. Now lacking spiritual support for their own guardian rights, the human members of the donor patrilineage cease to be concerned with the land and ritual in question so that the change in name and status causes no ill will in either realm of the cosmos, human or superhuman.[9] I illustrate this in Figure 10, albeit in somewhat ideal terms. As I have already argued in Chapter 3, the process may be retarded or hastened by at least a generation because of the vagaries of genealogical knowledge.

Religion and the Socioeconomic Order

As I stressed at the beginning of both Chapter 2 and this chapter, the Garia regard their cosmic order as an integrated system, which consists of two interdependent realms or networks of relationships co-existing in the physical environment. Man sees himself as the focal point of both. In the secular realm he is bound up with human beings: the economic and sociopolitical structure. In the superhuman realm he has putative ties with deities, ghosts and, in the view of some people, his sylvan double: religion. It is essential to consider religion in its complementary social and intellectual roles: as a fictive addition to but also endorsement of human society; and as a life of the mind that channels and even instigates a good deal of socioeconomic action.

In this chapter I have dealt exclusively with the first of these two roles. Religion or the superhuman realm of the cosmos, as an unseen addition to its secular realm, validates the human sociocultural order. As the deities created it, they must have given it the seal of their approval. Ghosts corroborate it by replicating it in the lands of the dead. Because of these considerations, the sociocultural order has to be as it is: there can be no further argument. Moreover, from this point of view, Garia religion gives practical expression to the flexibility of the social system in the way I projected early in the previous section. The gods held in common by the whole society or language group — the primal creators, and those for betel-nut, initiation, dancing and sorcery — represent its general cultural homogeneity. Yet bush and economic gods reflect a social order based on convergence and multiple interpersonal links. Rights to these deities, especially those in the economic field, tend to follow the same pattern as ties of descent and kinship, and the land titles associated with them. They are not restricted to a closed or corporate unilineal descent group but radiate throughout the ego-centred security circle. This is true also of relationships with spirits of the dead, who are, as I have argued, an invisible link between the two realms of the cosmos and, certainly in northern Garialand, are thought to be most important in the structural processes associated with land tenure. In the next and final chapter I examine the second role of religion, which I introduced above: as an intellectual system that shows men how to promote cosmic harmony by maintaining and, where necessary, even restoring their relationships with the inhabitants of the superhuman realm and that is, therefore, an absolute prerequisite of leadership.

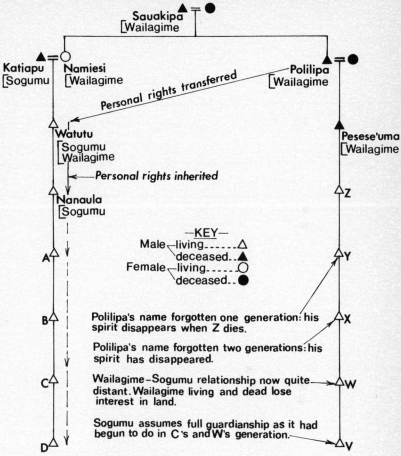

Figure 10 Ghostly custodianship of land

Should Nanaula change land name, ghosts of Polilipa and Pesese'uma would attack him. Should A change land name, ghosts of Pesese'uma and Z would attack him, even though Polilipa's ghost has disappeared. Ideally, at the level of the fifth descending generation (C-W) the land may be changed with impunity. A generation later (D-V), the change should be complete.

8

Religion: Putative Interaction between Human and Superhuman Beings

In studying religious ritual in any Melanesian society it is inadequate to base the analysis exclusively on what, in a previous publication (Lawrence 1965: 214), I have called the 'objective view of the outside observer', which tends to concentrate exclusively on its latent social meaning. I do not suggest that such an approach is wrong but only that it is bound to produce a limited answer: a mere statement about the factors that motivate the people's actions. Assuredly, it helps define what aspects of their total sociocultural order they value and regard as vulnerable: in a word, what causes them anxiety. The Garia see the burning issues clearly as economic and social: the success or failure of crops, human life and male sexual potency, for all of which they have elaborate myths and ritual. They tend to ignore or gloss over other aspects that they regard as of less importance. Yet to claim that this is a total exposition is to parade the part as if it were the whole. It does not tell us what the people believe they are doing when they perform religious ritual. Certainly the Garia, while acknowledging the values and anxieties I have suggested, would find unsatisfactory any explanation that claimed that their behaviour was designed to do no more than accentuate the one and allay the other. For a counterbalance we have to turn to what, in the same publication, I called the people's own 'subjective view', which emphasizes the intellectual assumptions underlying religious ritual: their interpretation of it as a means of achieving specifically defined ends.

At the very least, it is implicit in my whole argument that the Garia understand religious ritual in literal and straightforward terms: as a method of establishing with superhuman beings relationships that will bring them the greatest possible advantage. They believe that they are making compacts with gods, ghosts and possibly sylvan doubles that are ultimately in the interests of all parties concerned. Yet this assertion must rest on one premiss in particular: that they regard the existence of these superhuman beings as a matter not just of faith in the face of persistent doubt but of unquestioning conviction.

Anthropologists have debated this issue for many decades but I do not intend to review their arguments here. I merely put it on record that, after thirty years of research, I am satisfied that the Garia and other peoples of the southern Madang Province base many of their actions on the assumption I have outlined above. For them, gods, ghosts and demons are absolutely and physically real. This is a widespread Melanesian phenomenon, typified by Berndt's (1952-53: 262-3) seminal comment about the Kainantu people: that they do not merely 'believe' but actually 'know' that the spirits exist, just as they 'know' that the people in the next village exist, even if they cannot see them at the moment.

Garia informants expressed their view to me in these terms: *Oite'u pulina. Olo peläku pulina yaguna. Peläku pulina, pa'ati oite'u pulina* — 'The deity exists. Outwardly [literally, 'above all'] the myth exists and stands warranty. As the myth exists, so too must the deity exist'. Moreover, from the continual 'evidences' of nature it was incontestable for them, as it was for William Paley, that gods intervened in human affairs and that men could have pragmatic relationships with them. Two modern incidents support their argument. As described in Chapter 1, the Australian Administration and later the national Government initiated major road-building programmes in Garialand, abortively in the 1950s but successfully in the 1970s. On each occasion the people discovered that deity sanctuaries lay along the routes to be cleared. In their eyes the wanton destruction of these sancta would have caused divine wrath and widespread misfortune. The problem had to be solved by ritual experts who could induce the deities to establish themselves elsewhere. In the first case, near Kolu village in north-western Garialand, in 1952-53, I was told that a local big man entered the obstructing sanctuary and explained the people's dilemma to the god, who immediately and graciously volunteered to find a new home in the general vicinity. In the second case, informants told me that at Amapike in Yapa country, about 1974, three local deities vigorously resisted the road gang's attempts to dynamite the cluster of boulders they inhabited, and made their anger known by causing a tree to crash on and destroy the cabin of one of the engineering company's trucks. As it was recognized that the deities had originally emigrated from Mamunaku domain in Garialand to Amapike, the Garia accepted responsibility and sent a team of ritual experts to resolve the issue. The experts persuaded the gods to find another sanctuary nearby by means of a reasoned invocation (*sisi*) and an offering of kava (*isa,* Pidgin *koniak*),[1] cooked chickens and other food, and money. Later, when I asked the team's leader why he had provided money, for surely traditional gods had no stores of their own, he replied that they could go to Madang and spend it there.

Hence, as Garia are convinced that the existence of gods, ghosts and demons is indisputable, my analysis of religious ritual as a system of quasi-dynamic relationships between them and human beings must proceed along the same broad lines as for secular society. In Chapter 7 I showed that, from ego's point of view, not only the human but also the superhuman inhabitants of his political region can be divided into those who do and those who do not belong to his security circle. I indicated, in addition, that he sees these superhumans as the only possible source of the power that he must harness to overcome the dangers of a sometimes threatening environment. Without their co-operation, the apparently integrated cosmic structure I have described would be impossible. I now break this argument into three parts, which I discuss in the following sections. First, to preserve cosmic harmony, men must maintain positive relationships with superhuman beings or, if that is impossible, at least keep them at bay. Second, in the event of human transgression, they must try to neutralize their anger and ward off their retaliatory action. Third, it is in these two contexts that leaders assume paramount importance in popular estimation: as persons who can operate virtually outside human society and promote the general interest by achieving collaboration between the inhabitants of both realms of the cosmos.

Maintenance of Cosmic Relationships: Moral Obligation between Human and Superhuman Beings

The Garia believe that, as in the case of those between human beings themselves, effective relationships between human and superhuman beings depend on the principle of reciprocity: the mutually beneficial exchange of goods and services. They express the essence of these relationships in exactly the same terms as for those in human society: *oite'u/kopa*[2] *po nanunanu änikani eiyo änikani täbu/puluwobu* (Pidgin *kisim/pulim tingting na sari bilong masalai/tamberan*), 'to get or direct towards oneself the interest and concern of a deity or ghost'. They see this as tantamount to a sense of moral obligation between men and gods, and between men and spirits jof the dead, based on their own performance of ritual honour in return for benefits which I shall detail later. Broadly, although there are technical differences to which I shall refer in due course, they regard ritual as a substitute for face to face interaction between sentient beings: men use it in their dealings with deities and ghosts merely because in most instances they cannot see them.[3] Yet, just as in the case of human beings, there are some superhuman beings in ego's political region who are impervious to his approaches and invariably hostile to him. I examine this by reconsidering, in the context of ritual, the four categories of superhuman beings I described in Chapter 7. I present them in the same order as before: first and second, deities and spirits of the dead, with whom, as is implicit in my foregoing comments, the people believe that they can establish the satisfactory relationships I have outlined, and, third and fourth, demons and personal doubles, with whom their relations are often inimical and at best imponderable.

There are two kinds of ritual approach to deities, who, as mentioned in Chapter 2, revealed them to men in the period of antiquity. I have already referred to both in earlier contexts. The first is audible invocation (*sisi*), which is sometimes accompanied by offerings of food, traditional valuables and, as in the Amapike case, nowadays money. This is the accepted technique for Obomwe (when she is needed to ward off pestilences) and bush gods who have no secret names or whose secret names the ritual operators have not been able to learn. The second and more highly valued form of ritual is the inaudible or breathed spell (*osa*), of which the most important ingredient is either the relevant deity's secret names (*wenum minikoro*, Pidgin *naen insaet*) as against his or her open name (*olo wenum*, Pidgin *naen antap*), by which he or she is known in public, or the secret names he or she is said to have bestowed on his or her specific item of culture. Although *osa* is used for bush gods only in some instances, it is the invariable approach to the two initiatory gods, Maulemu and Wese Oite'u, the gods of Uluai and the dances introduced from the coast, the god of sorcery, Yeyaguliba, and the economic deities, especially those for agriculture. As already described in Chapter 7, rights to *osa* are complex and jealously guarded, each patrilineage claiming exclusive secret names for the deities in its security circle, which its members reveal, with the strictest safeguards, only to those enates (mainly true sisters' sons) they can trust. It would be to court disaster to reveal these names to unrelated or distantly related persons, who would use them to impoverish the original owners by stealing the deities' sense of moral commitment (*nanunanu* and *eiyo*).

This stresses the people's essentially pragmatic attitude towards ritual: the quality of the relationship between man and god on the one hand, and the range of the moral obligation involved in it on the other. In the first place, as stated, they regard ritual as a proxy for direct interaction with superhuman beings whom they cannot see, as another form of the exchange of goods and services: ritual honour in return for success in raising crops and livestock, dancing and so forth. Their aim is to create with the deities in their security circles the same kind of relationships that exist between themselves. Unless they are guilty of sacrilege, which I discuss in full later, they have no automatic assumption of their own dependence on deities whom they cannot at least manipulate through ritual. In large measure they believe that *osa* especially is almost spontaneously effective: provided a god's secret names are used correctly, he is bound to grant a propitious outcome, so that failure is due only to human ignorance or incompetence in reciting the spell. This was impressed on me by two incidents. I was being shown how a man should prepare a love-potion: rolling a cigarette, bespelling it with the secret name of Yabapunaku (also the god of love) and then giving it to the lady of his choice. When she smoked it, the god would arouse her desire for him. My informants described this as very powerful ritual, which they had used successfully in Madang. When I commented that Madang was a distant place and had its own gods, and that I wondered that a Garia deity could be effective there, they replied: *'sini nubo nanunanu tinuku'* (Pidgin *mipela gat tingting bilongen*) — broadly, 'we can get him to "think on" us [and grant our desires because we have breathed his secret names correctly]'.[4] Again, Watutu [Sogumu] explained to me how to perform planting ritual, the essence of which was to breathe the secret names of the goddess Ibinime over specially selected taro shoots and place them in already prepared holes in every strip in the garden. She would then make the crop grow. 'But', I asked, 'what if she does not wish to?' He replied: 'She will do so because I perform the ritual and repeat her secret names without mistakes'. In both these cases the implication was that, there being no human error, the deity had to honour his or her obligation to the ritual expert. Yet the issue needs qualification and I review it at the end of this chapter.

In the second place, as we have seen, a properly educated man who has completed the initiatory cycle may include within his superhuman security circle a wide range of deities: primal creators, several bush gods, initiatory deities, dance gods, the god of sorcery and economic deities. Yet, just as with the members of his human security circle, the moral commitment between these deities — especially bush and economic gods — and himself is determined by his group membership only to a limited extent and is, in many cases, based on purely individual ties. Thus, as an agnate, ego shares with other members of his patrilineage common bonds with the bush god(s) in whose domain(s) the landholdings over which they assert guardian rights are situated, and with those economic deities for whom they have hereditary sets of secret names. Yet, as an enate in other cognatic stocks, he may have purely personal ties with other bush and economic deities. Thus, in Table 16, Labi and Naguni, as Sogumu agnates, claimed Iwaiwanaku as their patrilineage bush god and Ibinime, Liyu and Unaile as their patrilineage taro deities. After adopting agnatic status in Limau in 1980, they can claim at least Malainaku and Kamai'asa as additional bush gods, and Teteine and Iniburi as additional taro goddesses. In the same way, had Ālitolo remained in the Uria area, he could have reinforced his rights to Ulilainaku as an additional bush god, and established them in the case of Siliguku and Apai as additional taro deities. Once again, agnates can be differentiated not only by enatic ties but also by land and ritual rights associated with them.

Furthermore, as in human society, ego should never assume that a deity will voluntarily help him merely because of a nominal relationship: a right inherited as an agnate or acquired as an enate. He has to win the god's moral commitment and support through his own effort by performing ritual. Thus an inhabitant of Unoba domain had rights to two taro goddesses, Iniburi through his father and Unaile through his mother. For several years he carried out careful experiments: eventually he decided that he had closer rapport with Unaile because she seemed to give him better crops and that he should concentrate on her thereafter. Deities as individuals respond only to ritual performed by human beings as individuals, so that ego regards the members of his superhuman, like those of his human, security circle as a general reservoir which he can tap for support according to the circumstances of the moment.

This helps clarify the paradox I discussed in Chapters 2 and 4: that common residence in a bush god domain does not in itself create political loyalties between persons who do not already belong to each other's security circles. As the deity may preside over any form of serious conflict in his domain, we might assume that he would be embarrassed by potential discord among its inhabitants, who should be his followers, and therefore insist on unity. Garia see it otherwise: they argue that he is morally committed only to those who have fulfilled their obligations by performing ritual in his honour. They interpret his reactions in terms of the forces governing disputes in human society. Thus, if inhabitants of his domain attack outsiders without invoking his support, he will be completely disinterested and do nothing to aid them. If two unrelated inhabitants of his domain, A and B, fight, his attitude will be determined by their individual behaviour towards him. If neither of them invokes him, he will stand aside. If A invokes him but B does not, he will help A — or vice versa. But if A and B both approach him with equal ritual skill, he will remain neutral and use his superhuman power to arrange a compromise solution.

I illustrate Garia ritual honour to deities with two examples from the long agricultural cycle to which I have continually referred. There are eight ritual exercises necessary for the preparation of a new garden: ritual to drive away Sikikiba before the site is cleared; ritual to ensure successful tree-felling; ritual to ensure successful fence-building; planting ritual; *sä'orumu* (Pidgin *het bilong suka*), or planting the leaf of the sugarcane; *wulu,* the croton planted to promote the growth of broad and shady taro leaves, to ensure the growth of adequate taro shoots (*mäposi,* Pidgin *pikanini bilong taro*) for the next season, and to prevent the theft of crops by sorcery (*oi'oi osa*);[5] ritual to promote the growth of sugarcane; and, finally, the planting of a cordyline (*o'ai,* Pidgin *tanket*) to permit the gardeners to harvest the new crop. The examples I have chosen are *sä'orumu* and *wulu.*

Sä'orumu is performed at any time from early October until December depending on the maturity of the new taro, which by now should be about 60 centimetres high. The aim of the ritual is to ensure that the crop reaches a proper size for harvesting at the end of the wet season. There are three elements: symbolic association, homoeopathic magic and the esoteric spell. Symbolic association is represented by *musa,* a concoction of bush herbs sacred to Ibinime,[6] and by veiled allusions to a sulphur spring she created by urinating. The element of homoeopathic magic is the planting of lengths of sugarcane (about 120 cm) complete with leaves in each strip in the garden. As the cane grows taller, it will incite the taro to emulate it. But neither symbolic association nor homoeopathic magic is effective without the spell (*osa*), by repeating which garden leaders claim to induce the goddess to 'think on' them and lend her power to the undertaking. Only then will she endorse the symbolic association and homoeopathic magic.

The teams that perform *sä'orumu* vary according to a garden's size. A garden with fewer than ten strips needs only a leader and a helper; a medium garden of about twenty strips, a leader and two or three helpers; and a large garden of up to thirty strips, three leaders and between six and ten helpers. Women may not participate. The proceedings last about three hours. They begin when leaders and helpers have assembled the necessary impedimenta and ingredients to be used at the edge of the garden.

The leaders first prepare *musa* and other potions. *Musa* consists of scraped roots of wild plants, chopped taro shoots, wild taro stalks, and spinach, pit, yam and croton leaves (including *wulu*), all mixed together in a wooden bowl or plate. Meanwhile, the helpers — generally youths serving their ritual apprenticeship — burn dried banana palm bark previously soaked in Ibinime's sulphur spring and mix the ashes with the *musa,* over which they now pour water (another reference to the goddess's act of urination). The leaders then cover the prepared *musa* with a wild taro leaf and concoct a second potion: ashes of burnt bandicoot fur, chopped roots and leaves, liquid drained from the *musa,* and more water. At this stage, they have breathed no spells but have merely used a number of substances closely associated with Ibinime.

The serious part of the ritual now begins. Leaders and helpers carry the two potions, lengths of sugarcane and digging sticks into the garden. As a team, they move from strip to strip across the garden. In each strip they choose a large taro plant, clear away any weeds, and dig a hole at each side of it. They breathe Ibinime's secret names into the second potion which they sprinkle over the plants nearby, especially taro. They then breathe her secret names into the *musa* and put spoonfuls of it into the holes they have dug. Finally, each leader takes a length of sugarcane in each hand, again breathes her secret names into them, and plants them in the prepared holes. They repeat this in every strip so that the goddess will give her support to every gardener.

Wulu ritual may be performed at any time from mid-December until the end of January, again depending on the crop's maturity. The taro should be a metre high. As noted, the aim is to ensure shady taro leaves, promote the growth of taro shoots and prevent theft of taro by sorcery. *Wulu* has the same general pattern as *sä'orumu,* with the three elements of symbolic association, homoeopathic magic and the esoteric spell (*osa*), which is again the vital element for success.

As in *sä'orumu,* the leaders and their assistants prepare two potions, *musa* and *komai,* near the garden. The *musa* now consists of scraped bananas, yams, and taro, and red powder, mixed together in a wooden bowl or plate. The *komai* is a long bundle made from the bark of a tree of that name and daubed with *kole* (an indigenous ochre). They prepare as many *komai* as there are strips in the garden. They then bind *wulu* sprays and fasten bundles of *musa* at the bottom of the stalks, and finally make an *o'api,* a length of pit stalk and *wulu* leaves, with which they conclude their ritual. They claim that all the above ingredients are in some way connected with Ibinime.

The party now enters the garden, going to each strip in turn. The leaders again choose a large taro plant, clean its roots of weeds and stones, stretch out the stalks, cover them with red paint, breathe Ibinime's secret names into a *komai,* and place it in the middle of the plant, above the corm. They then uncover a few taro shoots and daub them with red paint, and take a *wulu* spray and *musa* bundle, into which they breathe her secret names. They next place the spray on top of the *komai* inside the taro plant, remove it, pass it round the base of the plant, and breathe a second spell into it and also a short digging stick, with which they make a hole. In this they finally plant the *wulu* spray. Then, once again breathing the goddess's secret names, they clear away any remaining loose earth and stones from the base of the taro corm — an act of homoeopathic magic intended to give the shoots space in which to grow. They repeat the ritual in every strip so as to benefit all members of the garden team. As they leave the garden, they plant the *o'api* near the stile over its fence to announce that they have performed *wulu* ritual and placed a taboo on the traditional crops in it until further notice.

Of the two categories of ghosts I ignore *kaua* (spirits of those killed by violence) in the present context because, as I have already hinted and shall show in the next section, they are invariably inimical, often to their own kin. I refer solely to *kopa* (spirits of those who have died from natural causes, including sorcery): they are always potentially benign to their own surviving relatives. Although, like those with deities, the relationships human beings enjoy with spirits of the dead within their superhuman security circles should be based on reciprocal moral obligation and concern (*nanunanu* and *eiyo*) — services rendered in return for services received — their quality or content is somewhat different because of the special position of ghosts as against deities within the cosmic order. This introduces the technical differences in ritual to which I have already referred. Although in the period of antiquity a number of deities lived for a time with men to teach them secular and religious knowledge, and were thus always part of the total cosmic moral order, they were never properly part of human society. Hence the content of ritual performed by humans in their honour is bound to be relatively esoteric. Ghosts, however, were once part of human society: indeed, as I have suggested, they are seen as an extension of human society into the superhuman realm of the cosmos. Thus their putative interaction with men and women has much of the quality of the dealings between living human beings themselves. Their supposed behaviour towards their surviving relatives and their surviving relatives' ritual responses to them can be regarded as quasi-social behaviour, intelligible in terms of purely secular relationships between human beings.

As protectors of their interests, spirits of the dead are of the greatest importance to their living relatives. They are believed to perform many services for them. As we have seen, youths are formally brought under their protection when they enter the initiatory cycle by witnessing Abaiwala for the first time. Provided that they obey the rules laid down for the ceremonies, the ghosts of their forebears see that they complete them without harm, especially the operation of penile incision which, although less severe than in other societies, is bound to be fraught with some risk because of the generally insanitary conditions. Ghosts protect their living kinsmen in battle: they help their arrows or spears reach the mark but deflect those of their enemies. They bring up game for their living relatives to shoot in the bush. In particular, they raise and herd wild pig, which they may send as gifts to hunters, telling them where to find and how to corner them, and which they prevent from invading kinsmen's gardens. In addition, they protect gardens from natural disasters, especially landslides during the wet season, and so help bring crops to maturity. They ward off ill luck and disease, and promote good health. They are especially important as purveyors of information: during dreams or even waking hours they bring messages to their living relatives about future important events — not only hunting but also disputes, visitors from other settlements and so forth. They may also bring them material gifts (axes, knives and valuables), which they steal from persons unrelated to and out of favour with them.

Finally, the dead perform the service for the living described in Chapter 7, as the ultimate custodians of patrilineage estates. This belief influences the lending and leasing of land. Where a man seeking temporary cultivation rights is closely related to the landholder, especially if the latter is an agnate of the stock whose name the strip bears, usually there is no question of rent. The ghosts will approve the arrangement as it concerns only close kinsmen. Yet should he seek such rights from a more distant relative, he should ponder carefully his relationship with him, and especially his standing with the relevant guardian patrilineage, lest the spirits of the dead should think that he is trying to take advantage of one of their descendants. Unless he is sure of his position, he would be wise at least to offer rent so as to ward off their resentment. As this suggests, ghosts, like deities, retaliate against those who offend them. I discuss this in the next section.

By the same token, of course, the living can expect these benefits from the dead only if they create bonds of moral obligation by performing comparable services for them. Although these services are religious in form, they are, as mentioned, more akin to ordinary social behaviour than is the ritual performed in honour of the deities. They belong to two categories: those which are fortuitous and those which are tied to focal or multivalent activities. Fortuitous ritual services, such as occasional food offerings and invocations to ghosts when wild pig have persistently invaded a garden, need no elaboration. The focal or multivalent activities which operate to co-ordinate serious ritual honour to the dead are: funerals, pig exchanges, dancing and initiatory ceremonies (Abaiwala, Oitu and formerly Nalisägege). I devote some attention to each one.

As soon as a death occurs, the news is relayed from settlement to settlement by slit-gong and then by messengers, who bring precise details. Immediately,

all available members of the deceased's security circle — as previously indicated, at least three hundred in the case of an important person — assemble
at his or her settlement. Their purpose is certainly to comfort the bereaved
and see to the disposal of the corpse but also to express their respect and sense
of loss so that the ghost will fulfil his or her obligations to them after arriving
in the land of the dead. The women form a separate group and engage in
formal keening, while the men sit quietly on their own. Meanwhile, kinsfolk
from the settlement prepare food for the mourners, while others dig a grave
either in the local cemetery or, as is more common, in the bush nearby. The
company then escorts the corpse to the grave and, after the burial, returns to
the settlement to eat. Next day there is another gathering. The closest kin
send pigs to those persons with whom the dead has not completed exchange
commitments so that his reputation among the living is not tarnished (see
pp. 158-9). The ghost is now expected to set out for the land of the dead.
But the journey is hazardous, for the monster Kesene lurks along the track
ready to ambush and devour any unwary spirit. Some surviving kinsmen try
to buy off Kesene by placing part of the dead person's property by the grave
as a placatory gift. Others in elaborate regalia, which I describe in greater
detail below, perform minatory ritual to drive him away. If sorcery is suspected, yet others, also specially dressed for the occasion, try to divine the
culprit and plot revenge.

Pig exchanges help cement ego's relationships not only with members of
his human, but also with ghosts belonging to his superhuman, security circle.
They are the most important occasions for paying ritual honour to the dead.
Garia do not practise animal sacrifice in the conventional sense by killing pigs
as offerings to ghosts, but they do send them to partners 'in the names of'
specific forebears to show them that they still remember and 'think on' them.
Moreover, in the past before the substitution of inhumation for exposure of
corpses, principals at pig exchanges used to cover with red ochre the skeletal
remains — especially the skulls and jawbones — of the dead still kept in
their houses, and either carry them on their persons or place them in prominent positions on the food poles set up for display.

Again, as I have made clear in Chapter 7, all dancing is said to please the
dead. Although ghosts are not specifically invited to pig exchanges, they are
nevertheless expected to attend and watch them of their own free will. They
should be particularly interested in their living kinsmen's dance regalia: the
shell and bone ornaments, the bird of paradise head-dresses and the various
face paints and herbal scents rubbed into their skins to give them 'new bodies'
(*oma mubikomu,* Pidgin *niupela sikin*), whose physical glory they flock to
witness. The same applies to the initiatory ceremonies, during which novices
and initiands come under the special protection of the spirits of the dead. The

Abaiwala and Oitu singing pleases ghosts as well as gods, as does the regalia worn to haul the new slit-gong and for the Nisiri dance. Finally, in the past, the Nalisägege was the special ceremony in which the living invited the dead to visit their settlements and paid them honour, by means of music and feasting, in return for all the benefits they conferred during the previous year. All participants in these ceremonies are supposed to 'think on' their departed relatives as they dance or sing throughout the night, thereby impressing on them that they still recollect and value them. It is a reciprocal communion between human beings and ghosts.

The role of demons is unambiguous. The people exclude them entirely from the superhuman security circle: in Burridge's (1965) terms, they regard them as outside the moral order. It is impossible to have with them equivalent, mutually beneficial relationships based on 'interest' and 'concern', for their sole aim is to destroy, kill, maim or cause disease. All men can do is to drive them away or keep them at arm's length. Thus before women and children begin clearing a new garden site, its leader must perform ritual to exorcise the snake god Sikikiba, whose continued presence would cause the crops to wither. Again, at a funeral, kinsmen use the two techniques I have mentioned to foil the monster Kesene, who hopes to ambush and devour the ghost as it journeys to the land of the dead. They place items of personal property with the corpse to be used to buy off the demon. Yet they have greater faith in aggressive ritual designed to repulse him. Kinsmen decorated in black paint and cassowary plumes (*uwi negei,* Pidgin *bilakpela bilas*), and carrying spears and wooden shields, burst in on the ceremony, yelling and making threatening gestures obviously intended to frighten him. Finally, non-specific bush demons, 'wild men and women' (*norugoiba* and *sigiasi*), are habitually inimical, causing death, ill fortune, and epidemics such as the outbreak of dysentery that led to the disintegration of Uria village in 1950. There are no effective countermeasures: victims can do no more than withdraw from the scene, as did the Uria people when they moved to new settlements.

As indicated in Chapter 7, there is a measure of disagreement about human personal doubles (also called *norugoiba* and *sigiasi* according to sex). Some informants insisted that these beings were uniformly and invariably dangerous, especially in their attempts to entice men and women to sexual encounters that could lead only to their destruction. Others, however, asserted that ego's own double was potentially friendly and could be manipulated to help him by means of special ritual, particularly offerings of betel-nut and tobacco. These informants argued that, although personal doubles were believed to steal human children and rear them as their own, the reverse process also could occur. At least one cognatic stock claims that the woman who married its founding ancestor was a *sigiasi* child, whom human beings captured when it strayed too near their settlement, reared, and eventually educated.

Retaliatory Action in the Superhuman Realm

In so far as they harbour Utopian beliefs, Garia would be more at home with Dr Pangloss than with ordinary western millenarian thinkers. They belong to a cosmic order which is as good as it can be, for they know no other with which to compare it, and, certainly before the arrival of the Europeans, they do not seem to have looked towards a future state of social perfection, after which there would be no further change.

Nevertheless, they would not go all the way with Dr Pangloss and argue that all was for the best in the best of all possible worlds. Many events are clearly disastrous. However hard he tries to shore up his security circles, both human and superhuman, ego still has to realize that he inhabits a cosmos that, as I stated in an earlier context, is only partially clement and at times irrevocably threatening. He has to reckon with disease, death, occasional earthquakes and periods of famine, and other adversities, all of which he tries to explain and forestall or neutralize. He has to seek out the responsible agent from among the miscellany of gods, ghosts, demons, personal doubles and men who live almost side by side in his political region.

For some deaths at least, Garia have the standard answer that Obomwe's unseemly impatience in the original act of parturition condemned all human beings to mortality. Yet, as they are not passive fatalists, they accept it only in the case of the aged. When the young die, people assume that they have been killed either by malevolent human beings who have harnessed super-human forces or by superhuman beings acting on their own volition. Although I made no systematic examination of Garia basic personality, those who know the people well would support my view that three concepts beyond any others express their character: introversion, suspicion and personal inse-curity. This, too, reflects their elastic, unstable cognatic system. In a previous joint publication (Lawrence and Meggitt 1965: 17), I have suggested that their obsession with sorcery is precipitated by their cognatic social structure and kaleidoscopic local organization. Especially in the north, although less so in the south, ego lacks the personal surety afforded by membership in a politically united and residentially concentrated corporate group. Because of the heterogeneity of the human population of his political region, he can never be sure who and where his potential enemies are. Hence suspicion and accusation of sorcery are inevitably almost everyday events. People quarrel, commit offences against each other and die. The next of kin examine personal histories and hold guilty those bearing grudges. If they cannot come to a satisfactory conclusion through discussion, they resort to various forms of divination. It is the combination of a socially conditioned conscience with a socially conditioned belief in the operation of specific cosmic forces.

Nevertheless, sorcery is not invariably a sufficient explanation of everyday problems. Not all deaths can be attributed to it, and death is not the only human misfortune. There are the other potential misadventures which I have already enumerated and which ego cannot always attribute to his human enemies: illness, deformity and so forth. He may search his own conscience and those of his close kinsmen, and yet find no secular fault that he can present as the motive for the harm done him. Hence he looks for an other than human author of his suffering. This introduces the concepts of sacrilege (specified in Chapter 5) and what is often, but certainly in the Garia context, erroneously called the 'supernatural sanction':[7] the fear of retaliation by gods, ghosts and demons which, in my experience, does achieve a very high degree of conformity in this field. This deterrent is especially effective in the case of deities. Although men claim that, in the past, they put to death women who had witnessed the secrets of the Male Cult, they have always left other offences of this order for gods and ghosts to bring to book: sexual indulgence near gardens, non-observance of initiatory taboos and the disruption of ritual exercises. They themselves take no direct action.

Retaliatory action by deities after the above offences is immediate and irreversible. Gods have only ritual bonds with human beings, who therefore automatically forfeit their sense of moral obligation when they break the rules they laid down in antiquity. As they were never genuinely part of human society, they owe men nothing beyond their formal contracts. Human beings have no way of circumventing their wrath. This is particularly true of training given youths in sorcery and general ritual in the Male Cult. In the case of sorcery training, youths who flout the initiatory injunctions against sex, certain foods, water and food cooked in water are subjected to a superhuman version of the rule of reciprocity. Yeyaguliba withdraws from them the benefits he would normally confer. He sees that the medicines (*naguli* and *a'au*) turn 'cold' in their stomachs so that they will never become sorcerers and healers but always remain *mä'apu* ('just like women'). Nowadays, this is less of a disadvantage but, in the past, before the *Pax Australiana,* it took away an important skill that could advance youths to big man status, and left them and their kinsfolk open to attack by their enemies in their political regions.

In the field of general ritual education, divine retribution is said to be more severe. The gods of the two initiatory ceremonies, Maulemu and Wese Oite'u, and the economic deities take more drastic action against youths who flout the taboos on sex, food and water, and against children who secretly witness their arcana before their time. Not only do they prevent the culprits from becoming proficient in the use of esoteric spells for agriculture, pig-raising, dancing, initiation and so forth, and condemn them to be nonentities all their lives. They may also stunt their growth, and afflict them with grave illness, deformity (the antithesis of physical maturity), and even early death. Big men pointedly represent those with withered limbs and other bodily defects, who are still found in many settlements, as drunken Helots: they impress on novices from the beginning that such persons angered and were justly chastised by the deities because, long before they were due to be initiated, they crept into the cult-houses and watched the Abaiwala or Oitu secrets.

The impossibility of deflecting deities from courses of retaliatory action on which they have embarked by means of invocation, food offerings and other forms of ritual distinguishes them clearly from the spirits of the dead. Although ghosts are often thought to associate themselves with the gods and goddesses in acts of retribution against those guilty of sacrilege, they are far more amenable to human intercession. As noted, the putative reactions of the dead to the living must be understood, in part at least, in terms of secular social relationships. In the main, ghosts observe the ordinary rule of reciprocity: when they are angry with their living kin, they withdraw from them the benefits they would normally confer; and they have no moral obligation to those to whom they are not closely related and hence attack such persons whenever they infringe the rights of their living relatives. I deal with their behaviour towards each of these categories of people in turn.

When ego has to attribute his misfortune to the anger of a ghost rather than to the malevolence of a sorcerer or deity, he must turn again to his kinship computer: he must search through his genealogy for the identity of the departed spirit responsible and examine carefully the nature of his offence. He must distinguish between the two kinds of ghosts I have described. He must always be on his guard against *kaua,* who are invariably, as mentioned, aggressive and dangerous. They roam the bush seeking their enemies and those of their relatives who have not tried to avenge them. They can turn into wild pig and devour both crops and people, even their own kin. They are, like demons, virtually in every way outside the moral order: they are obliged to nobody, and their attacks are incessant and undeviating. Men have no ritual techniques by which to repulse them.

Kopa, however, are initially and normally friendly towards their surviving kinsmen, to whom they are bound by a continuing sense of moral obligation, and for whom they will always perform services provided they are not molested and are ritually honoured. Yet they will make reprisal against human beings who do not meet these conditions: both living kinsmen and unrelated persons. They can be harsh towards their living relatives. They will not protect youths who misbehave during initiation: this, as noted, is a threat to those who are about to undergo the operation of penile incision and for whom septicaemia is an obvious risk. They desert their living kinsmen in battle, and obstruct them in the hunt by driving away wild pig and other game. They send wild pig to destroy gardens, especially those of persons who abduct widows and show no respect for their secondary affines (*oyopei*) by planting near land used by the first husbands, as was illustrated by the case of Waguta [Kulosi] of Yabapunaku-Eimanaku domain. They promote — or at least do not prevent — landslides, illness and general bad luck. Finally, they insist on their custodian rights over their patrilineage estate. They discipline sisters' sons who have purchased permanent usufructuary rights but do not show proper regard for the donor agnates by offering them the first birds of paradise they shoot or fish they catch on the land they have acquired. They are particularly angry with such a man who tries to transfer to his own sister's son the cultivation and ritual rights he has purchased from his own maternal uncle without having first obtained the guardian patrilineage's permission. At the very least, they destroy his crops and, if they think it warranted, resort to even harsher measures.

I have already made it clear that *kopa* always protect the interests of their living kinsmen who pay them proper honour against depredation by unrelated persons. They do not tolerate trespass of any kind on their land, so that non-kin who plant it should always feel obliged to pay rent as insurance against the destruction of their crops and the other forms of misfortune which I have outlined above and which would be particularly severe in their case. As I have already indicated, they make their anger against such persons obvious by stealing valued artefacts from them and giving them to their own living kin. If a man cannot find an axe, knife or dance ornament, he will exclaim: '*A, kopa pä'etai*' — 'Ah, a ghost has stolen it!'

Retaliation by *kopa* is not regarded as invariably irreversible. Especially in the case of former close kin, ego can terminate it by making proper amends for any offence he has caused. He can win back a spirit's favour with a food offering and a verbal apology. Should this prove ineffective, he will then undertake to send out, at the next exchange in which he himself is to be a principal, a pig in the ghost's name as a mark of special ritual honour. Also, in the past, he would have decorated and displayed to public view the ghost's skeletal remains. In the case of ghosts of persons formerly unrelated or only distantly related to him, he has to take such measures to even greater lengths. Above all, he must come to terms with their living descendants if he has offended them. Thus, if he is a second husband, he can escape the wrath of his predecessor's spirit only by taking his new wife to a settlement in a different area and paying adequate bride price to his secondary affines.

Finally, when ego cannot attribute misfortune to sorcerers or the anger of either deities or ghosts, he has one other possible explanation: an attack by demons. In this context Sikikiba is of little importance because his sole function is to cause crops to wither unless the leaders use ritual to evict him from garden sites, while Kesene is totally irrelevant in that he attacks not the living but only the recent dead. This leaves the impersonal wild men and women of the bush and, to some extent, human doubles or alters. Of these, Garia generally regard impersonal wild men and women as the more dangerous. As I have argued previously, they describe them as, like *kaua,* outside the moral order: no ritual can deflect or neutralize their assaults. Their attitudes towards personal doubles, however, are ambivalent. As noted, while some asserted that these beings were equally ominous and implacable, others assured me that they could be conciliated as well as manipulated by means of suitable offerings and other marks of attention.

The Leaders as Cosmic Persons

My central argument can be restated in these terms. In Garia eyes the cosmic order is an essentially anthropocentric system composed of two interdependent realms (one human and the other superhuman) or networks of relationships (secular social structure and religion), both of which are fixed squarely in the natural or physical environment and are completely positive. Hence, man's values are intrinsically materialistic and pragmatic. The cosmos exists for his benefit: he is not concerned with abstract or nominal relationships but with those that promote his welfare. This has been apparent in the interpretation of both cosmic realms.[8]

Sociopolitical structure has to be understood from an egocentric standpoint: in terms of constellations of interpersonal relationships that I have called human security circles. I have described the content of these relationships as the exchange of goods and services. A pure relationship in itself has little value. What counts is that each party is made to 'think on' the other by the fulfilment of the social obligations specific to it, as in kinship, affinal, initiatory and exchange commitments: these demand automatic and equal returns at the risk of losing personal reputation and mutual advantage. In this context focal or multivalent activities and institutions are of supreme importance. More generally, material wealth, apart from its primary utility, has the secondary and perhaps greater value as the content of social relationships. Its existence enjoins co-operation between, and its abundance confers prestige on, both individuals and those who support them in vital undertakings such as pig exchanges. Where there is no exchange of goods and services, there is likely to be no relationship — certainly no positive relationship — to promote reciprocal moral obligation, but only suspicion and the risk of conflict.

By the same token, religion must be understood in terms of ego's putative relationships with a number of gods and spirits of the dead, who represent his superhuman security circle. The deities made and gave him his culture as a concomitant of living, while his ancestors, although not creators, help him enjoy it. Yet the persistence or maintenance of these relationships and of the material benefits they guarantee depend once again on the exchange of goods and services: gods and spirits, like human beings themselves, respect no tie that is not reinforced. Man has to show them that he 'thinks on' them and is concerned for them before he can expect reciprocal acknowledgement. He must fulfil his obligations to them by respecting their sanctuaries, observing the taboos they instituted and, above all, performing ritual, somewhat arcane for deities but quasi-social for ghosts. In short, as I have said of the southern Madang Province generally (Lawrence 1964: 29), in McAuley's (1961) terms, religion for the Garia is 'above all a technology' by which man can maintain his central position in the cosmic order.

Nevertheless, expressed in these terms, the Garia cosmic order would appear to be entirely self-acting, as if all its members — gods, ghosts and men — responded to each other as virtual automata. Clearly, this is not a complete representation. One feature remains: the big men or leaders, who are the nerve-centre of the whole system because they mobilize both human and superhuman beings for joint undertakings. As I have stressed, they operate in both realms of the cosmos. It is essential to consider their actual and conceived roles in each.

Little more need be said about the leaders' roles in the secular realm. I have portrayed them as central figures in garden teams, pig exchanges and initiatory ceremonies, as determinants of settlement formation and migration and, although they lack judicial authority, as primary negotiators in the resolution of disputes. At the height of their powers, they are like magnets: they attract people to themselves on the basis of interpersonal rather than group relationships. For this they need substantial property in land so that they can lend or lease plots to others who wish to work with them. Yet large patrilineage estates in themselves give them no special standing: men like Watutu [Sogumu], Yerema and his son Kasumala [Nali A], and Imoguli and Papoku [Nali B] enhanced their own importance by augmenting their holdings through enatic links — in Imoguli's case, by adopting a new agnatic status.

In other words, leaders have to be men of achievement (*sainatua'apu*, Pidgin *man bilong wok*). Initially, their reputations rest on four factors: their self-confidence; their oratorial powers (as *kunatua'apu*, Pidgin *man bilong tok*); their ability to assemble wealth for exchanges; and their proven capacity to take charge of several different kinds of undertakings — agriculture, dancing, initiation and so forth. As I have said, like their social system, of which they are microcosms, leaders must be generalized. The narrow specialist wins only moderate renown. Yet, as must be clear from previous analysis and discussion, in the people's eyes, these factors of personality and accomplishment in the secular field are of little account unless the leaders can demonstrate their effectiveness in the superhuman realm of the cosmos as well.

Any consideration of the leaders' wider cosmic role must introduce the Garia concept of knowledge. As in the epistemological systems of other peoples in the southern Madang Province (Lawrence 1964: 29-33 and 1965: 216-21; cf. McSwain 1977), outside observers may define two broad categories of knowledge: secular or empirical knowledge, which the Garia actually possess and, presumably, in fact discovered for themselves; and sacred knowledge, which has no empirical foundation but which they believe was revealed to them by their deities.

Although their material culture is less sophisticated and diversified than that of other Papua New Guinean peoples, especially in coastal areas, in relation to the resources at their disposal the Garia have a sound body of secular knowledge, especially for agriculture and pottery, and use it with great efficiency. Their agriculture demonstrates a high degree of mastery over their physical environment, and their coil-made pots have aroused the admiration of others well outside their own borders. Yet they do not interpret and value their secular knowledge in the same way as do Europeans. This can be seen in two contexts. In the first place, although they distinguish between the two· categories of knowledge, they do not regard them as having separate origins. They do not acknowledge the importance of the inquiring secular, human intellect as against revelation by deities. Indeed, they attribute all knowledge, both secular and sacred, to the second source. They believe that, at the time of the creation, the deities either lived with human beings or came to them in dreams and taught them both kinds of knowledge. Thus Ibinime showed men how to clear land, fell trees, plant taro and other crops, and at the same time perform the rituals that would ensure the success of these purely physical activities.

In the second place, as I foreshadowed in Chapter 7, the Garia, like other peoples in the southern Madang Province, do not accord secular knowledge high prestige as do Europeans. Within the total complex of knowledge claimed to have been derived from the deities, they regard sacred knowledge as paramount. They do not use empirical knowledge as a system of explanation *in its own right:* as a process of arguing from substantiated fact to further discovery. Purely secular techniques represent a low level of intellectual achievement that is expected of virtually everybody without any particular effort. The hard core of knowledge is myths and spells, which are not easily acquired. This was illustrated for me by two incidents. On one occasion I was talking with Imoguli [Nali B] of Yabapunaku-Eimanaku domain, who was mending an arrow-head. When I asked him about the manufacturing processes involved, he disclaimed all knowledge of them. In view of his expertise in repairing arrows, I expressed surprise. He replied that *technically* he could 'make' perfectly good arrows but that they would never be accurate because he had not learnt the relevant myth and ritual. On another occasion I initiated a general discussion about agriculture with several young men in a garden who had been felling trees with consummate skill. They told me that they 'knew' nothing about agriculture. They referred me to an elderly, balding, and not outwardly prepossessing man sitting under a tree by himself and eating betel-nut. He *'knew'* about agriculture: he was, in fact, a most prominent garden leader, whose expertise in the relevant myths and ritual was widely recognized.

This emphasis on sacred as against secular knowledge is, as I have already shown, a marked feature of the education of males, especially those aspiring to leadership, during and after initiation. It is then that a youth begins to learn through an elaborate process of instruction not about practical skills, which he has previously acquired by imitation, but about religion: myths and esoteric spells. Those who excel in this training eventually may become *sibatua'apu* (Pidgin *saviman*), 'men who know'. They will be more than scholars in the western sense: they will understand how to get human and superhuman beings to co-operate for the common good. The attainment of this status is not immediate but comes only after years of careful apprenticeship and experiment. Those who aspire to knowledge and leadership — which are essentially the same thing — cannot expect immediate recognition. As we saw in the case of agriculture, they must begin in a small way and gradually demonstrate by continuing success in increasingly ambitious enterprises that they have mastered the relevant techniques. This is particularly important in the context of relationships between man and his deities. It is only when he has demonstrated this mastery that ego can be said to 'know' and be 'known' by them: to become their intimate, as it were. This is a gruelling novitiate, which by no means all men complete. Many do not even attempt it: they have not the self-confidence to shoulder the responsibility. Others drop out along the way because of failure in unforeseen circumstances (such as unexpected drought), bad luck, the inability to memorize spells (which are often most intricate), or lack of nerve for any other reason.

This, as I have argued elsewhere for the whole southern Madang Province (Lawrence 1964: 31-3 and 1965: 218-20), signifies a high degree not of mysticism but rather of pragmatism in Garia thought. I demonstrate this by reconsidering yet again — even at the cost of repetition — the people's understanding of the cosmos in terms of space and time. In spatial terms I have consistently presented their view of the cosmic order as two systems of relationships between human beings themselves on the one hand, and between human and superhuman beings on the other, co-existing in the same physical environment. Gods, ghosts and demons are as much a part of nature as are ordinary men and women. They are terrestrially real rather than mystical: their co-operation with, or retaliation against, human beings has the same degree of physical authenticity as when men co-operate with or retaliate against one another.

The people's views about chronology are in keeping with their ideas about geography. They lack a historical tradition in the western sense. They conceive two broad periods: genealogical time, which they measure by tracing descent and kinship links into the past but which can have little depth because of the loss of generations as names of forebears are forgotten and ghosts disappear from the lands of the dead; and the period of antiquity or the creation of the sociocultural system, which is chronographically vague in that, as mentioned at the beginning of Chapter 2, myths present the emergence of food-plants, artefacts, domestic animals and important institutions in no discernible order, and describe each part of the culture as if it had originated in its final form, ready made and ready to use, without further modification or elaboration. Although no doubt changes did occur, even the most drastic and traumatic events, such as the earthquake mentioned in Chapter 1, were probably compatible with the sociocultural system and thus easily or eventually absorbed by it. Hence Garia mythology offers a picture of the eternally static cosmic order to which I alluded in Chapter 5: unless deities introduce new knowledge by further acts of revelation, relationships between human and superhuman beings are immutably fixed. All have their determinate obligations to each other: there is no room for mysticism.

This belief in the permanent reciprocal duties between human and superhuman beings is the final expression and validation of what I have called the dual cosmic role of the Garia leaders. Yet, as I have forecast, it is essential to reconsider the nature or quality of these duties, especially in the case of putative relationships between men and deities. This was a matter of great concern for anthropologists in the nineteenth and early twentieth centuries, although it has received less attention since the rise of so-called structural-functionalism in the 1920s. In my early research I considered the problem in the context of two diametrically opposed concepts: human dependence on superhuman powers with freedom of choice and action, whom Tylor (1903) and Frazer (1971) unhesitatingly set in the field of religion; and human control of impersonal or non-spiritual occult forces, which they saw as the basic criterion of magic. But the dichotomy seemed untenable as a general proposition. Frazer (1971: 67-71), an impeccably honest scholar, concluded that there were many cases in which the two concepts were hopelessly confused: in which men appeared to control their deities. Thus:

. . . in India at the present day the great Hindoo trinity itself of Brahma, Vishnu, and Siva is subject to the sorcerers, who by means of their spells, exercise such an ascendancy over the mightiest deities, that these are bound submissively to execute on earth below, or in heaven above, whatever commands their masters the magicians may please to issue. There is a saying everywhere current in India: 'The whole universe is subject to the gods; the gods are subject to the spells (*mantras*); the spells to the Brahmans; therefore the Brahmans are our gods' (Frazer 1971:68).

Again:

. . . French peasants used to be, perhaps are still, persuaded that the priests could celebrate, with certain special rites, a Mass of the Holy Spirit of which the efficacy was so miraculous that it never met with any opposition from the divine will; God was forced to grant whatever was asked of Him in this form, however rash and importunate might be the petition (Frazer 1971:69-70).

In Lawrence (1954), *mutatis mutandis,* I implicitly endorsed this assumption, when I wrote that Garia big men, by breathing secret names, had 'direct control' over their deities. I now regard this interpretation as too mechanistic. It ignores the phrasing of these putative relationships. To assume direct human control of gods is to suggest that men can make them do anything they desire, as is explicit in the foregoing quotations from Frazer. This cannot be so: a Garia deity's area of competence is strictly defined by his myth, and no leader could persuade him by ritual or any other means to operate outside it. (In addition, of course, even big men cannot control *kaua* and impersonal wild men and women of the bush.) The Garia position is probably closer to other cases described by Frazer and Codrington. Frazer (1971: 110-11), relying on 'a native account', says of Melanesian 'chiefs' that the 'origin' of their power lies 'in the belief that they have communication with mighty ghosts'. Codrington (1969: 46) says that the power of 'chiefs' in eastern Melanesia is believed to be derived 'from the spirits or ghosts with which they [have] intercourse'. By the same token, Garia big men — as I have, in fact, consistently portrayed them — try to achieve the same end: to create and maintain relationships with deities and spirits of the dead on the same basis as those they enjoy with other human beings, that of strict *quid pro quo*. They claim to establish and preserve a set of morally binding contracts. This, I believe, is a more exact interpretation of the phrase *oite'u/kopa po nanunanu/ eiyo tābu/puluwobu* (Pidgin *kisim/pulim tingting/sari bilong masalai/tambaran*): 'to gain the interest and concern of gods and ghosts'. It is implicit in the Garia words *tābu* and *puluwobu,* and the Pidgin *kisim* and *pulim,* which mean respectively 'to get' or 'to win' and 'to pull' or 'to attract', and which are used as synonyms in this context.[9] These words imply *not* control but persuasion on the basis of mutual advantage. (This is particularly true in the case of human dealings with spirits of the dead, who, as I have reiterated, are in a sense an invisible extension of secular society and still respect its moral precepts.) As far as they can, leaders meet gods and ghosts to settle cosmic issues as co-residents of the same physical environment and almost as peers.[10] In brief, as human and superhuman beings have their stereotyped roles to play towards each other, the function of big men is to fulfil the social obligations and perform the ritual that will promote collaboration between both, and so help to maintain the integrated cosmic structure to which I have continually referred.

Yet, as I have consistently made plain, the leaders' success in co-ordinating the activities of other human beings depends less on secular socioeconomic skills than on their experience and self-assurance in the superhuman realm of the cosmos. Although they certainly attract followers because they offer material advantages, as Garia see it, they cannot provide such services efficiently unless they have the backing of deities and spirits of the dead. Mastery of ritual is the road to cosmic effectiveness: in fact, authority and status expressed in these terms are possibly more important in an individualistic cognatic society than in one based on strong, corporate political groups, which of their very nature enforce social conformity to some extent. Leaders are essential as what I have already called the catalysts of social action: they get things done and prevent inertia. Left to themselves, my informants continually asserted, ordinary people would do nothing in the economic and sociopolitical fields. They need the initiative of big men, who can give them confidence by winning the support and protection of gods and ghosts, and without whom the cosmic order would in all probability grind to a halt.

Epilogue: the Garia and the Modern World

This book is, in part at least, a sociocultural history of a small society in Papua New Guinea. Although I have concentrated on the Garia as I knew them between 1949 and 1953, when I carried out the bulk of my research, in some fields — especially local organization and land acquisition — I have continued the inquiry until 1980. Primarily, of course, I have addressed the work to professional anthropologists. Yet must it be restricted to this narrow audience? Had it appeared, as it should have done, twenty years ago, this question might not have arisen. At that time, when it was evident that colonialism was fast coming to an end, anthropological monographs served the important public function of informing expatriate administrators and other experts about the peoples for whose lives and welfare they had assumed responsibility, and thereby helping them prepare for the establishment of new nation-states. In the southern hemisphere alone, they were read by officers in training at the Australian School of Pacific Administration in Sydney or serving in the field, where they found places in libraries in towns, at District Headquarters, and on out-stations. In addition, there were always lay persons interested in or critical of metropolitan powers' conduct of affairs in their dependent territories.

Colonialism in Papua New Guinea died nearly a decade ago with the proclamation of self-government in December 1973. Since then, books of this kind have had to search for new readers outside the academy in two closely related areas: first, among those indigenes who have received western secondary and tertiary education, and have inherited the complex task of governing their own country; and, second, among the foreign diplomats, journalists, businessmen, representatives of aid programmes and the United Nations Organization, and specialists under contract to the Government who, in a sense, have replaced the former Australian administrators. For people in both these categories, basic information about traditional societies should be of value: indigenous public servants because, such is the degree of cultural variation throughout the country, they very often have to work among peoples whose usages are markedly different from their own; and the new expatriates because, like their predecessors, they have to come to terms with behavioural and epistemological systems with which initially they are totally unfamiliar. Yet such persons — especially the foreigners — will not readily appreciate the relevance of this kind of information unless it can be made to shed light on the problems rural villagers face as they become citizens of the new nation-state and are progressively incorporated in the international community. In earlier works I have discussed this issue in wider contexts: in Lawrence (1961) for the people of the whole country; and, in Lawrence (1964), Harding and Lawrence (1971), and Lawrence and Lawrence (1976), for the inhabitants of the southern Madang Province generally. In these last few pages I consider the Garia alone from this perspective.

When I first visited them, the Garia had been under Australian influence and direct rule for about twenty-five years, except for the brief interlude of the Japanese invasion. Like most young field workers of the period, I had wanted a society as near to pristine conditions and as little 'contaminated' by western contact as possible, so that I was apprehensive that I should find only the remnants of a traditional way of life. Yet, as I got to know the people, I came to realize that their sociocultural system, like those of many other Melanesians, had proved remarkably durable in the face of considerable external pressures. They still carried on largely in their own style despite the suppression of traditional fighting, their concentration in villages under appointed headmen, their nominal conversion to Christianity, and their experiences during and immediately after the Pacific War. In fact, as I have made clear in Chapter 1, my arrival coincided with a cultural renaissance: the reintroduction of traditional religion in 1948 in response to propaganda attributed to Yali of the Rai Coast; and, a little later, the gradual abandonment of the pattern of local organization imposed by the Australian Administration and return to the old system of scattered hamlets. The ease with which the people could resume so many of their old ways demonstrated that they had never really lost them. As a result, once I had been accepted, I was able to observe a great deal of the traditional sociocultural system and, helped by reliable eye-witness accounts, reconstruct — with the main exception of the Nalisä-gege — those parts that were defunct. In spite of the building of the Usino airstrip and highway in the 1960s and 1970s, the situation had changed but little by 1980. Like steel tools after 1871 (Lawrence 1964: 226-7), air and motor transport has speeded up but not so far revolutionized the socioeconomic system. The people can travel farther and faster than in the past, but they still gain their living and fulfil their social obligations mainly by traditional techniques and through traditional social relationships.

Yet it is arguable that this sturdy sociocultural continuity is a mixed blessing in the late twentieth century. On the one hand, quite obviously, it has offered the people a viable and more satisfactory alternative to economic dependence on European and other foreign employment: it has saved them from the shock that would have been caused by the complete destruction of their own way of life (cf. Lawrence 1968: 5). This was both apparent and important before the Pacific War: once they had adjusted to the colonial order, they did not regard it as an intolerable burden because, in most instances, they were allowed to follow their own customs with little interference. On the other hand, the persistence of the traditional sociocultural system, especially in the economic and epistemological fields, is clearly an obstacle to the people's successful assimilation to the programmes of modernization that their government is now offering them. This was implicit in their reactions to early colonialism through the Cargo Movement until 1949 (Lawrence 1964) and is perhaps even clearer in their responses to general development policies since that date. In both cases their behaviour has been consistent with traditional religious beliefs and social values.

In the Cargo Movement the Garia tried to achieve a *modus vivendi* with Europeans and get access to their goods. They still conceived the cosmos as a single physical realm, although they expanded it spatially so as to include Sydney, Australia, which they identified as Heaven, the geographical source of the new wealth, manufactured by God and Jesus Christ with a certain amount of help from the spirits of the dead. (Older informants believed that Europeans could meet and talk with Jesus in Sydney: they had seen 'photographs' of him in mission publications.) So far, white men owed their privileged economic position to their monopoly of religious techniques through which they could contact the two cargo deities. Hence the people hoped that conversion to Christianity and assiduous church attendance would place them in a profitable relationship with God or find them Europeans who, remembering mankind's shared descent and kinship ties through Adam and Noah, would show a sense of moral obligation and concern, and see that they also got a fair share of cargo. They would then have discovered *Anut/ausi'apu po nanunanu/eiyo* (Pidgin *tingting/sari bilong God/wetman),* 'the interest and concern of God or Europeans'.

By 1949, after a brief experiment with the pagan cargoist propaganda relayed to them from Madang, Bogati and Dumpu, the Garia, by their own decision, ceased to participate in the Cargo Movement. But they began to be caught up in the purely secular policies that the Australian Administration initiated, that I outlined in Chapter 1, and that set the stage for self-government and independence in the 1970s. These policies, more feasible after the construction of the Usino airstrip, patrol post and highway, were based on development in the fields of economics (cash crops, trade stores and so forth), politics (the Local Government Council and participation in elections for the House of Assembly — now the National Parliament — in Port Moresby) and education (access to primary and secondary schools, universities, and teachers' and technical colleges).

There is now an extensive literature on post-war development in Papua New Guinea. For the southern Madang Province, McSwain (1977) has written the best account. She has argued cogently that among the Karkar islanders, some of the most advanced and sophisticated inhabitants of the whole region, although there has been a considerable degree of success, progress has been impeded by the contradiction between the institutions we have introduced and the indigenous sociocultural system. This is even truer of the subcoastal Garia, who have had fewer traditional advantages and, because of the difficulty of communications until recently, fewer benefits from contact with the west than the peoples of the seaboard.

Economic development has had only moderate success in Garialand. Rice was a poor cash crop: it never prospered in the mountains and even in the Ramu Valley, with easier access to the Madang market afforded by the airstrip, it failed. Coffee has done marginally better. Yet, even where he has the incentive, the individual grower is hampered by the complexities of land tenure. In the north, where personal holdings are fragmented, it is hard for him to concentrate his trees in a single area large enough to be economically viable. Moreover, because of the pressure on him to be migratory, he cannot live permanently near all his coffee gardens at the same time and supervise them efficiently. In the south, where fragmentation of holdings is less likely, there is always the problem of a substantial permanment economic crop claimed by an individual grower but planted on land held under communal title. His profits may be whittled away by cash payments to neutralize complaints from kinsmen that he has exploited their rights in the joint estate. Hence, although cash crops have brought the Garia more ready money for European goods, they have not promoted the accumulation of the capital necessary for major economic undertakings. In the same way, kinship obligations erode the economic viability of modern trade stores: proprietors generally have no knowledge of accounting and may set their prices by the varying degrees of relationships between themselves and their customers with the frequent and inevitable result of bankruptcy. Again, if, as is normal, a motor vehicle is purchased by a kin consortium without proper written records of the original financial contributions, it is impossible to define individual rights in it precisely, so that it may be used, and abused, by any number of people for their own idiosyncratic purposes until its engine seizes for lack of maintenance and it is left derelict along the road.

By the same token, their cognatic sociopolitical structure and kaleidoscopic pattern of local organization have influenced Garia reactions to political development in the field of local government. The Usino Council Area, of which Garialand is one part, is divided into a number of geographically defined wards, each of which returns its own member. The main difficulty that emerges in this situation is virtually the exact antithesis of that in regions with large language groups divided into strong local units, as in the Highlands: traditional sectionalism. This occurs when the language group represents the whole or at least a significant part of a council area, so that its smaller units, such as clan-parishes, the traditional fighting groups bound up in networks of kinship, affinity and shifting military alliances and enmities, become the voting wards. A council chamber may become a microcosm of traditional politics: councillors support or oppose each other on the basis of traditional alignments rather than of modern interests (Lawrence 1971a: 28). This situation cannot obtain in Garialand, where the problem is to stabilize the voters in each ward. With their long tradition of migration, there is no guarantee that they will live for any length of time within the geographical boundaries drawn up for them by government officers. Mobo village, founded in the early 1970s, is a prime example: it has attracted inhabitants from at least three separate wards. This poses three issues. First, should these conditions prevail, some councillors could be left to represent 'rotten boroughs': they should be prepared for the temporary but periodic return of people whose only interest is to vote and for whom they cannot provide services because they are living elsewhere. Second, other councillors may be expected to provide services for some residents of their neighbourhoods who cannot reward them with their votes because they are registered in other wards. Third, to meet this problem of the intermittent flux of local populations, government officers must be prepared to review each ward in Garialand at regular intervals, carefully recensusing its inhabitants and, if necessary, redrawing its boundaries.

Even though Garia society may be Langness's 'extreme case', its essential individualism may help us understand modern urban residential and political behaviour. As elsewhere in the Third World, cities and towns have grown rapidly since the Pacific War in Papua New Guinea. A marked feature of this expansion has been the establishment of compartmentalized ethnic enclaves rather than the random mixing of the populations of these urban centres. On arrival, an immigrant's initial needs are obviously housing and personal security: the first has always been scarce and the second is a most serious consideration because, certainly in Port Moresby and Lae, violence is increasing and barely controlled by the authorities. Hence he must rely on what is popularly called the *wantok* ('one talk') system, turning to persons from his own language group who have already settled in the town. As far as he can, he tries to re-create his home community. If he comes from a unilineal society, he prefers to live with members of his lineage or clan. Yet, for obvious reasons, this is by no means always possible, so that he has to make use of a wider range of cognatic and affinal ties (Oram 1968; Levine and Levine 1979: 40-74). He builds round himself a *de facto* security circle of the kind I have described in this book. This is particularly important if he has aspirations for a career in the Public Service or national politics. He must maintain a network of relationships on which he can invariably depend. For this he uses any relationship that is available: in fact, he will deliberately create and foster associational ties to this end. Clearly, urban living tends to widen his sociopolitical horizon in his home society.

Moreover, this structural flexibility that we now recognize as inherent in all Papua New Guinea societies is at least consistent with the unabashedly volatile alignments in the National Parliament in Port Moresby. The Parliament is based on the so-called Westminster system. So far, despite occasional grumbling when it has conflicted with their interests, relatively few of its members or the electors have expressed any strong wish to replace it, and it has confounded the early arguments of academic experts that it would collapse because of the lack of strong political parties. We should not forget our own history. In both Britain and Australia, Parliament commanded greater respect before party lines were indelibly drawn, partisan colossuses began to hammer on each other's skulls, Cabinet came to use it purely as a rubber stamp, and debates became mere exercises in already programmed numbers games.

European observers of the Parliament in Port Moresby are still puzzled by the absence of political procedure they take for granted at home and by the mercurial quality of voting patterns. The Government of the day cannot invariably rely on ready-made party support and has to work to gain majorities in the House. The process typifies, albeit at the domestic level, Lord Palmerston's enunciation of wise foreign policy: no permanent friends; no permanent enemies; only permanent interests. This was apparent in the fortunes of the governments led by the Rt Hon. Michael Somare from 1972 until his defeat early in 1980. The whole period was marked by almost continual and unpredictable changes of allegiance. During the debate over the Constitution in 1975, Mr Somare did not enjoy the unequivocal loyalty of his own Pangu Pati but eventually carried the day because those who opposed him were no more efficiently organized (Griffin, Nelson and Firth 1979: 217-30). Again, in November 1978, the first Coalition Government disintegrated when the People's Progress Party withdrew to join the Opposition. Yet Mr Somare retained office because the United Party left the Opposition to form a new coalition with Pangu. Finally, this government failed when Mr Somare, forced to dismiss several ministers after a series of crises, lost support in the House to be toppled by his former Deputy Sir Julius Chan, Leader of the People's Progress Party and Papua New Guinea's second Prime Minister. It is significant that these events took place without even a call for Mr Somare to go to the country.

To westerners — especially those bred in the British tradition whereby confrontation and defeat are followed by a general election — this is strange politics. But the so-called Melanesian Way tends to eschew confrontation as long as negotiation and compromise can achieve desired ends, so that these parliamentary manoeuvres in no way surprised Papua New Guineans. Mr Somare, Sir Julius Chan and other members of the House merely adapted to another arena the tactics of traditional politics and dispute settlement that I have analysed: those of adjusting alliances as the fortunes of big men wax and wane, and of taking up neutral stances that help protect the social order from undue strain by preventing conflict from going too far. This process, at the national level, was typified for me by a discussion during the 1968 election campaign with a distinguished indigenous parliamentarian who had been returned unopposed. I asked him if he intended to give open support to any particular candidates in neighbouring electorates. He replied: 'No, I shall support them all'. When I asked why, he said, 'I should be stupid to back only one person and thereby risk the enmity of any other who defeated him!'[1]

Finally, in this context, my analysis of the politics of neutrality among the Garia may be pertinent to the current marked revival of traditional warfare in the much larger arena of the Central Highlands since the end of Australian rule. The cases at issue appear to be more difficult to contain than in the past. Some are based on pre-contact land claims frozen by the Administration, but others are initiated by motor accidents along the modern highways. Strathern,

A. (1974: 266) has commented that 'groups which formerly had nothing to do with one another may now be brought into conflict as a result of increased mobility'. In other words, some disputes now occur at a social range far greater than before (cf. Case 5, Chapter 6), so that traditional forces of control are lacking: the parties are not linked, and hence restrained, by intermediary kinship networks. It is possible that more detailed studies of the roles of political neutrals in the area might shed light on what is happening at present and help government officers devise a substitute process of conflict resolution for cases in which such persons or groups do not exist.[2]

Western education so far has made little impact on the Garia. Several boys and girls have gone as far as secondary school but none, as far as I am aware, to a university or other tertiary institution. Although they have not participated in any cargo cult since 1949, the villagers still tend to use traditional values and beliefs to interpret the modern world in ways that sometimes verge on cargoism. In 1971 the Australian Administration was preparing the people for self-government and independence, an inevitable issue in the forthcoming national election. At village meetings in the inland area, officers used the analogy of a tractor driven by an indigene under European supervision. This was self-government. When the European could allow him to operate the machine on his own, there would be full independence. During discussion, the Garia and their neighbours regularly asked one question: 'Yes, when do we get tractors?'[3] Again, in 1978, Garia informants told me that, after living with them as an impecunious youth nearly thirty years before, I was now in comfortable circumstances and an important person because I had been taught their religious secrets: although I had not used my knowledge to impoverish them, I had clearly turned it to my personal advantage. A significant feature of these remarks was that the ideas on which they were based had been brought back to Garialand by students at Tusbab High School in Madang, who clearly were little weaned from traditional epistemological assumptions.[4]

Whatever the future holds for Papua New Guinea, one thing is certain. Like many other old dependent territories, it will not remain a facsimile of its former metropolitan power but become its own kind of nation. Although most of the institutions the Australian Administration left behind still retain their external forms, the people are adapting them to suit their own bent. This is inevitable but, as is implicit in the foregoing discussion, not without considerable risk. The sketch I have given above and the more detailed analyses of other scholars suggest that the establishment of national politics— certainly from the operational point of view — has been relatively successful, although there are serious difficulties at the local level, particularly in urban communities. Nevertheless, any purely political achievement at whatever level is bound to ring hollow unless the country can overcome the problems in the two other fields which I have discussed — the economy and education — and in which the Garia performance is by no means another 'extreme case'. Papua New Guinea's interest is to rely less on royalties from trans-national companies and Australian aid. To this end the people must produce more for the cash market and so make a greater contribution to their country's budget. Similarly, villagers must become better informed about the modern world than, quite obviously, many of them are at the present time. Unless local government councils, provincial governments and, above all, the national Government can rely on a vigorous, viable indigenous economy and have to answer to a discerning indigenous electorate, politics — especially politics in the capital Port Moresby — could degenerate into the vicious game of personal aggrandizement at the expense of public service that we have seen in other parts of the Third World. The conservatism of the Garia and other peoples like them may retard the resolution of this issue for much longer than we have so far supposed[5] and, ideally, the Government should allow. Indeed, such a resolution may well necessitate the progressive atrophy of their traditional sociocultural systems as entities in themselves. If that happens, it remains to be seen whether they can be spared the strain and trauma which northern Europeans experienced during and long after the capitalist and scientific revolutions of the seventeenth century, when they also had to make a comparable leap into a new and unpredictable era.

NOTES

Introduction

1 My comments here and elsewhere in the text do *not* attack the African Model (segmentary theory) itself or question its validity in its country of origin. Indeed, I suspect that, had its original antipodean devotees applied it with moderation and humility, it would still be recognized as relevant in important respects to certain types of society in Papua New Guinea.

2 In Lawrence (1971a: 8), relying on Chowning (1962) I wrongly classified the Bwaidoga of Goodenough Island as a cognatic society. For scholarly comment, of which I was unaware at the time, see Young (1968).

3 This literature is now too extensive to cite *in toto*. Much of the Papua New Guinean ethnographic corpus published since 1945 (and even earlier) is concerned with traditional exchange economics and sociopolitical structure. Those unfamiliar with the material should begin by reading Epstein, T. S. (1972) and Strathern, A (1971) for exchange economics, and Langness (1972) and Lawrence (1971a) for sociopolitical structure. In particular, they should consult the bibliographies in these works.

4 As much of this book's argument hinges on Garia cosmic beliefs, I cannot ignore Needham's (1972: 3) recent sophisticated discussion of my (Lawrence 1964) and, by implication, other social anthropologists' use of the term: '[Lawrence] does not find it necessary . . . to specify what he means by belief or how it is known that men in New Guinea believe what they say. The tacit assumption is that [belief] denotes a common human capacity which can be ascribed to all men'. I acknowledge the criticism but reply that it is an old academic chestnut about which there has been much wasted abstract speculation: a problem insoluble until we understand the human mind in physical and chemical terms. For the moment, I refer Needham to Lawrence (1971c: 146): 'I accept as sociolog-

ically valid those statements about religion and cargo cult which ordinary people clearly act out not only in formal ritual but also in their daily lives'. I remind him also of Dr Samuel Johnson's comment on the freedom of the will.

Chapter 1

1   These co-ordinates correct those which I gave in Lawrence (1955: 1; and 1967: 93) and based on inaccurate post-war cartographical evidence. I thank Mr Edgar Ford for drawing this to my attention.
2   The names of the linguistic groups listed are those used by the Garia. In some cases their members may designate themselves differently. In border areas bilingualism is so marked that the Australian Administration, understandably but probably wrongly, classified the inhabitants of the north-western tip of Garialand as Sopu-Garia. Yet this raises the obvious question: Who is a Garia? I answered this by accepting as Garia those who claimed to speak Garia as their primary language. Yet, as will appear in my argument, it is possible that some people at least periodically change their linguistic status to suit their sociopolitical advantage.
3   I use Garia and Pidgin words and phrases mainly where translation into English is difficult.
4   The official rule of one shotgun for each 100 persons does not, in my opinion, protect valuable wild life, especially the bird of paradise. Highlands traders are said to have been active in the Garia area by the early 1970s. The temptation to sell them plumes must have been very great.
5   Since 1945 three currencies have been used in Papua New Guinea: until 1966 the Australian pound; after 1966 the Australian dollar; and after 1975 the country's own kina. Comparative values are: £A1 = $A2; and, until about September 1982, K1 = c.$A1.25, although with the depreciation of the Australian dollar since that date, K1 = c.$A1.37 (November 1982). In the text I refer to the currency in use at the time of the event described.
6   This was the starting point also of the Garia oecological calendar, which, even in 1949, only a few informants could explain. The people had adopted (and to some extent understood) the European system of reckoning months, introduced by the Lutheran Mission. The traditional calendar divided the year into about twelve named periods, some equivalent to lunar months and others marked by seasonal phenomena.
7   This eruption has been incorporated in at least one important myth along the seaboard: the Kilibob-Manup cycle around Madang (Lawrence 1964: 22).
8   I discuss the difference between *kaua* and *kopa* in Chapters 7 and 8.

Chapter 2

1   I indicate all classificatory kinship relationships by quotation marks.

² I put the names of bush god domains with which ego is associated in round brackets.

³ I put the descent name which ego inherits exclusively patrilineally (as *sawaibopi*) in square brackets after his personal name. Where I hyphenate two descent names in square brackets, the second refers to ego's mother's patronymic.

⁴ Fortes, following Justinian, uses the concept of enation to cover only ego's sister's children. I extend it to include all persons linked to his patrilineal descent line, or claiming membership in his primary cognatic stock, through females.

⁵ I have adopted the foregoing terminology after many years of contemplation. To those who object I can say only that they are at liberty to substitute other terms but that they should not allow disagreement with me over this issue to cloud their judgement of my total argument.

⁶ I have written this paragraph largely in the present tense because, as mentioned in Chapter 1, although the content of traditional trade has been considerably diminished, the network of ties is still remembered.

⁷ I was told that the true mother's brother should initiate a boy into the Nalisä-gege. But, as the ceremony was defunct by 1949, I cannot vouch for the truth of this.

⁸ See Brookfield and Hart (1971: 237) for a reinterpretation of this figure in geographical terms.

Chapter 3

¹ The following account repeats but amplifies and corrects Lawrence (1955-67). It incorporates material which I have collected since 1972.

² Cf. Allen (1971), who analyses a comparable situation among the Nduindui of Aoba, Vanuatu, in which the availability of land influences the solidarity of unilineal descent groups.

³ The following emends Lawrence (1955-67).

⁴ As informants admitted, in northern Garialand, these conventions are open to abuse by the congenitally dishonest. I am unable to say how often such abuse occurs.

⁵ I describe the history of Nali linked patrilineage in Chapter 4.

⁶ I refer here, of course, to Labi's and Naguni's decision to accept agnatic status in Limau. By August 1980 they had made no attempt to establish permanent usufructuary rights on Limau land in Siliwanaku, Pukusakunaku, Iwaiwanaku and Yabapunaku-Eimanaku. Limau holdings in these domains are in northern Garialand and hence are mainly small strips, the rights to which are vested in individuals. Labi and Naguni would have to acquire them on a personal basis. In view of their joint rights over the huge southern estate, this would hardly be worth their while.

⁷ The Pidgin *wanwok* (literally 'one work') is the accepted translation of the Garia *saina'omei*, although I have heard it used more often in the context of European employment.

Chapter 4

1   Since the early 1950s there has been a gradual relaxation of these taboos. In 1952-53 I noted four cases in which husband and wife cohabited in a single room. By 1965 the number had increased. Also, in the 1960s, women began to chew betel-nut, which they had never done before.

2   I am indebted to the late Emeritus Professor W. E. H. Stanner of the Australian National University for this phraseology, which neatly summarizes the innumerable ethnographic accounts I presented in seminars.

3   In this context I ignore events before the 1940s, which I could not observe and therefore cannot present in detail.

4   In Lawrence (1955-67) I mapped this settlement wrongly as Ugalimu.

5   It is perhaps significant that Waburu became the main local centre of the Seventh Day Adventist Mission, which has always encouraged its followers to be exclusive.

6   These outliers are the Oyesinō strips which Sogumu bought in the past but whose designation was equivocal in the 1950s (p. 73). I refer to them as Oyesinō in Table 4 and throughout the text.

7   On the basis of informants' general assertions, I treat Kamai'asa as one of the twelve domains whose inhabitants claimed political solidarity because of the concentration of internal interpersonal relationships. For reasons I have reiterated I cannot substantiate or refute their claim.

Chapter 5

1   The following account fulfils a promise in Lawrence (1955: 31, fn. 31).

2   Ghosts can die a second time. Decomposition of the body refers to the traditional practice of exposing corpses on tree-platforms. I discuss these matters in Chapters 7 and 8.

3   I discuss the significance of this in Chapters 7 and 8.

4   Cf. Burridge (1965: 246) who refers to a comparable belief among the Tangu near Bogia in the northern Madang Province: human beings are believed to be derived from pigs but not the reverse, as in Garialand.

5   By general Papua New Guinean (especially Highlands) standards, this is minuscule. Yet it should be remembered that it was about a quarter of the total Garia population.

6   Keisa was Wowoli's true son. In 1949 he commuted between Araka and Igurue, the area of his mother's land. He later settled permanently at Igurue, where he had been a temporary refugee at the time of the cargo prophecies of late 1947. During the exchange he identified with both Araka (Ubesuanaku domain) and Igurue (Mubu domain).

[7] For details of Nisiri and Abaiwala see Chapter 7.

[8] For details see Chapter 7.

[9] By the same token, I recorded only one case of a man buying usufructuary rights from distant kin in this broad category. As we saw, Apuniba [Nali B] sent pigs to Wowoli [Muli] partly to cement an exchange partnership and partly to acquire title to parcels of his land.

Chapter 6

[1] Leach (1977), whose work I read long after I conceived and drafted this passage, makes a comparable observation, although in more general terms.

[2] The Garia term *kununapu* means literally 'men talking' and is translated into Pidgin as *kot,* derived from the English 'court'. In previous publications (Lawrence 1969: 31 and 1971b: 87-8), I have variously used the English terms 'assembly' and 'court', which are not really satisfactory. I now follow Strathern, M. (1972) and substitute the term *moot* in its general sense of 'meeting, encounter' *(O.E.D.).*

[3] See also Lawrence (1969 and 1971a). I am not concerned here with minor disputes which are settled out of court and in which the impetus to negotiation derives from the same forces of self-regulation as I describe in Chapter 5 (cf. Sawer 1969: 12; and Brown, B. J. 1971).

[4] Since about 1925, of course, cases of physical homicide have been referred (officially at least) to Administration and now Government courts.

[5] A comparable, although more elaborate, example of this is cricket, which Methodist missionaries introduced to the Trobriand Islands but which the people recast to fit their own sociopolitical processes.

[6] For details see Chapter 7.

[7] I discuss initiatory taboos in Chapters 7 and 8.

[8] This claim contradicted the previous prediction that Yelibubu's early sexual experience had prevented him from using any ritual successfully. In the heat of the moment, nobody noticed this.

[9] Yerema [Nali A] was an aggressive man who, as noted (p. 116), threatened to kill his fellow agnate Yolekauma and also stole his wife.

[10] Later, by marrying Yaboi's widow Kisianalu, Labaia became also an affine of Ukapu. This case gives an interesting example of cross-linking relationships. Tupalia [Mosoli], who nominally supported his Ukapu matrikin in the mock battle, had been brought up by Yerema [Nali A], his close 'father' (Chapter 4). Labaia also was Yerema's close 'son'.

[11] Usegiliba and Libupu had refrained from calling on geographically distant kin and affines for the obvious reason that they did not need to do so. In view of this, had Wila taken such a step without adequate excuse, he would have lost face and sympathy.

[12] See Chapter 7.

13 At this time women rarely accompanied their menfolk to European employment and homosexuality was rife in labour compounds. In keeping with the attitudes of the day, the Australian Administration treated offenders severely.

14 This was a traumatic experience for Watutu, who said to me in 1952: 'I myself took Äbalia to the Supreme Court in Madang — me, my own "brother"!' His comment represented a struggle between his duty as an Administration official and his loyalty to a kinsman.

15 A fully grown pig was worth £A5 between 1949 and 1953. The return requested by the Sogumu agnates represented six pigs already paid out as bride price plus one sent as compensation to Kuauba.

16 According to Mattes (1969: 76), the Court for Native Affairs was replaced by the Local Court (by Ordinance 1963-66).

17 For the vengeful ghost (*kaua*) see Chapters 7 and 8.

18 For an even more extreme case from the eastern Highlands see Watson (1971).

19 Two comments are relevant. First, in Lawrence (1955: 10) I wrote: 'The Garia are not a political society'. This is, of course, nonsense: it reflects my own mindless but temporary capitulation to the so-called segmentary theory of the period as if it were the only political model that could be used for traditional Papua New Guinean societies. I allowed the statement to be republished in Lawrence (1967: 101) as a drunken Helot. Second, a distinguished English jurist, Lord Porter of Emmanuel College, Cambridge, with whom, after my return from the field in 1950, I discussed informally much of the material in this chapter, commented that Garia social control was almost an embryonic form of international law, certainly before the establishment of the Court at the Hague.

Chapter 7

1 This corrects 'Warua' in Lawrence (1954), an early ethnographic error.

2 This contrasts with beliefs in other areas of Papua New Guinea, especially the Highlands, where there is a clear distinction between recent and remote dead. In a survey of Melanesian religions (Lawrence and Meggitt 1965: 1-25), I carelessly omitted to mention this Garia belief.

3 During Australian rule Europeans were addressed as *kanaba* as well as *masta* (Pidgin). The two terms are now used for indigenous public servants.

4 See also p. 145. The general Pidgin equivalent for Nisiri throughout the whole area between the Gogol and the Ramu rivers is Kaima. I use the Garia name in this book.

5 I did not witness this operation and rely on informants' accounts, which were consistent with information from Dr P. L. McLaren, who worked near Bongu, and Drs L. Conton and D. Eisler, who worked at Usino (Sopu country). All three confirmed the use of the miniature bow and arrow for this purpose in their areas.

6   I adopt here the Pidgin *mas* (mast), taken from seamen's jargon. It is the most accurate term I can find, and also the Garia themselves use it. Youths put on shorter 'masts' than adult males.

7   Throughout the text I have hyphenated Yabapunaku and Eimanaku whenever I refer to their joint domain. I do not do so here because, in themselves, they are separate gods (see p. 34 above).

8   For details of the use of deities' secret names see Chapter 8.

9   Leach (1956) challenges my veracity on this point, claiming that Garia surely cannot argue in this way. In my turn, I challenge him to live in a southern Madang Province village for a year and then repeat his assertion.

Chapter 8

1   A toxic drink made from wild ginger.

2   I ignore *kaua* here for reasons which will be apparent in this chapter.

3   Conversely, if beings they regard as gods or ghosts settle among them, they communicate with them not by means of ritual but by means of ordinary social techniques. This is corroborated by the cases of Maclay at Bongu (Lawrence 1964: 249; and Mikloucho-Maclay 1975) and Yali of the Rai Coast (Lawrence and Lawrence 1976: 70), both of whom were regarded as gods but treated with no ritual honour.

4   Garia also believed that Yali had *Anut po nanunanu* (Pidgin *tingting bilong God*): the ability to get God to 'think on' him and lend him his aid (Lawrence 1968: 23-4).

5   'Theft' of crops by sorcery, which makes them 'walk out' of a garden, is reported from other parts of Melanesia: for example, Dobu Island (Fortune 1932).

6   I cite only Ibinime here because the leaders I watched perform *sä'orumu* all claimed to use her rather than the other taro deities. This applies also to the *wulu* ceremony described below.

7   I have already stressed that Garia, like many Melanesian peoples, have no concept of the supernatural and transcendental.

8   My argument here repeats a good deal of Lawrence (1964: 28 ff.; and 1965). I use this material again because it is essential for my portrayal of the total cosmos that the Garia conceive.

9   The Garia *puluwobu* and the Pidgin *pulim* are so similar as to suggest that the first is derived from the second. Yet informants assured me that this was not so: that *puluwobu* was a traditional Garia word.

10 I have cited two cases of Garia leaders who 'relocated' deities believed to be obstructing the construction of motor highways. I was given a comparable example by Yali for the Ngaing of the Rai Coast in 1974. His father, a big man, met and was entertained by a local god, who sent him home with valuable presents. His father's brother, a man of small consequence, tried to match this experience. He roamed the bush in search of the deity, who obviously regarded him as presumptuous and kept out of his way.

Epilogue

1 In this context it is significant that in the 1982 national election, which returned Mr Somare to power, several successful candidates were endorsed by more than one political party and that recently it has been reported that Mr Somare plans to introduce legislation to prevent this happening in future. His aim apparently is to tie Papua New Guinea practice more closely to the Anglo-Australian model so as to promote more efficient government.

2 I have discussed this issue independently with Professor A. Strathern and Mr R. A. Hiatt, M.B.E., a distinguished Australian still serving with the Government of Papua New Guinea. Both have long experience and extensive knowledge of the Highlands. Both agree that this suggestion may well have substance.

3 In coastal areas the officers used the analogy of a ship crewed and captained by indigenes but still made fast to a wharf by a hawser supervised by a European. That was self-government. When the European loosed the hawser and let the captain take the ship to sea, there would be full independence. Many villagers asked: 'Yes, when do we get ships?'

4 In my own defence, I must say that in my study of Garia religion I concentrated on understanding the principles underlying it rather than on collecting examples of esoteric spells regarded as the expression of its power. Out of respect for Garia belief, I have never revealed to other people the secret names for the deities I did learn. The same applies to my work among the Ngaing.

5 McSwain (1977) has cogently argued this case for the Karkar. I am indebted to her analysis.

BIBLIOGRAPHY

Allen, M. R. 1971. Descent groups and ecology among the Nduindui, New Hebrides. In L. R. Hiatt and C. Jayawardena eds.

Barnes, J. A. 1961. Law as politically active: an anthropological view. In *Studies in the sociology of law*, ed. G. Sawer. (Mimeo). Canberra: Australian National University.

1962. African models in the New Guinea Highlands. *Man*, 62, 5-9. Republished in *Readings in Australian anthropology*, eds I. Hogbin and L. R. Hiatt. Melbourne University Press.

Beck, C. von. 1911. *Das überseeische Deutschland: Die deutschen Kolonien in Wort und Bild* (compiled by C. von Beck *et al*.). Stuttgart: Union Deutsche Verlagsgesellschaft.

Berndt, R. M. 1952-53. A cargo movement in the Eastern Central Highlands of New Guinea. *Oceania*, 23, 40-65, 137-58, 202-23.

1964. Warfare in the New Guinea Highlands. *American Anthropologist*, 66, 183-203.

Berndt, R. M. and P. Lawrence eds. 1971. *Politics in New Guinea*. University of Western Australia Press.

Blong, R. J. 1982. *The time of darkness*. University of Washington and Australian National University Presses.

Brookfield, H. C. and D. Hart. 1971. *Melanesia*. London: Methuen.

Brown, B. J. ed. 1969. *Fashion of law in New Guinea*. Sydney: Butterworths.

1971. Outlook for law in New Guinea. *Oceania*, 41, 244-54.

Brown, D. J. J. 1980. The structuring of Polopa kinship and affinity. *Oceania*, 50, 297-331.

Brown, P. 1971. Non-agnates among the patrilineal Chumbu. In *Melanesia*, ed L. L. Langness and J. C. Weschler. Chandler Paperback. First published in *Journal of the Polynesian Society* 1962 (71: 57-69).

1978. *Highland Peoples of New Guinea.* Cambridge University Press.

Burridge, K. O. L. 1960. *Mambu.* London: Methuen.

1965. Tangu, Northern Madang District. In P. Lawrence and M. J. Meggitt eds.

Chowning, A. 1962. Cognatic kin groups among the Molima of Fergusson Island. *Ethnology,* 1, 92-101.

Codrington, R. H. 1969. *The Melanesians.* Oxford University Press.

Colson, E. 1951. The Plateau Tonga of Northern Rhodesia. *In Seven tribes of British Central Africa,* ed E. Colson and M. Gluckman. Manchester University Press.

1953 Social control and vengeance in Plateau Tonga Society. *Africa,* 23, 199-221.

Conton, L. and D. Eisler. 1976. The ecology of exchange in the Upper Ramu Valley. *Oceania,* 47, 134-43.

Craig, R. 1969. Marriage among the Telefolmin. In *Pigs, pearlshells, and women,* eds R. M. Glasse and M. J. Meggitt. New York: Prentice Hall Paperback.

C.S.I.R.O. 1976. *Lands of the Ramu-Madang area.* Land Research Series No. 37. Melbourne: Commonwealth Scientific and Industrial Research Organisation.

Durkheim, E. 1954. *The Elementary Forms of the Religious Life.* London: Allen and Unwin.

1964. *The division of labor in society.* Glencoe: Free Press Paperback.

Epstein, A. L. ed. 1974. *Contention and dispute.* Canberra: Australian National University Press.

Epstein, T. S. 1972. Economy, Indigenous. In *Encyclopaedia of Papua and New Guinea.* Melbourne University Press. Republished as Economy. In *Anthropology in Papua New Guinea,* ed. I. Hogbin. Melbourne University Press Paperback, 1973.

Evans-Pritchard, E. E. 1940. The Nuer of the Southern Sudan. In M. Fortes and E. E. Evans-Pritchard eds.

Fortes, M. 1970. *Kinship and the social order.* London: Routledge and Kegan Paul.

Fortes, M. and E. E. Evans-Pritchard eds. 1940. *African political systems.* Oxford University Press.

Fortune, R. F. 1932. *Sorcerers of Dobu.* London: Routledge and Kegan Paul.

Fox, R. 1967. *Kinship and marriage.* Pelican Paperback.

Frazer, Sir J. 1971. *The golden bough.* Macmillan Paperback.

Freeman, J. D. 1961. On the concept of the kindred. *Journal of the Royal*

Anthropological Institute, 81, 192-220.

Glasse, R. M. 1968. *Huli of Papua.* Paris: Mouton.

Gluckman, M. 1954. *The judicial process among the Barotse.* Manchester University Press.

Griffin, J., H. Nelson and S. Firth. 1979. *Papua New Guinea: a political history.* Heinemann Australia Paperback.

Hannemann, E. F. n.d. *Village life and social change in Madang society.* (Mimeo). Lutheran Mission, Lae, Papua New Guinea.

Harding, T. G. and P. Lawrence. 1971. Cash crops or cargo? In *The politics of dependence,* eds A. L. Epstein, R. S. Parker and M. Reay. Canberra: Australian National University Press.

Hempenstall, P. J. 1978. *Pacific Islanders under German rule.* Canberra: Australian National University Press.

Hiatt, L. R. and C. Jayawardena eds. 1971. *Anthropology in Oceania.* Sydney: Angus and Robertson.

Hogbin, I. 1939. *Experiments in civilisation.* London: Routledge and Kegan Paul.

—— 1967. Land tenure in Wogeo. In I. Hogbin and P. Lawrence.

Hogbin, I. and P. Lawrence. 1967. *Studies in New Guinea land tenure.* Sydney University Press Paperback.

Inselmann, R. 1944. *Letub, the cult of the secret of wealth.* (Mimeo). Kennedy School of Missions. Hartford Seminary Foundation.

Keesing, R. M. 1971. Descent, residence and cultural codes. In L. R. Hiatt and C. Jayawardena eds.

Lane, R. 1965. The Melanesians of South Pentecost, New Hebrides. In P. Lawrence and M. J. Meggitt eds.

Langness, L. L. 1972. Political Organization. In *Encyclopaedia of Papua and New Guinea.* Melbourne University Press. Republished as Traditional political organization. In *Anthropology in Papua New Guinea,* ed. I. Hogbin. Melbourne University Press Paperback, 1973.

Lawrence, F. and P. 1976. The Southern Madang Regional Electorate. In *Prelude to self-government,* ed. D. Stone. Canberra: Australian National University and University of Papua New Guinea Presses.

Lawrence, P. 1952. Sorcery among the Garia. *South Pacific,* 6, 340-3.

—— 1954. Cargo cult and religious belief among the Garia. *International archives or ethnography,* 47, 1-20. Republished in *Melanesia,* eds L. L. Langness and J. C. Weschler. Chandler Paperback, 1971.

—— 1955. *Land tenure among the Garia.* Canberra: Australian National University Press. Republished in I. Hogbin and P. Lawrence.

—— 1956. Lutheran mission influence on Madang societies. *Oceania,* 26, 73-89.

—— 1959. The background to educational development in Papua and New

Guinea. *South Pacific,* 10, 52-60.

1961. Some problems of administration and development in Papua and New Guinea. *Public Administration,* 20, 305-14.

1964. *Road belong cargo.* Manchester and Melbourne University Presses. Reprinted as paperback by Melbourne University Press 1967, Manchester University Press 1971, and Humanities Press 1979.

1965. The Ngaing of the Rai Coast. In P. Lawrence and M. J. Meggitt eds.

1967. Land Tenure among the Garia. In I. Hobgin and P. Lawrence.

1968. *Daughter of time.* University of Queensland Press. Republished in *Cultures of the Pacific,* eds T. G. Harding and B. J. Wallace. Glencoe: Free Press, 1970.

1969. The state versus stateless societies in Papua and New Guinea. In B. J. Brown ed.

1971a. Introduction to R. M. Berndt and P. Lawrence eds.

1971b. The Garia of the Madang District. In R. M. Berndt and P. Lawrence eds.

1971c. Statements about religion: the problem of reliability. In L. R. Hiatt and C. Jayawardena eds.

1973. Marriage rules and kinship terminology among the Ngaing. In *Festschrift Zum 65. Geburtstag von Helmut Petri,* ed. K. Tauchmann. Köln, Wien: Böhlau Verlag.

Lawrence, P. and M. J. Meggitt eds. 1965. *Gods, ghosts and men in Melanesia.* Melbourne: Oxford University Press.

Leach, Sir E. R. 1956. Review of Lawrence (1955). *Man,* 56, 32.

1977. *Custom, law and terrorist violence.* Edinburgh University Press.

Levine, H. B. and M. W. 1979. *Urbanisation in Papua New Guinea,* Cambridge University Press Paperback.

McArthur, M. 1971. *Men and spirits in the Kumimaipa Valley.* In L. R. Hiatt and C. Jayawardena eds.

McAuley, J. P. 1961. My New Guinea. *Quadrant,* 19, 15-27.

McSwain, R. 1977. *The past and future people.* Melbourne: Oxford University Press.

Maine, Sir H. 1965. *Ancient law.* London: Dent.

Malinowski, B. 1926. *Crime and custom in savage society.* London: Kegan Paul, Trench, Trubner and Co.

Mattes, J. R. 1969. The courts system. In B. J. Brown ed.

Meggitt, M. J. 1965. *The lineage system of the Mae Enga.* Edinburgh: Oliver and Boyd.

Mikloucho-Maclay, N. N. 1975. *New Guinea diaries, 1871-83.* Translated by C. L. Sentinella. Madang: Kristen Press.

Morauta, L. 1974. *Beyond the village.* London: Athlone Press.

Moses, I. 1977. The extension of colonial rule in Kaiser Wilhelmsland. In *Germany in the Pacific and Far East, 1870-1914*, eds J. A. Moses and P. M. Kennedy. University of Queensland Press.

1978. The extension of German colonial rule in Kaiser Wilhelmsland. Unpublished M. A. thesis. University of Queensland.

Nadel, S. F. 1951. *The foundations of social anthropology.* London: Cohen and West.

1953. Social control and self-regulation. *Social Forces,* 31, 265-73.

Needham, R. 1972. *Belief, language, and experience.* Oxford: Blackwell.

Oram, N. D. 1968. The Hula in Port Moresby. *Oceania,* 39, 1-35.

Radcliffe-Brown, A. R. 1940. Preface to M. Fortes and E. E. Evans-Pritchard eds.

1952. *Structure and function in primitive society.* London: Cohen and West.

Radcliffe-Brown, A. R. and D. Forde eds. 1950. *African Systems of Kinship and Marriage.* London: Oxford University Press.

Read, K. E. 1955. Morality and the concept of the person among the Gahuka Gama. *Oceania,* 25, 233-82.

Rowley, C. D. 1958. *The Australians in German New Guinea, 1914-21.* Melbourne University Press.

Sack, P. and D. Clark eds. 1979. *German New Guinea: the annual reports.* Canberra: Australian National University Press.

Sawer, G. 1969. Introduction to B. J. Brown ed.

Scheffler, H. 1965. *Choiseul Island society.* University of California Press.

1971. Dravidian-Iroquois: The Melanesian Evidence. In L. R. Hiatt and C. Jayawardena eds.

Stanner, W. E. H. 1953. *The South Seas in transition.* London: Australasian Publishing Co.

Strathern, A. 1971. *The Rope of Moka,* Cambridge University Press.

1974. When dispute procedures fail. In A. L. Epstein, ed.

Strathern, M. 1972. *Official and unofficial courts.* New Guinea Research Unit Bulletin No. 47. Canberra: Australian National University Press.

Tylor, Sir E. B. 1903. *Primitive culture.* Vols 1-2. London: John Murray.

Watson, J. 1971. Tairora: the politics of despotism in a small society. In R. M. Berndt and P. Lawrence eds.

Williams, F. E. 1930. *Orokaiva society.* Oxford University Press.

Young, M. 1968. Bwaidogan district groups. *American Anthropologist,* 70, 333-6.

Zelenietz, M. and J. Grant. 1980. Kilenge *Narogo. Oceania,* 51, 98-117.

Index